Jean-Claude Martineau

The Arada Pledge

A historical novel

NEW EDITION

Trilingual Press

PO Box 391206, Cambridge, MA 02139

Tel. 617-331-2269

E-mail: trilingualpress@tanbou.com

Typographic composition:

David Henry, www.davidphenry.com

Cover illustration by Reginald Martineau

ISBN-13: 978-1-936431-36-6

ISBN-10: 1-936431-36-X

Library of Congress Control Number: 97819364313

New edition: October 2021

Jean-Claude Martineau
The Arada Pledge
A historical novel
NEW EDITION

Trilingual Press, Cambridge, Massachusetts (USA)

Other books by the author (among others)
Haïti en six leçons, essays, 2012.
Flè Dizè, poems, 2002.

Contents

Introduction 7

Chapter One
The Sacred Field 9

Chapter Two
Ganiloa 27

Chapter Three
The Footprints without Toes 49

Chapter Four
The Drums of Kalame 59

Chapter Five
The Centaur 77

Chapter Six
The Education of Bambolo 101

Chapter Seven
And The Sky Caved In 121

Chapter Eight
The New Kalame 141

Chapter Nine
The Curse of the Pledge 165

Chapter Ten
Three Abolitionists on a Slave Ship 199

Chapter Eleven
Flag Day 227

Chapter Twelve
Eladjo 245

Chapter Thirteen
A Ship Renamed Haïti 259

Epilogue 275

Introduction

I never held in my hands a book entitled "History of France." However I think I know French history as well as the average French citizen. I didn't learn it at school. It came to me through songs, articles, magazines, films and novels. With d'Artagnan, Lagardère, Jean Valjean and Quasimodo, people from the former French colonies, Haiti included, learn not only the history of France, but more importantly its culture. The result is that their French educated elites come to know and love France better than their own countries. This is how France and Europe established and still maintain their cultural domination. As a result, a large portion of the so-called elite in the former colonies have adopted the European heroes as their own, not the fictional ones mentioned above, but the real, historical ones like Christopher Columbus, Napoleon and Washington who never had but contempt for any race but their own.

If Europe, more precisely France, can use its culture to glorify its heroes who were nothing but enslavers and authors of genocides, why can't we do the same to glorify the leaders of our resistance? In Haiti, the resistance was victorious and we are still paying for it. Haiti is one of the most vilified countries in the world. Almost everything you know about Haiti has been thought by her enemies. Now it is our time to speak about our struggles, our failures and our successes. This book is a story to explain history.

—J.C. Martineau

Chapter One

The Sacred Field

As suddenly as it had started, the rain stopped. The children had continued walking because they knew that this misty drizzle wouldn't last. Even though the sky still had some tears to shed, the dry season was approaching.

Twenty boys were walking in two parallel columns with a little herd of goats running helter-skelter between them. The animals were kept together by the long sticks carried by some of the boys. While the group didn't seem to be in a hurry, the pace of the march was steady because they knew they were going far. As they crossed the savannah, the two men in the lead knew exactly where they were going although there were no paths to follow. On the horizon they could see the beginning of the forest.

"How much further do we have to walk?" asked one of the children.

Without turning around, one of the men answered, "It takes a whole day to walk from our village to the sacred field. It's midday now, so we have half a day to go. We'll reach there before sundown."

"Have you been there before?" another boy asked.

"Of course, many times. The first time I was about your age. I was in a group like this, carrying fruit and vegetables to feed the people gathered at the sacred field."

"I'd rather bring goat," said the last child in the column. "At least we don't have to carry them."

The boys started laughing but stopped at a gesture by one of the men.

"It isn't good to make noise while crossing the savannah," he warned.

When they reached the first trees of the forest, the men signaled the children to stop.

"We're going to stay here for a while to rest and eat. Bambolo and Nguele, take care of the goats. Make sure they don't run away."

From the sacks hanging from their shoulders, the men distributed ripe fruit and boiled vegetables for the children's lunch. The group sat quietly at first, but little by little, they started talking. Bambolo and Nguele used their long sticks to gather the goats together in a tight bunch and then sat a little away from the others.

They were known in the village as the Mischievous Pair. Not that they were disrespectful to adults—that would be unheard of in the Arada tribe. It was an affectionate name bestowed because of their direct questions and their practical jokes. They'd go out of their way to make people laugh.

At fourteen years, these two were the oldest of the boys. Like most Arada children, they had strong, well-nourished bodies because the tribe lived in a fertile area where vegetables and fruit grew in abundance and game was plentiful. In addition, the Aradas had domesticated goats and cows, not so much for their meat as for the milk they provided.

Bambolo and Nguele were the most inquisitive of the children. As usual, they wanted to know where they were going and why. Though it was considered bad manners in the Arada tribe for children to ask too many questions, they couldn't suppress their curiosity.

"Bao," asked Bambolo, "are we going to see the king?"

"Maybe," the man replied. "Tomorrow is going to be the day of the griot—the storyteller. The king doesn't conduct this ceremony, so he may or may not come."

"Who is the griot?"

"His name is Adegba. He's an old man who has the whole story of the tribe in his head, and tomorrow he's going to tell it."

"Do you know the story?"

"Yes, I do, but I can't tell it as well as the griot. I heard the story some years ago when I took the pledge. You see, during the ceremony, the story of the tribe is told by the griot in order to explain all the laws we have and why we have them."

"Is that when you chose Eladjo as your companion?" Nguele asked, pointing to the other man.

"Yes," Bao nodded.

"When I grow up, I'll choose Bambolo as my companion," Nguele stated firmly.

"I think it's too early for you to think about having a companion. It's a very important decision to make, because your companion will be for life. You'll hunt with him, fish with him, tend the goats or cows with him. So since it's such an important choice, why rush? You still have a few years to think about it."

"Do you mean that everywhere you go, Eladjo has to be with you?"

"Only when we have work to do outside the village. But as you know, inside the village we have our separate families and homes, and we don't always have to be together."

It was time to continue the journey. The adults stood, stretched a bit, and the children instinctively rose and imitated them. The boys gathered the goats and joined them with a single long rope stretched from one animal to the next, tying each to the others with a loop around the base of their horns.

Bao addressed the group. "The danger of the savannah is different from the danger of the forest. In the savannah we have to worry about lions, wild dogs and other flesh-eaters. They won't follow us into the forest, but here we have to watch for poisonous snakes in the dead leaves on the forest floor."

The men took the lead, clearing a path with their long sticks, and entered the forest.

The goats were tied together because it would be easy to lose them among the trees and dense underbrush. In the savannah, the children could run after them and gather them back. But in the forest, two or three steps in a different direction and they'd never be seen again. There was a path, of course, but it wasn't well traveled. Only the experienced eyes of the adults could see and follow it. Where the children had been asked to keep quiet in the savannah, here they were encouraged to talk and make noise freely.

Eladjo explained, "The creatures on the savannah attack because they're hungry. Although they won't attack people, the goats attract them. Here in the forest, the creatures strike out of fear. So if we make a lot of noise, they'll clear out of our path when they hear us approaching."

Bambolo was extremely happy to hear this; he had so many questions. Since he was walking at the back of the group, he had to yell to the adults at the front of the march.

"Eladjo," he shouted, "how does someone become a griot?"

"I don't know," Eladjo replied. "I guess he has to have a good memory and must like to tell stories."

"I mean," continued Bambolo, "does the king choose the griot?"

"In a way, yes. If the king calls on a storyteller to answer a question, that makes him an acknowledged griot."

"I don't understand," Bambolo said. "Why would the king ask the griot about anything?"

Eladjo explained, "Let's say a sickness is killing our cows and the healer can't find what is wrong with them. The king may ask the griot if anything like that has happened in the past. If the griot remembers, he may also remember what was done to get rid of the sickness: for instance, if it had come from the spirits as a punishment to the tribe, or if it came from bad water or bad grass where the cows were grazing."

"Oh, so the griot is very important?"

"Very important. Everyone listens to the griot, even the healer."

"That's what I'd like to be," said Bambolo. "I'd like to know everything."

This statement was received with a burst of laughter.

"Yes," one of the children teased, "you like to talk a lot, but do you have the memory you'd need?"

Nguele came to his friend's defense. "Yes, he does! He remembers everything we do, even things we did when we were very small, things that I don't remember myself."

"That's fine," said Bao, "but you can easily recall now because you're young and what has happened to you wasn't so very long ago. But can you remember stories of things that occurred before you were born, or before your grandmother was born?"

"Where can I learn those stories?" Bambolo asked.

"From an older griot, and this is how the stories pass from generation to generation."

"Does that mean that I would have to live where the griot lives?"

"There are plenty of storytellers in our village, too. They haven't been consulted by the king, but they are still griots. It isn't a very easy thing to learn," Bao continued. "You would have to be able to listen and to know which stories are important to remember, and you would have to travel from village to village asking questions and listening to people. If an older griot happens to like you, he might train you. He would take you wherever he goes and teach you how to recall things. The last time Adegba came to our village, he had four young men with him. He went around talking and listening to people. At sundown he asked these young men to tell him what had happened during the day. This is the way the griots are trained."

"That's what I want," Bambolo said. "I want to be a griot. I want to know everything."

There was a certain determination in the way he said it. This time no one laughed.

As they continued to walk, Bao explained that Adegba was the main griot, the griot of the entire tribe. That made him a member of the king's council. When he died, or if his memory were erased by old age, the king could replace him either by asking the advice of another griot or by appointing one to conduct the ceremony of the pledge.

When they reached the sacred field late in the afternoon, the sun had already disappeared. But from its hiding place behind the mountains, it was still sending rays high into the sky.

Clouds hanging over the horizon glowed red with the last light of day. Everything was cast in red and black.

The sacred field was a small savannah within the forest, a clearing about the size of Bambolo's village. Under the trees surrounding the field were campfires, but there was no one in the field itself. The children felt a certain strangeness as they approached, perhaps because they'd been told that every dead Arada still roamed this place. Besides sensing that they were being watched by their ancestors, they knew that they were forbidden to set foot on the field until the ceremony. The solemn atmosphere was heightened further by the fact that no one was speaking aloud; if people had to say something, they communicated in whispers.

The boys strolled around the circle, meeting with people, seeking others from their village, and when they found them, joining their campfires. Many temporary shelters of branches and leaves had been built already. Bambolo felt that he was experiencing the greatest day of his life. He had heard so much about this spot—the sacred field—so important to the cultural life of his tribe.

This was the only event where he could meet Arada children from other villages. He wanted to talk with them, to tell them about places he had seen, places that he had explored, and places where he could not go, such as a certain mountain near his village, an area taboo to the Aradas. They couldn't step on that ground unless they were in danger and had no other place to find shelter, because the first known king of the Aradas, Gaou-Guinou, was buried there. He wanted to tell them about his curiosity about Gaou-Guinou's Mountain and his desire to explore it. He wanted to ask them if there were places like that near their villages, and whether they had tried to sneak into them without other Aradas knowing.

When he saw the sacred field, he had symptoms of fear—cold sweat and shivering—but he wasn't afraid. On the contrary, he was excited to be there, so happy that for the first time he would witness the ceremony that would take place the next day although he had no role to play in it. But he knew the griot would be there and he would, as he did every year, tell the story of the tribe.

Bambolo didn't know the story very well. He had heard parts of it in conversation with people in the village but he wanted to hear it in its entirety, and he intended to remember it all and tell it back to Nguele on the way home. He anticipated this as his first lesson toward becoming a griot. Filled with these thoughts, he fell asleep later than almost everyone else.

When the sun awoke him, he realized that he had overslept. He stretched and came out of the shelter built by men from his village. Most of the children were already up and running about, but still no one entered the sacred field. Smoke floated up from campfires and the smell of food cooking was delicious. It was certainly not as silent as it had been when they had arrived. In fact, it was becoming quite noisy as some people were already dancing to the beat of drums. Bambolo searched for a familiar face and found Eladjo's.

"What's going to happen now?" he inquired.

"People are going to eat, dance and celebrate most of the day. Then in the late afternoon, when the sun starts to go down, the griot will enter the field. He'll call on the young men who are going to take the pledge to approach him. He'll stand right there on that mound and they'll kneel two by two and take the pledge. Then he'll invite everyone to enter the field to hear the story of the tribe. You may go now and meet the children from the other villages, but don't forget that you have to avoid stepping on the holy ground without first going to the river and thoroughly cleaning yourself."

Bambolo circled the field, encountering groups of playing children. Some trying to push others onto the field while those being pushed tried their best not to violate the sacred space. He saw groups of girls dancing or whispering in each others' ears, commenting on the boys and young men passing by. Their giggling followed him and made him feel embarrassed. Finally he met up with Nguele.

His friend was among a group of young men trying their skill at throwing spears at a target carved into the trunk of a large tree. He quickly joined the contest although he couldn't hope to win against Nguele, who was the best spear thrower he'd ever seen. A skillful young man from another village gave his name as Gaouno. He was two or three years older than Bambolo, but the three—Bambolo, Nguele and Gaouno—became fast friends.

From time to time a few young men left the contest to look for food. These three would go together and be welcomed at any campfire where there was something to eat. Then they'd rejoin the contest.

They passed the entire morning playing, eating and joking. Once, when Bambolo hurled his spear and missed the target by more than a foot, Gaouno said, "You'd be a very poor defender of your village if the pink men attacked."

Bambolo had heard that expression, 'the pink men', before and assumed it was one of the many legends of the Aradas. But now he was eager to talk about his overwhelming desire to become a griot.

"If you want to be a griot," Gaouno advised, "you'd better hurry. Look! Adegba is ready to enter the field."

People were leaving whatever they were doing to gather at the edge of the clearing, where they stood and watched the griot walk onto the field alone.

Led by the older boy, the three friends raced to the river, frantically washed their heads and faces, hands and feet, and just as quickly as they had come, they ran back to the sacred field.

The griot had stepped up onto a central mound that was about two feet tall. Around his waist he was wearing a white wrapper that hung down to his feet. His upper body was bare except for a string of beads around his neck from which a round wooden amulet hung onto his chest. He extended his arms, remaining in that position for a few seconds, and then slowly dropped them. It was the signal for the drums to begin.

Three groups of young men, each coming from a different direction, entered the sacred space dancing. Rhythmically they made their way slowly to the mound. Reaching Adegba, they sat at his feet. He extended his arms again and the drumming stopped. At that moment, everyone else entered the field, forming a large circle about ten paces from the troupe of young men.

Bambolo, Nguele and Gaouno arrived and wiggled their way through the crowd, trying to find a place as close to the griot as possible. The disturbance they created was noticed by Adegba, who stopped to look at the three young men as they burst forth from the circle.

"Quiet," he said, but there was no anger in his voice. Then a look of surprise crossed his face as he recognized Gaouno. "Son of the king," he said, "I am pleased that you came to hear me today."

Without saying a word, Gaouno bowed his head slightly.

"But why are you causing this commotion?" the old man asked.

Gaouno crossed the space separating the rest of the Aradas from the young men and explained, "I'm with a friend named Bambolo. He wants to hear the story of the tribe because he hopes to become a griot."

"Then come forward. Come and sit right here at my feet where you will not miss a single word."

Bambolo couldn't believe he was being given this privilege, but nevertheless he crossed the space between the two groups, passed between the candidates for the pledge, and sat at Adegba's feet. With order restored, the griot began.

We were not originally from this area. We came here many, many years ago, long before my great-grandmother was born. We were living near the great salty water, and our king was Gaou-Guinou. The Aradas were not a very big tribe. We had only one village, but we lived in harmony with the other tribes in the area: the Fons, Mandingos and Ibos.

King Gaou-Guinou was a very fat and lazy king and there was nothing at first to indicate that he would become our greatest king and our greatest hero. But all the laws that we have in our tribe today came from him. He became great because of a tragedy that struck the Arada tribe.

One morning the Aradas woke up assuming that they had in front of them a day as peaceful as the day before and the day before that. But then they saw something strange floating on the salty water. King Gaou-Guinou and the council of elders went to the shore to find out what it was. Many people followed them.

When it came closer to the shore, they realized it was a floating village. There were people on it, but these people were pink, at least their faces were. No one could see the rest of their bodies because they were completely covered up. These pink people put out on the salty water small canoes like the ones we use for fishing, and they came ashore. They were carrying some strange tools in their hands.

As the pink men landed, the Aradas realized that those tools were weapons. They made great noise, as loud as thunder, and threw invisible arrows. People were falling, people were bleeding, but no one could see the arrows wounding them.

King Gaou-Guinou was wounded and almost all the elders were killed on the shore. Those who survived ran back to the village but the pink men pursued them. There was panic as the Aradas tried to run from the village to seek shelter in the surrounding forest. But from the forest came the noise of hundreds of voices. The Fons—their friends, their neighbors—were attacking. The people couldn't run back to the salty water and couldn't flee to the forest. They were trapped. Many Aradas were taken alive, even the son of King Gaou-Guinou. The healer was killed, the griot was killed, and that's why the memory of the Aradas doesn't go back beyond the day of the tragedy. The memory of the Aradas was lost.

In spite of the panic, King Gaou-Guinou gathered everyone he could, and fighting the Fons back, a group of Aradas broke away and disappeared into the forest. Before the pink men and the Fons left, they burned the village—every last hut—to the ground.

Days later, King Gaou-Guinou and the survivors returned to the burned village to survey the damage and decide what to do. Some wanted to rebuild at the same site, but the king said, "No, we are going to remain in the forest for now until we're sure that it's safe to construct our village here."

He thought about the Fons, a friendly tribe that had lived in peace with the Aradas for generations. In fact, many Fons women had married Arada men, and many Arada women had married Fons men. What had happened to change that friendship?

He called on two Aradas who spoke the language of the Fons and sent them out to spy. He instructed them to gather all the information they could without putting themselves in danger: Why had the Fons turned against the Aradas? Who were the pink men? Where were they taking the people they captured? Who were their gods, and were they more powerful than the Aradas'?

The healer was dead, but fortunately the healer's wife, who knew a few of her husband's secrets, had survived. She gathered roots, herbs and bark and took care of the king's wounds. By the time he was healed, the spies had returned.

The king gathered a few of the elder men and women, and with the spies, they went into the forest and sat at the foot of a big tree.

"What have you learned?" he asked.

A spy stood and replied, "We've learned a lot, but perhaps not enough to know what to do. If we had your permission to go and talk to the Fons, we might have been able to learn more. But we could only listen to people who were passing near our hiding places."

"Well, who are these pink men?"

"They're from different tribes, and these tribes aren't friendly to one another. Sometimes they fight among themselves with their terrible weapons. There was a fight near the Fons' village and many pink men died."

"Where do they come from? What do they want?"

"When they first appeared, the Fons thought the pink men were living on the floating villages, but they are not. They're from other lands where they have wives and children."

"How did the Fons determine that they are from different tribes?"

"Some of them have been around the Fons for a long time, and some Fons have learned words from their languages."

"But what do they want?"

"We don't know. They come and take people away. In the beginning, the Fons thought that people like us were the pink men's food, but this isn't so."

An old man stood and demanded, "I want to know why the Fons turned against us. We've lived peacefully with them for many years. My wife is a Fons."

"The Fons haven't turned against us. They were threatened with being taken away themselves if they didn't cooperate in the capture of our people. Not being able to resist the awful weapons of the pink men, they had to comply."

"Nevertheless," the king said, "they have become our enemies, and I was right to ask you not to show yourselves. You would have been taken away, too."

"No," replied one of the spies, "they are only after young people: mainly young men, fewer girls, and still fewer children."

"What makes them so powerful?" the king asked. "Do they have mighty gods protecting them?"

"We don't know for sure, but it seems they have only two gods: a good one that they praise, and a bad one that they obey. These gods are too powerful for us. There is no way we can resist or fight back. The Fons have tried and have failed. And I heard also that other tribes living further away, so far that we've never met them, were also victims of attacks."

After hearing the spies' report, King Gaou-Guinou formed a council with the elders and they deliberated very late into the night. The plan they made was laid out by the king the next morning when he gathered what was left of the tribe.

He ordered the Aradas to move inland as far as they could, taking whatever could be salvaged from the ruins. No one remembers how long they marched, crossing or skirting the territory of many tribes: the friendly Bakas, who use poisoned arrows and don't grow bigger than our children; the fierce Kaplaous, who refused passage to the Aradas; and the Congos, who indicated to the king that there was a vast and uninhabited territory beyond the great swamps.

One night after passing the swamps, the Aradas arrived at a clearing in the forest and slept there. When they woke up, they found themselves right here where we are today.

The king stood on this mound and said, "We have arrived. All during our journey I've been thinking about where and how we should live. We're going to have three villages instead of one, and the tribes will be separated into three groups, each with a chief of my choosing. The groups are going to march from this point in three different directions. They'll walk for a whole day and then rest for the night. The next morning, they'll build a village at that place.

"Each year, at the end of the rainy season, we will come here and a griot will tell the story of our march so we will always remember that the pink men attacked us without provocation, and that a tribe of people like us helped them.

"From this day on, no Arada should go alone when they leave the villages, but neither should they venture out in large numbers. They must go in pairs, except for children, who should be protected by at least two adults. Each Arada man will be free to choose his own companion, and that companion will be his for life. We're going to remain here a few days, and during that time I want all the young men in our tribe to choose a companion. Before we separate, I want them to take a pledge to be faithful, to defend each other, and if one dies outside the village, the other must bring his body back to the village to be buried according to our customs. The body shouldn't be left to be eaten by wild animals. When a man dies, the surviving companion is responsible for the welfare and protection of his companion's family. Every year we will come back to this place, gather our young men, and they will choose companions and make the same pledge to each other."

Eight days later, King Gaou-Guinou gathered the people and summoned the young men to come forward. The tribe was so decimated that only sixteen men remained to take the pledge. The women, old people and children of various ages stood as witnesses. With the eight pairs before him, the king called on an old man whom he had asked to conduct the ceremony. The elder told the youths to kneel two-by-two facing each other, to put their right hand on their companion's left shoulder, and to repeat after him:

'I have chosen you as my companion. We will work together, we will fight side by side. I will bring your body to the village if you die outside of it, and I will take care of your family if you die before I do. I will never lie to you nor keep a secret from you.'

Then, instructed by the king, each pair chose a design that would identify them, such as a circle, a broken line, straight line, tree or snake. They were free to apply the design to their shoulders, arms, the backs of their hands or their cheeks. One young man would draw the design on himself with a sharpened stick, and then it would be applied to the same place on the body of his companion so the two would be identical.

When the ceremony was over, King Gaou-Guinou chose two chiefs and told them in what direction to walk the next day. He would lead the third group himself.

The next morning, the Aradas were ready. The chief of the first group was named Ba. His group built the village of Kilou. The second group was led by Chief Shelon. After marching a full day, they built the village of Weewa. And the third group, led by King Gaou-Guinou, built Kalame.

At the end of the story, the griot called on the young men to approach. This time there were at least two hundred pairs.

In two rows they knelt, one in front of the other, each one putting his hand on his companion's shoulder, and at the griot's direction, repeated the same pledge their forefathers had taken many generations ago. Bambolo was so impressed that he would have taken the pledge right then and there with Nguele as his companion, but he knew he had to wait a few more years.

After the ceremony, the griot continued telling the tribe's stories until nightfall. Most of the children were already asleep and many adults were yawning, but Bambolo never lost interest in his people's history. Sitting at the griot's feet, he heard the story of Gaou-Guinou up to his death and burial on the mountain near Bambolo's village, Kalame. Now he understood why it was forbidden for an Arada to set foot there. He listened to the names of all six kings who succeeded Gaou-Guinou and realized that they all had 'Gaou' in their names. He also realized that Gaouno, his newfound friend, was probably the next king of the Aradas.

But he was also troubled, because he had already trespassed on Gaou-Guinou's Mountain. When he was hunting for birds recently, he followed one and was on the mountain before he realized that he was on forbidden ground. Hearing voices, he quickly hid in the underbrush. The two men who passed without noticing his presence weren't Aradas, and he couldn't understand their language. When they disappeared, he ran back to the village and told no one, not even Nguele.

When Bambolo rejoined his friends the next day, he went straight to Gaouno. As the son of the king, he would know what the punishment was for stepping on holy ground. Bambolo bowed as he should before royalty, but Gaouno laughed.

"I'm not the king," he said. "I am only his son, and I may not become king if Father changes his mind and names someone else the *Gaou*, the heir."

"Well, then, I have a question. If someone entered the sacred field without washing first, what would happen to him?"

"He would be shunned by the tribe and isolated for a few days."

"And what about Gaou-Guinou's Mountain?"

"Gaou-Guinou's Mountain is different. I heard that an Arada can enter there if he is hiding to protect his own life or that of his companion—for instance, if he is attacked by a wild animal. But no one can go there without a pressing reason."

"Oh. Then I can tell you what happened. I was following a bird and I found myself on the mountain. I didn't do it on purpose. And I saw two men there who weren't Aradas."

"Did you report this to your chief or your elders?"

"No."

"You should have. You see," explained Gaouno, "we are isolated and safe here between the swamps, the river and the forest. The neighboring tribes respect us, and we've been living peacefully with them. They'd never violate our sacred places. But if those men did, they must be enemies. You've just heard the story from the griot. What happened long ago with the Fons could happen again. When you get back to Kalame, I urge you to tell your chief and your elders what happened."

"Will I be punished?" Bambolo worried.

"Maybe, but the safety of the tribe is more important than a few days of isolation. Do you promise to report it?"

"Yes, I do."

A few minutes after this conversation, the three friends seemed to have forgotten about it. They were too busy eating, talking, participating in contests of strength and skill, and watching the young women. Bambolo was impressed and a little envious to see how the young people approached Gaouno and bowed their heads before him. Then Gaouno would place his palm on the top of their heads. This was the normal way for children to approach their elders, but it was the first time Bambolo had seen this custom used for a young man just a few years older than himself. He was even more impressed by the fact that Gaouno didn't seem conceited about his position. He in turn would bow to the elders so they could greet him by touching the top of his head with their palms.

The ceremony of the pledge wasn't the only reason the Aradas gathered at the sacred field. In fact, eight days after the ceremony they were still there. It was a time of intense cultural activity. From each village came dancers, storytellers and musicians, each eager to show their talents and skills to people from the other villages. It was not a competition, but rather a display of colors, motions and sounds.

Food was cooked and consumed all day long. Besides the roots and vegetables that the Aradas had brought from their respective villages, a wild pig or an antelope was brought from the forest from time to time by the young men. These animals were immediately skinned, gutted and put on the fire. The elders loved these festivities and went around tasting food from different campfires. Again, there was no competition. No group, no village was trying to outdo the others.

It was a very special time for young men and women of marrying age, since many inter-village marriages originated from these gatherings at the sacred field. The young men tried to present themselves at their best by participating in games that showed their strength and skills with the spear, in races and in hunting. And the young women would respond by dancing to the beat of the drums that were alternately slow and languorous, then fast and complex. They showed their charms with one, their strength and agility with the other.

Understandably, Gaouno was the center of the young women's attention, not so much because he was the king's son, but because he was an outstandingly handsome young man. He was tall and slender, with broad shoulders, and his skin was dark and smooth. He wore his hair long and braided, tied in a knot on top of his head. His teeth were white, creating a contrast with his black skin that the Aradas found beautiful. In spite of the girls' attention, Gaouno remained friendly, but proper and distant.

"Have you found your queen yet?" Nguele asked.

"Yes, but I'm not completely free to choose the woman who will live in my hut. My father and the council of elders may approve my choice and they may not."

"What?" Bambolo asked. "They choose your wife for you?"

"I didn't say that. I just said that they may or may not approve."

"But if you were free to choose whomever you please, tell me, who would it be?"

Gaouno said simply, "Follow me."

They walked around the edge of the field until they reached a campfire where women were busy cooking.

"Look," he said to his friends.

Nguele and Bambolo took a sweeping look at the group of women, and their eyes fell on one of them, a young woman sitting on log and peeling manioc. They knew it was she without Gaouno even having to point her out. She was round and strong; her breasts were full and shiny like polished mahogany. When she notice Gaouno, her face lit up in a smile as beautiful as the sunny morning that follows a rainy night. Then she quickly lowered her head and went back to her chore.

"She is the one I would choose. He name is Maile and, like me, she is from Weewa. I have known her all my life, and I have liked her all my life. This must be a secret, so don't repeat it to anyone."

Chapter Two

Ganiloa

Life among the Aradas was simple. They had mastered the art of survival in their environment. They knew the savannah and the forest, and had learned the migration patterns of big animals. Their lives were adapted to the rainy and dry seasons. Their limited agriculture consisted of a few roots planted around the village, tended by the women and children. Between their hunting, herding, gathering and farming, they kept their villages well supplied. There was no need for accumulation except for one dry season at a time. In a life like this, in a society so simple, there was little room for personal ambition.

In general, young people don't think about the future, since they feel that the present is eternal. In the Arada tribe, the children were even less inclined to speculate about what their lives would become. There was no need, since they would be what their parents had been before them and their grandparents before that: hunters, gatherers and herders.

Nevertheless, Nguele was thinking about the future, not because he had some special ambition, not because he wanted to add some excitement to his life, but because his two best friends, Gaouno and Bambolo, each had a plan. One would be the king, and the other wanted to become a griot.

It was the last day of the festivities. In the same small groups in which they had come, the Aradas were heading back to their villages. Nguele was sad that their trio was going to break up, with Bambolo and himself returning to Kalame and Gaouno, to Weewa. Having nothing to add to the conversation, whenever his friends had talked about their future in the last few days, he had always felt left out. He had to come up with a future of his own.

He considered the possibilities and decided that when they met today, he would announce that his dream had always been to become a healer. He knew this would impress them, because the healer was probably the most powerful of the Aradas, even more powerful than the king or griot. The healer cured the sick, and more importantly, had to maintain close contact with the gods who healed through him. So the healer was also a priest. That was it! He was going to become a healer, or at least that was what he'd say.

He found Bambolo and together they set out to find Gaouno among the villagers from Weewa on the other side of the sacred field. They met the older boy coming to say goodbye to them.

"Wait," Nguele said, "I have something to say. You never asked me what I wanted to be, but I've realized that I've always wanted to be a healer."

"No," Gaouno said in a determined voice. "If I become king, I want you to be a defender."

"A defender? What's that?"

They sat down on the grass and Gaouno explained. "When King Gaou-Guinou told the young men to become each other's companions, he also created a group that would defend the villages in case of attack. That was one of the functions of the companions. Each village would have a chief defender who would organize its defense."

"I've never heard of that," Bambolo said.

"No, you haven't heard about it because we haven't had conflicts with other tribes for generations, and little by little, the practice of training together and preparing to defend the villages has disappeared. Our friendly competition during the celebration of the pledge is the only thing left of this tradition. Even here at the sacred field, many companions should have been posted far away to serve as sentries. By being all together on the savannah we are very vulnerable, and if we had enemies, this would have been a logical time for them to attack. We would have been defenseless. And the young people in each village who haven't come to the sacred field should also have formed defense groups in case their villages were attacked. If I become king, I'm going to form a group of defenders for each village, and I want you, Nguele, to be the chief defender of Kalame. You're good with the spear, you're an excellent hunter, and you'll become a great warrior."

Nguele was stunned.

"I have to go now," said Gaouno. "My group is leaving."

Bambolo asked, "When will we see you again?"

"I'll talk to my father about forming the groups of defenders. If he agrees, I'll be visiting Kalame soon. I also have to check on you to see if you told the elders about the two men you saw on Gaou-Guinou's Mountain."

Gaouno placed a hand on each boy's head, turned and walked away.

"I don't like it," Nguele said.

"What don't you like?"

Nguele was surprised he'd spoken loud enough for Bambolo to hear. "I don't like this talk about becoming a warrior. I like life the way it is. I lied when I said I wanted to become a healer. I'd never thought of these things before. When I thought about the future, I only thought of myself becoming your companion and about... something else."

"What?" Bambolo exclaimed. "You've kept a secret from me?"

"Yes, I did. But you also had a secret. You never told me about the two men you saw on Gaou-Guinou's Mountain."

"You're right. I was wrong to keep that from you. Now that you know my secret, you have to tell me yours. Companions aren't supposed to have secrets."

"But we aren't companions. We're too young."

"We are," Bambolo agreed, "but the only thing we haven't done is to take the pledge, and we can do that any time we want. Come with me."

They walked to a secluded area, knelt before one another, each with his right hand on the other's left shoulder, and repeated the pledge as they had heard it a few days before. Then they chose a symbol. Bambolo was the first to scratch a circle on his left cheek. He pressed it to Nguele's left cheek, and on the line of blood, scratched his friend's skin.

"Now we're companions," said Bambolo. "So what is the secret?"

Nguele hesitated, then said, "When I think of the future, I always see myself sharing a hut with Ganiloa. I like her. It pleases me to hear her voice. When I wake up in the morning knowing that I have some chores to do with her, it pleases me. I like to hear her laugh when we fetch water at the water hole. I've always liked her, but I've never told you because I know you like her, too."

"Yes, you're right. I like her. I think she's more beautiful than Maile. But we're companions now. We can't quarrel. We must find a way to decide who will be Ganiloa's husband when we grow up."

"Nguele! Bambolo!" Eladjo was calling.

"We're over here."

Eladjo found the boys still kneeling. Noticing the circles on their cheeks, he exclaimed, "Ah, you've taken the pledge on your own."

"Did we do something wrong?" Nguele asked.

"No, many boys do it after seeing the ceremony, but it has no value for the tribe, and you'll have to take it again when you come of age. I only hope the scars on your cheeks won't be deep enough to stay. What would you do if you decided to choose other companions when your time comes to take the pledge?"

"Oh, don't worry about that," Bambolo said. "We'll always be companions."

"Perhaps. Now it's time to go. Almost everyone from Kalame has already left and we're the last group."

They joined the rest of the boys who were waiting with Bao, and tied up the remaining goats. Besides the ones that had been eaten, some animals had been offered as gifts to Aradas from the other villages.

When they reached the edge of the forest at midday, Nguele and Bambolo still hadn't exchanged one word. Bambolo was concerned with what would happen to him when he told the chief about his transgression. He was trying to decide what to say and what to avoid saying. Which was the more serious violation: not telling about the two men he had seen, or stepping on forbidden ground? He concluded that the latter was the more important, so he would mention the men without saying exactly where he had seen them.

Nguele's thoughts were different. He was thinking of Ganiloa and wondering how to determine whether Bambolo or himself would marry her.

The marchers stopped to eat and rest. Although they weren't talking, Bambolo and Nguele sat together, away from the others. Bambolo broke the silence.

"Nguele, since my father is one of the elders, perhaps I should tell him first what happened."

"No, you have to go straight to the chief."

"But he'll punish me."

"How many times has anyone been punished in the village?"

"Never, in my memory. But I know the story of a man who was sent away from the village."

"I know the story too, but that was different. That man went to work outside the village with his companion. The companion died, and he failed to bring the body back to be buried. That was very serious. It wasn't like stepping involuntarily on sacred ground."

Nguele was right. Leaving your dead companion to be eaten by wild animals was the most serious offense in the tribe. The Aradas believed that animals would find human flesh better tasting than any other meat, but a god had convinced them that it was foul-tasting and tough. If by chance an animal actually tasted human flesh, it would realize how mistaken it had been, and people's lives would be in danger if it communicated its discovery to other beasts. Thus the Aradas also believed that such an animal had to be killed immediately. This was why it was so important that a body be buried in or near the village.

This conversation reassured Bambolo. His punishment wouldn't be so terrible since his offense was not. He had started to relax when Nguele presented him with another problem.

"How are we going to decide who will marry Ganiloa?"

"Well, I haven't been thinking about that. Maybe she should decide. Let's agree that when we get to Kalame, the first one to see her has the right to talk to her first."

"Agreed."

While they were resting, Bambolo searched his memory for a clue as to which of them would stand a better chance of winning Ganiloa's favor, but no matter how many ways he looked at the question, he couldn't find an indication. She was equally friendly to both. In fact, they formed a trio of mischief makers. Whenever the boys weren't engaged in their practical jokes or doing their chores, Ganiloa was usually with them. Bambolo couldn't count the times she had tended to the cuts and bruises the boys had sustained from some daring deed in the forest or savannah. From practicing on her two patients, she had even gained some knowledge of healing herbs, leaves and grasses.

Since she liked them equally, Bambolo thought, the first to speak with her would have a serious advantage. He thought hard about a way for him to meet her first.

"If we arrive in Kalame by nightfall," he said to himself, "I won't enter the village, but I'll go straight to the water hole where the women will be filling their pots."

His thoughts were interrupted by Nguele saying, "I have an unfair advantage over you. When we arrive in Kalame, you'll be going straight to the chief, and I'll be free to look for Ganiloa. So I'll go to the chief with you, and then we'll look for Ganiloa together."

By late afternoon they had crossed the savannah and entered the wooded area beyond which Kalame stood. In another half-hour they passed Gaou-Guinou's Mountain on the left. Now on familiar ground, the boys no longer needed to remain together under the supervision of Bao and Eladjo. In a cascade of laughter, the group broke and ran toward home.

The men quickened their steps to keep up with them. Bambolo and Nguele alone kept the same pace, so they were the last to arrive at the village.

"I see her," Nguele said.

"Where?"

"Standing beside the first hut."

There she was, waiting for them. When they reached her, she asked, "Why are you the last ones? What were you doing?"

Then in the fading light, she noticed the circles on their cheeks.

"Oh, you've taken the pledge."

"Sort of," Nguele mumbled.

"But you're too young to take the pledge. You're always doing something wrong."

In spite of her words, she wasn't angry, but laughing and shoving them. Usually they would push her back, but not today.

She stopped, put her hands on her hips and asked, "What's wrong?"

Standing in the sunset, tall and slender, she wore a single piece of blue cloth wrapped around her waist and falling to her knee. The other end wound over her right shoulder, covering one breast and leaving the other bare.

"Are you going to tell me what's wrong?"

"Bambolo has to talk to the chief," Nguele replied. "Let's go with him."

At Bambolo's call, the chief came out of his hut. He was a short stocky man, already graying.

"What is it?"

The three children approached with lowered heads so the chief could touch them in greeting.

Bambolo began, "About fifteen days ago I saw two men, and they weren't Aradas."

"Were they Bakas?"

"No, they were tall."

"They must have been Kaplaous."

"I don't know. I didn't understand their language."

"That's strange," the chief said. "Some men from other tribes come around here to hunt—the short Bakas, the Kaplaous and the Congos—but they usually come to the village first. Were the two men hunting? Where did you see them?"

Bambolo hesitated briefly before answering, "On Gaou-Guinou's Mountain."

"What were you doing on Gaou-Guinou's Mountain?" the chief demanded. "Don't you know it's forbidden to go on that holy ground?"

"I was hunting for birds and I accidentally followed one onto the hill."

The chief looked pensive.

Timidly, Bambolo asked, "Are you going to punish me?"

"Yes, of course," the chief replied absently. He had never dealt with anything like this since he had become the leader of Kalame.

"What do I have to do?" Bambolo asked. "Are you going to expel me from the village?"

"Yes, yes," said the chief, still confused about what punishment to impose.

"For how long?"

"Well, I... I... I order you to walk until the sun is down. Then you will sleep outside, and you can come back in the morning."

"May I tell my mother?"

"No, you have to start now and be far away from the village by nightfall. Nguele and Ganiloa will tell your parents."

As Bambolo turned to leave, the chief warned him, "Don't go near the water hole. Some animals may be drinking there now."

The boy lowered his head and walked out of the village. It wasn't a harsh punishment. Bambolo was capable of spending a night alone in the open. He knew what to do, what dangers existed, and how to avoid them. What saddened him was the fact that he was the first Arada he knew to be punished this way. Of course, he had heard stories told by old people on clear nights during the dry season, stories of people who were forced out of the village for weeks or even months. He remembered the story of that woman, whose crime he didn't recall, who was shunned by the tribe for a very long time. He wondered whether, upon his return, no one would talk to him.

At the moment, only Nguele, Ganiloa and the chief knew about his crime; the only other person, Gaouno, was far away in his own village. And by now, his mother must know too. Were they going to tell everyone or would they keep it a secret to protect him from shame?

But Bambolo had something else to worry about now—where to spend the night. He knew it should be in a tree because at night the ground belongs to the flesh-eaters. He chose a tree whose branches criss-crossed to form a platform, and quickly made himself a bed of branches and leaves.

He lay down with his hands behind his head and let his thoughts drift toward Ganiloa. He knew that she was lost to him, for by now she would know of Nguele's intentions. How could she refuse, since the two of them had been friends for as long as he could remember? He had made a mistake. He and Nguele should have talked to her together and then let her make her choice. But now it was too late. Ganiloa would never know about his feelings.

Maybe it was better this way. Now he could concentrate on being the best griot possible, providing that his trespass didn't become common knowledge. Yes, it was better this way. And his friendship with Nguele would be safe forever.

Before falling asleep, his mind floated over the events of the last few days. He saw the griot's face, the sacred field, Gaouno, Maile... but after walking all day, he was very tired. He sank into a sleep so deep that even his dreams didn't follow.

Awakened by the first rays of the sun, he rubbed his eyes, stretched and looked around to see if it was safe to slide down the tree. He picked up a familiar scent, the scent of danger.

Often, at the height of the dry season, the savannah caught fire. Animals would run berserk in all directions to escape the burning tall grass and bushes. Bambolo looked for smoke but saw nothing. After hesitating, he slid to the ground, and still unable to figure out where the burning smell was coming from, cautiously started toward Kalame.

He was in an area where the grass was short and the trees fairly distant from each other. He ran from one tree to another, stopping at each to scan his surroundings. When he reached the wooded area surrounding Kalame, he felt more secure. Here the trees were dense and the grass reached almost to his waist. He could easily climb a tree or hide in the tall grass at the first sign of danger. He turned one last time to try to detect smoke or a stampede. Everything was calm, so he proceeded toward the village at a quick pace.

"Young man," said a voice that seemed to fall from the sky.

Bambolo stopped. "Who said that?"

"I did, up here in the tree."

Bambolo looked up and saw an old man sitting on a lower branch of a tree. He recognized him immediately as Nabo, the singer.

"What are you doing there?" asked Bambolo.

"I spent the night here," Nabo answered.

"Do you want me to help you down?"

"No, I think it would be better if you joined me up here."

What could Nabo have done to be punished, Bambolo wondered. Nabo was one of the most respected elders in the village. He was the sacred singer, very different from those happy singers who encouraged the Aradas while they labored in the fields. Nabo worked alongside the healer, maintaining contact with the gods and spirits with his songs and his drums while the healer attended the sick. What was this important personage doing in a tree looking like a baby zebra separated from its mother?

Bambolo couldn't help feeling some anger toward the chief or the healer or whoever had forced this venerable man to spend a night out of the village. An old man might not be able to climb a tree and survive, or he could easily fall prey to some flesh-eating animal.

With the agility of a leopard, Bambolo scaled the tree and sat near the singer. Then he saw that Nabo was looking in the direction of Kalame with empty eyes and tears rolling down his cheeks. However, he made no sound and his face was as stone.

The boy thought that Nabo was feeling the shame of being sent from the village, but he didn't want to ask him what he had done.

Overtaken by a wave of compassion, he put his arms around the old man's frail shoulders and asked, "How did you get up here?"

"Bao helped me up," Nabo answered. "He told me to wait for daybreak and he would come to get me."

"I'll help you down if he doesn't come," Bambolo promised.

"Thank you. You're a very nice young man, you and the other one who is always with you."

"Nguele."

"Yes, Nguele. Do you know if he escaped?"

"Escaped from what?"

Nabo turned and looked at Bambolo with an expression the boy couldn't read. It spoke of profound sadness, yet there was a question in his raised eyebrows.

"Escaped from what?" Bambolo repeated. But Nabo didn't answer. He was listening to something else.

"Someone's coming!" he said. "Prepare to run!"

"Run for what?"

"For your life!"

"What about you?"

"I have no strength to run, and my life is already spent."

Nabo was right; someone was approaching. Bambolo's keen hearing picked up the sound of a twig snapping nearby.

"Who's there?" he called.

"Me."

And Bao appeared. Bambolo leaped from the branch and ran to him.

"Bao," he whispered, "something is happening to Nabo. He's talking like his mind doesn't belong to him anymore."

"What did he say?"

"He's acting as though we're in great danger."

"We are! We're still in great danger!"

Bambolo was further confused as three people—two men and a woman—emerged from the bushes and joined them.

"Go back!" Bao urged them.

The three slipped back into the shrubbery without a word, like bodies without souls.

"Come with me," Bao directed Bambolo. "Let's get Nabo down from that tree."

Very gently they lowered the old man to the ground. Then they went to the bushes where the three had just disappeared, and Bambolo realized that there were others hiding there also. One of them, another old man, was bleeding from a wound in his abdomen.

Before Bambolo could ask questions, Bao said, "I need your help. Follow me." Without waiting for an answer, he started walking toward Kalame. At the foot of Gaou-Guinou's Mountain, Bambolo stopped.

"Bao, where are we going?"

Bao turned and again ordered, "Follow me!"

"No," Bambolo said. "We need to stop and talk. Last night when we returned from the sacred field, I told the chief that I had trespassed on this mountain without a good reason. He punished me by sending me to spend the night out of the village…"

"You spent the night out of the village? You weren't in Kalame last night?"

"Yes, that's what I said."

Slowly Bao sank to the grass.

Bambolo continued. "I realize that something happened last night. When I woke up this morning, I smelled burning, but I couldn't see where it was coming from. Then I found Nabo in a tree. I thought he had been punished like me, but there are all these other people also outside the village. And one of them is wounded. What happened last night in Kalame?"

Bao searched for words, then started slowly.

"I feel so sad that I am the one to tell you. Kalame is no longer. We were attacked last night by men like us and pink men together. I don't know how many huts are still standing in Kalame, but most were burned down. Many people were killed and many young people were taken away."

"What?" The question erupted from Bambolo's throat as loud as the scream of a charging elephant.

"Keep your voice down," Bao said calmly. "The attackers might still be around and we have lost enough people already."

"My mother, my father...?" asked the boy, tears filling his eyes.

"I don't know. I know that my parents and the healer are dead. I don't even know where my wife or my companion are."

At the word *companion*, Bambolo remembered that he also had one.

"Nguele?" he whispered. "Do you know where he is?"

"No."

"Ganiloa?"

"I don't know."

"What are we going to do?" The question wasn't directed to Bao; it was rather an expression of despair. But Bao answered anyway.

"At first, I wanted us to hide near the village and observe what's going on, but now I think I have a better idea. Go to the top of the mountain..."

"No! No!" Bambolo interrupted. "I'm not going on sacred ground again!"

"Listen, if we go near Kalame, we'll have to move from one hiding place to another to observe the whole village. That could be dangerous, since we don't know who is still there. But from the mountain, you can see the entire area without having to move."

"But I was punished for stepping on..."

"You had no reason to go there then! It's different now!"

"Let's talk to the chief about it."

Bao realized that the magnitude of the tragedy hadn't yet sunk into Bambolo's understanding.

The Arada Pledge

"Why do you think the chief is alive?" he asked. "I don't know where he is and we must bury our dead before nightfall. If we let wild animals eat their flesh, all of us will be cursed by the gods."

Reluctantly Bambolo accepted to go. When he inquired if Bao were going with him, the man answered no.

"You've been to the mountain and the gods didn't touch you. They allowed you to come back. If I go, they may disapprove and strike me or both of us. Besides, I have other things I must do. Listen to me: Go find a spot where you can see the whole village. Observe the area until the sun is in the middle of the sky. Remember that our enemies may by lying in ambush, waiting for the survivors to return. Don't make noise, no matter what you see. Be as silent as a hunting leopard. Afterwards, rejoin me where you found Nabo in the tree. We'll decide what to do next. Do not enter Kalame for any reason."

Gaou-Guinou's Mountain was covered with tall trees and thick undergrowth. Undisturbed for generations, a variety of animals lived there, some of them quite dangerous. Bambolo knew this and proceeded with great caution. With no tool to clear his path, he progressed slowly, taking about half an hour to reach the summit.

In other circumstances, he would have marveled at the breathtaking view. On one side, he could see past Kalame all the way to the water hole. On the other, he was able to see the wooded area surrounding the village, and beyond to the savannah. He would have admired the mountains on the horizon made blue by the distance. But Bambolo only had eyes for Kalame lying in ruins at his feet.

Of the fifty or so huts making up the village, fewer than a dozen were still intact. The others all showed degrees of destruction: some completely burned, some partly destroyed, others with walls still standing but roofs collapsed. In the spaces between the huts, bodies were lying motionless. Bambolo's impulse was to scream, but remembering Bao's caution, he muzzled himself with a hand over his mouth.

He remained there for several hours, watching for any movement in the village. When the sun reached the middle of the sky, he went down looking for Bao.

"Is it safe to go back?" the man asked.

"I think so. I saw no pink men, there are many dead Aradas, and after a while, I saw some people coming out of the ruins. Most of them seemed wounded."

"Very well," said Bao. "It's time to bring our people back."

"How are we going to gather them?"

"I have an idea. We'll go to Kalame and search the main hut for the sacred drum. We'll bring it to Nabo, and when our people hear Nabo's drum, they'll understand that it's safe to come back."

As they were about to enter the village, Bao advised, "Don't look at the dead. We'll return for them later. We must first get the drum."

At the partially destroyed communal hut, Bao stopped. The body of the chief lay across the threshold. They had to step around it to enter. What they saw inside brought sobs that they tried to suppress. The floor was littered with the bodies of village elders lying in grotesque positions, their robes soaked with blood.

Bao and Bambolo picked their way between the corpses to get to the area where the healer kept his materials. This part of the structure had collapsed, with the beams that had supported the roof now hanging askew. The drum was intact in its place on a post that was still standing, although it had nothing to hold up. Bao took the drum and they left the hut and the stench of death as quickly as they could. Passing among the burned huts, they looked straight ahead, trying to avoid the bodies that lay everywhere. They made no attempt to identify anyone. With the veil of tears clouding their vision, it wouldn't have been possible anyway.

They passed the outskirts of the village and went around the base of Gaou-Guinou's Mountain before they stopped. Although it was only a short walk from the village to the mountain, they were breathless and sweating as if they had been running for a long time. They sat facing away from each other, not wanting to confront the pain in the other's face. After a few minutes, Bao had his emotions sufficiently under control to speak.

"Let's go. We have a lot of work to do. Our people have to be buried before sundown."

Bambolo rose and followed Bao without a word. They walked silently for a while and then Bambolo asked, "Did you see the healer's body?"

"No, but I know he's dead. Last night, when we returned from the sacred field, I went straight to my hut where I found my mother attending my father, who was ill. He was complaining of a stomach pain. We spend a good part of the evening trying to comfort him. My wife and my mother made beverages for him to drink to make the pain go away. It wasn't working, so they asked me to go and bring the healer, and I did. He touched my father's stomach, turned him in all directions, and finally told me to go and tell Nabo to bring the sacred drum. When I woke Nabo up, he grumbled that one should not awaken an old man in the middle of the night. I explained what was happening, and we went to get the drum from the communal hut. We were almost there when the attack occurred. Hundreds of men from another tribe invaded the village, yelling and setting fire to the roofs of the huts.

"Our people ran from their huts and fled in all directions. The invaders captured as many young people as they could grab. Nabo and I ran back to my hut, but it was already in flames. Since he couldn't run very fast, I picked him up and ran out with him. I left him hiding at the edge of the village and came back to try to rescue my family. I saw the healer come out of my hut. A pink man stabbed him with a long knife. I don't know if he came out to cover my family's escape, but it was becoming too dangerous for me to stay. The whole village was burning, and our people were running, trying desperately to escape. Some young men and women were caught in huge nets held by groups of the other tribesmen. Then the pink men came with their long knives and long sticks that made deafening noise, killing the elderly and anyone who tried to resist. I was discovered and chased, but I outran those who were pursuing me. I picked up Nabo, we fled to the woods and I helped him up into the tree where you found him. A lot of our people escaped, but I don't know who or how many, except for that group you saw with me this morning, because we fled together."

"If the healer is dead," Bambolo asked, "who's going to take care of the wounded?"

"If Ganiloa is still with us, she could do it. You know that she's been helping the healer a lot lately."

When they reached the place where they had left Nabo earlier, they found that the wounded old man had died. Bao told two other men to carry the body to the village and gave Nabo the drum.

"Sit under that tree and beat the drum to gather our people."

"What rhythm should I play?"

"The rhythm of the dead."

Nabo sat, put the drum between his old legs, and slowly started to play. The rhythm was the slowest and saddest the Aradas had. It was the beat played at funerals, the rhythm that begged their ancestors to accept a new soul among them. The sound of the drum rose in the afternoon sky. If sounds could be seen, these would look like smoke, rising, twisting, curling around trees and branches, and stretching over the entire area and onto the savannah.

People started arriving, drawn to sound of the drum as if it were a magnet. They came in small groups, in large groups or alone, and all had the same end-of-the-world look in their eyes. There were wounded people; there were young girls carrying babies from other families that they had grabbed up in their flight. Old men and women leaning on young shoulders, all were coming. But Nabo was getting tired. He was too old to keep up the drumming for long.

When he stopped, Bao took advantage of the silence to tell the people, "We aren't staying here. We're going back to

Kalame. Many people are dead and we have to bury them before nightfall."

Without protesting or asking questions, the Aradas followed Bao. Bambolo, carrying the drum on one shoulder and supporting Nabo on the other, brought up the rear of the group. As they entered what had been their village, each survivor went immediately toward where their homes had stood, in search of parents, husbands, wives, children.

An eerie clamor rose from the ruins of Kalame. Screams filled the air as loved ones and friends were recognized. Bao was one of the few who seemed to have control over his emotions. He gathered a few men and they went from hut to smoking hut, picking up hunting spears. They distributed them, urging the survivors to start digging graves immediately. Amid the crying and wailing, the work began.

Like everyone else, Bambolo had run to his home. Like everyone else, he screamed when he discovered his mother's and father's bodies on the dirt floor soaked with their blood. Running to Nguele's hut, he found that his friend's parents had been slain outside their home. Unlike his own parents, who seemed to have been killed in their sleep, Nguele's father and mother had started to make a run for it. He went inside anyway. It was one of the few dwellings still intact in Kalame.

"Bambolo," a voice said the moment he crossed the threshold. It was a voice he knew too well, although coming in from the bright sunlight he couldn't see much. It was Ganiloa. She came from a corner and embraced him. They remained there for a while, grieving and sobbing softly. Eventually they came out from the hut, still holding on to each other.

"I'm going to bury my parents," he said, "and after that, I'll come back here and bury Nguele's. Where are yours? I didn't see their bodies when I passed by your hut."

"My parents are alive," she replied. But before Bambolo could rejoice at the news, she added, "They were taken away."

At Bambolo's hut—or rather, what was left of it—they found Bao already digging graves.

"What are you doing here?" Bambolo asked. "What about your own parents?"

"I'll take care of them," Bao said. "Now I need you to do something else. Nabo is tired and has stopped drumming. I want you to learn the rhythm from him and take over. We have to keep the drum beating in honor of our dead and to continue calling the survivors to come home."

"You can go," Ganiloa said. "I'll stay here and help Bao."

"No, Ganiloa. I have another assignment for you. Since you've been working with the healer, you must know how to take care of the wounded. Ask Nabo to help you. Now go, both of you."

By nightfall the work was done. All were buried, including seven tribal men who were not Aradas. They were interred in a separate grave. Some seriously wounded people were placed together in the ruin of the communal hut under the watchful eyes of Nabo and Ganiloa.

All during the burial, Aradas were still coming: by ones, by twos, by groups back to the village. But hours after the flow had stopped, Bambolo was still beating the drum. The moon was up in the sky and everything was silent except for the drum. Ganiloa left the main hut and went to join her friend.

Finally she said, "He isn't coming."

"He's coming," insisted Bambolo, and he continued beating the drum.

She waited a while longer before interrupting again. "He isn't coming."

"He *is* coming," Bambolo replied emphatically. "No one could catch him. He's too fast. He knows too many hiding places. No one can catch Nguele."

"I saw him being taken away."

The drum fell silent.

"You saw it? With your own eyes?"

"Yes."

"Tell me. Tell me how it happened."

Ganiloa took a deep breath and started.

"After you were sent away by the chief, Nguele and I went to tell your parents. We spent part of the evening together talking. Then he walked with me to my hut and I went to sleep. During the night, we were awakened by screaming. When we ran outside, we saw hundreds of strange men coming from all directions and setting fire to our roofs. As people came out of their huts, they were caught in big nets. I was so afraid I couldn't move. I stood there and saw our people being killed with clubs. Then the pink men entered the village behind the marauders. They were also killing people, but with different weapons—long knives and a stick that made a noise like thunder and pierced flesh without arrows. Most of the people they killed were old men and women, and also some young men who came out fighting. But their resistance didn't last."

"Eladjo," Bambolo interrupted. "Was he killed?"

"No, he was taken away. A pink man grabbed me. His hand on my arm infuriated me and I fought him, kicking and screaming and trying to free myself from his grasp. I got away and started running, and he ran after me. I heard someone call, 'Ganiloa, come here!' I don't know how I heard my name over the noise and confusion, but I recognized Nguele's voice. I ran toward the sound with the pink man after me. We were running behind the last row of huts overlooking the ravine. Suddenly Nguele came out from behind one of the huts with a spear. As I passed him, he threw it. Behind me someone screamed like a wounded animal. I turned around and saw Nguele being caught in a net, fighting against three men."

"What happened to the pink man who was chasing you?"

"I don't know."

"Why didn't they capture you?"

"I went down the ravine on that little path leading to the water hole and hid in the bushes. From where I was, I couldn't see the village and what was happening. But the attack didn't last long. After the noise died down, the attackers spent most of the night in the village. In the early morning they left, marching our young men and women out of Kalame. The Aradas had their hands tied behind their backs and long ropes around their necks. I saw Nguele, but I couldn't say anything for fear of being caught myself. Nguele saved my life, but we'll never see him again."

Bambolo and Ganiloa spent the night in the open, recalling their youth that had ended so abruptly. Then, overtaken by fatigue and grief, they fell asleep with the drum between them.

Chapter Three

The Footprints without Toes

The next morning, the surviving Aradas assembled in front of what used to be the main hut. There were about one hundred and fifty people sitting on the ground, waiting. They seemed to know that something had to be done, that decisions had to be made. What they didn't know was who was going to make them. So they all came: old people, young people, even babies waited before the communal hut. They were talking in small groupings, expressing their anger, fear and despair.

The destruction of their village was enough of a disaster, but the destruction of so many families was far more devastating. Not one family was unaffected. The very fabric of their society had been torn apart. The chief was dead. The healer was dead. Only a few members of the council of elders were still alive out of a group of twenty-four old men. A large number of the youth had been taken away. A village can be rebuilt, but how do you rebuild families? How do you re-weave the web of relationships that had been so violently ripped apart? How do you rebuild that sense of safety that had been so much a part of their lives?

All these questions and others had to be addressed that morning. But by whom? No one knew. No one, in fact, had summoned them. They had gathered spontaneously because decisions had to be made, including whether the Aradas were going to stay in the area or move away from it. Since no one had called for the meeting, no one knew how to start it. If fact, no one had the right to call it to order. So the groups continued talking among themselves, trying to absorb and make sense of the horrific events of two nights ago. The whole morning—in fact, the whole day—would pass in this way if Nabo hadn't had an idea. He picked up the drum and started playing. One by one, the groups fell silent and the drum took over.

When Nabo could see that all attention was on him, he stopped beating the drum and said, "My friends, we have to choose a new chief. I propose Bao." The crowd was taken by surprise. No one uttered a word.

Nabo continued, "During the attack, Bao saved my life, and he saved the lives of many of you. Then he gathered us together and directed the burial of our people who had fallen. I think that he acted like a chief, and since our chief has been killed and his sons taken prisoner, I propose that Bao replace him."

The recommendation was quite unusual because Aradas didn't choose their chiefs. When a chief died, usually his first son took over. If the chief left no male offspring or if they were considered unworthy, the council of elders would choose the next leader. There was no hurry, since the life of the tribe was so well regulated by tradition and habit that the presence of a chief was not a day-to-day necessity. Everyone in the village knew exactly how to conduct themselves.

Nonetheless, by tradition the power of the chief was almost limitless. Except for ordering the death of a villager, he could do whatever he pleased. But also by tradition, he had never found himself in the position of wielding his nearly unlimited power. The daily life of the tribe ran so smoothly that the power of the chief was used only for settling quarrels between spouses or other individuals or groups. However, in times of crisis, as at this moment, whatever the chief ordered would be obeyed.

After making his proposal, Nabo sat down. He didn't have long to wait for an answer. From one of the groupings in the rear, someone chanted, "Bao! Bao! Bao!" Like a wave, the name went through the crowd, repeated by dozens and dozens of voices.

The object of this spontaneous choice was the last person to have expected such an acclamation. Not knowing what else to do, he stood. Shouts of approval greeted him, immediately followed by questions.

"Shouldn't we warn the king?" asked a voice in the assembly.

"Are we going to leave this area?" asked another.

"Why can't we stay here?"

The Aradas were divided about what to do, and the duel of questions and answers bounced from one part of the crowd to another.

"We can't stay here! We cannot resist the terrible weapons of the pink men!"

"Yes, but this land has been good to us!"

"We should separate into two groups. One should go to Weewa, and the other to Kilou."

"The king should tell us what to do."

"Yes, Bao, send some messengers to the king."

All this time, Bao was trying to get a word in, but he couldn't be heard over the din. He made a sign to Nabo to start beating the drum again, and when silence was restored, he said, "My friends, I think the first thing I have to do is to choose a council of elders. We cannot make decisions when we're all talking at once. Let me and a new council discuss the situation and propose a solution."

Bao was a young man in his mid-twenties with well-defined muscles in his arms, shoulders, diaphragm and legs. He had developed his strong, lean body working with his companion, Eladjo, as the shepherds of a large herd of goats. Every day they had to guide the animals to new pasture, and many a night they had slept outside the village. Keeping the herd together and rounding up strays required a lot of walking and running. The strength and endurance of the two men were well known and appreciated among the Aradas. Thus, when Nabo proposed Bao as the new chief, there was no dissent.

After choosing twelve elders who would make up his council, he said to the crowd, "Go and find yourselves something to eat and bring us some, as we are hungry too."

Finding food was not difficult for the Aradas. They still had goats, cows, and a variety of roots planted nearby. Slowly the crowd started to disperse, discussing and disagreeing about what should be done. Bambolo and Ganiloa moved away with the others.

"Are you hungry?" she asked.

"No."

"Neither am I, but I have to cook something for the wounded. Do you want to come with me?"

"No," Bambolo said. "I need to be alone."

They went in opposite directions, Ganiloa toward the water hole and Bambolo toward the last row of huts before the ravine. There he looked for the hut where, according to Ganiloa, Nguele had been seen for the last time. The ravine was not very deep, just fifteen feet or so. On the other side, at a distance, was Gaou-Guinou's Mountain.

Bambolo stood there thinking about the games he used to play with Nguele and the other Arada children. During the rainy season, a fast-flowing stream ran through the ravine, carrying water from the mountain to the water hole. The children used to jump into the waist-high water and let themselves be carried downstream. At the end of the season, when the rains came less frequently, the water in the ravine receded. By the height of the dry season, the ravine was completely dry, leaving the water hole as the only source of water for the village.

The children's game would adapt to the new situation. Then it consisted of climbing down to the bedrock and back up again, hanging onto the bushes growing almost horizontally on the vertical wall of the ravine. The child who could do it fastest would be the winner. Bambolo was dreaming about those happy times and his friends, most of whom he would never see again. As he reminisced, he was instinctively climbing down, grasping the bushes as he had so many times as a child.

The rainy season had just ended. There was still a trickle of clear water flowing toward the water hole, and the bottom of the ravine was muddy. Bambolo sat on a rock and started weeping. He had wanted to be alone to reflect on the last few days and the tremendous changes that had occurred in his life. His father, his mother were no longer. He wouldn't have believed it if he hadn't seen their bodies himself. And Nguele, the other half of the Mischievous Pair—where was he now? Was he frightened? Was he injured? Was he fighting to get back to Kalame? Or was he dead?

And those pink men. What did they want? Why did they capture Aradas, and where did they take them?

Something else was bothering Bambolo. Nguele was his companion whether or not they had taken the pledge officially, and he had the circle on his cheek to prove it. The pledge bound him to bringing back the body of his companion to be buried in or near the village. How was he going to accomplish that? What would he do if the Aradas were to move out of the area? He was convinced that they would join the other two villages of Weewa and Kilou, and that it would be for the best. He didn't want to stay here, even though he had known this place for his entire life. Kalame wouldn't be the same. The sad memories would linger too long. He had decided that he would go to Weewa. At least there he knew someone: Gaouno. But he would have to make sure that Ganiloa would go to Weewa with him.

He didn't know how long he had stayed in the ravine when Nabo's drum abruptly awoke him from his reverie. He reached for a shrub to climb back up the ravine wall when he noticed something in the soft soil: tracks, many tracks. Bambolo asked himself why he hadn't noticed them before. They were human tracks, and they were everywhere. He let go of the branch and began to investigate. They were human tracks all right, and all going in the same direction—towards the water hole. Examining both banks of the little stream, he could make out the heels, the toes, and he started to figure out how many people had gone through. There must have been three or four, but there were two other sets of tracks that he didn't understand. They had the shape of a human foot, but they had no toes.

Bambolo followed the imprints downstream, and at a short distance from the water hole, where the walls of the ravine opened up and dropped to the level of the plain, he saw that the tracks turned directly away from the village. He wanted to follow them further, but Nabo's drum was insistent. Bambolo turned back towards Kalame.

The survivors were already sitting on the ground around the council of elders, who were themselves seated in a circle. After a few minutes, Bao came out of the big communal hut wearing the headdress of the dead chief. Now he had the imposing presence of a village leader. Nabo stopped playing.

Bao stood next to the circle formed by the elders and said, "My friends, those of you who wish to leave can do so. You may go to Weewa or Kilou, but we have decided that I, the chief, and the council of elders will stay. We would like some of you to remain with us, but we aren't asking you to stay against your will. Those of you who go to Weewa, tell the king what has happened. He'll decide if we should leave the area altogether, or if we can stay here and rebuild the village. Tonight we have enough huts for all of us. I would like some men to volunteer as sentries to take up positions around the village. Those who want to serve as sentries, raise your hands."

More than twenty hands appeared over the sitting crowd.

"Now," Bao continued, "I've decided to place a sentry at the top of Gaou-Guinou's Mountain."

"Sacrilege!" Nabo shouted. "It will bring disaster to Kalame!"

"We have discussed this," Bao answered calmly, "and we have decided that, under these circumstances, it is necessary for the protection of us all. But I will need a special volunteer. Who will be the sentry on Gaou-Guinou's Mountain?"

Not a hand was raised, not even among those who had already volunteered as sentries.

"I cannot force you," Bao said, "so I'll wait until one of you comes forward. Now you may go."

"Wait!" Nabo called.

By tradition, the decisions of the chief and the council of elders were final; no one challenged them. After hearing these decisions, the people would disperse silently. But this time they stayed to hear what Nabo had to say, thus giving legitimacy to his right to speak. After a tragedy of such magnitude, some traditions would have to be put aside.

"Wait," Nabo repeated. "I think we should all stay here, and the chief should send some messengers to inform the king of what has happened. Together we'll await his decision, and then we'll follow whatever he says."

"I agree," said Ganiloa from the crowd.

Another tradition fell.

Usually a child, and Ganiloa was not more than thirteen, would never be present, much less speak at a meeting. But everyone was listening.

"We should stay here," she said. "This is our home. We grew up here, and our ancestors are buried here. We should rebuild Kalame."

"And what will you do when the pink men come back?" asked a voice in the crowd. "They already know where we are."

"I don't know," Ganiloa admitted, "but maybe we should organize to defend ourselves."

"How can we defend ourselves against their terrible weapons?" someone yelled.

And then everyone wanted to talk at the same time, each person trying to shout louder than the next. Suddenly the boom of the drum silenced the commotion.

"My friends," Bao said, "as your new chief, I have done a very poor job. I didn't come before you with a clear decision. This is what I now propose. We're all going to stay here, and I'll send messengers to the king. They will travel two days to reach Weewa, and two days to return. I'll allow them a few days of rest in between. So in ten days at the most, I expect them to be back here."

Pointing to four young men, he said, "You are the messengers, and you will leave tomorrow morning. But I still need someone to serve as sentry on Gaou-Guinou's Mountain."

"I will," Bambolo said. "I'll go with your permission, and remain there as long as you want me to stay."

Bao dismissed the villagers. Bambolo found Ganiloa, who urged him to eat since he had gone without food since morning. They sat in the shade of a hut and he started eating the food she'd prepared.

"I have a question," he said. "The pink men—what do they look like?"

"Well, in all the confusion I didn't have a very good look, and their bodies were all covered."

"Covered with what?"

"Some kind of clothing. Only their hands and faces were showing. When the pink man put his hand on my arm, I looked at it. It was really pink. Then I looked at his face. It was pink, too, but mostly covered with hair. That was all I could see."

"What about their feet?" he persisted. "Because when I went to the ravine, I found some tracks. There were tracks of men, and others that have no toes. I imagine that our people tried to escape by jumping into the ravine, and they were probably followed by the pink men."

"Those are tracks of pink men," Ganiloa confirmed. "Their feet also were covered. Some people went down into the ravine after the attack, but they weren't Aradas. From where I was hiding, I could hear them, but I couldn't understand their words. They were carrying torches as if they were searching for something. When I saw the light coming around the bend, I was afraid they would see me in the bushes, so I climbed back up as quickly as I could and went to hide in Nguele's hut, where you found me. Those men were the last group to leave Kalame."

"Bambolo," said Bao, coming up behind them, "when you've finished eating, I want you to go and take up your position at the top of the mountain. I want you to stay there all day, every day. You may come down to sleep in the village at night."

"But the pink men came during the night," Ganiloa objected.

"At night we'll have sentries stationed far away from the village. They'll run back and tell us if the pink men are approaching."

"What will he eat?" asked Ganiloa. "May I bring him food?"

"No, he'll bring food with him."

"What would I do if I see pink men?" Bambolo asked.

"Nabo will give you a drum. You'll take it with you and at any sign of danger, you'll beat the drum."

"What will you do then?"

"We'll run for cover in the bushes. But if the king decides that we should stay here, we would have to make preparations to defend ourselves. We would set ambushes and traps in the pink men's way."

Bambolo said, "I wish we could capture some of them so they could tell us where they took our people."

"No," said Bao determinedly. "We wouldn't understand their language anyway. If we have the chance to kill them, we should kill them all."

Soon Bambolo was on his way to Gaou-Guinou's Mountain with the sacred drum hanging from his shoulder by a rope. When Bao had asked Nabo to make a drum for Bambolo, he was told that it takes time. A goat had to be killed, the skin had to be dried for days, and a special tree had to be found whose trunk would be the body of the drum. Since it was impossible to make a new one quickly, they decided to give Bambolo the sacred drum. But they cautioned him about its importance and the care he had to take not to damage it.

Instead of crossing the plain, Bambolo decided to go by way of the ravine again, because there was something puzzling about what he had seen there. At the bottom of the ravine, he followed the tracks upstream until he saw something even more baffling. The tracks stopped abruptly. Looking up at the ravine walls, he made out a pattern of broken branches that told him where the people had descended from the village.

And then he caught sight of a spear. Immediately Bambolo recognized it as Nguele's. Drawing it out of the bushes, he saw that the tip was covered with blood. He surmised that Nguele had wounded one of the assailants, who had then fallen into the ravine. Pink men and their tribal allies must have followed and taken the wounded man away.

Satisfied with his conclusions, he climbed the opposite side of the ravine. This was quite difficult, since he had decided to take Nguele's spear with him. Walking through the grass toward his observation post, Bambolo felt proud that his companion had fought and wounded one of the attackers. It must have been a pink man, because the raiders had left behind the bodies of the tribesmen who were killed by the Aradas. Yes, it must have been a pink man, and that's why they had come down into the ravine: to carry his body away. His companion was a hero who had been defending his village when he was captured.

With these thoughts playing in his head, he hadn't noticed that he had covered the distance between the ravine and the foot of Gaou-Guinou's Mountain. Without stopping, he started to climb. A strange feeling came over him. Was it because, once again, he was on sacred ground?

He began to feel he was not alone. He didn't stop walking, but he continued with extreme caution, watching his every step, avoiding dead twigs and lowering his head so as not to disturb any low-hanging branches. From time to time he looked in all directions. Almost to the top, he stopped suddenly. With his heart pounding, he tried to let out a scream but his voice abandoned him.

Twenty paces from where he stood, a pink man was sitting on the ground with his back against a tree. His clothing was stained brown with dried blood. Seeing Bambolo, he made a weak attempt to pull a long knife from his side. But as he tried to stand, he fell back to the ground, obviously with a broken leg.

And then, African and European, their eyes met.

Chapter Four
The Drums of Kalame

Since the departure of the messengers Bao had sent to the king, an idea had been taking shape in Nabo's head. Why shouldn't all the sentries have drums like Bambolo? In addition to the sacred drum, there were at least eight others of various sizes and shapes that the Aradas used for celebrations of marriages, births, deaths, and the coming of the rainy or the dry season. Also, their religion included dozens of gods who each had to be worshiped with a particular drum and rhythm.

Nabo's idea was to equip about twenty sentries and place them at various distances from the village. At the first sign of danger, a trail of sound would be relayed to Kalame. The first drummers should be far enough from the village to give the Aradas time to flee or to prepare a defense.

Nabo realized that it would take too long to make drums for every sentry. But if he could salvage some that had survived the fire and repair some that were partially damaged, he would save time. He went to the ruins of the main hut and after searching a while, he came out with three. The skins were completely gone and the wood had been warped by the heat, but Nabo was a skilled drum maker. He killed three goats, skinned them and put the hides out in the hot sun of the dry season. He knew that three drums were not sufficient to implement his plan; at least twenty were needed. Also needed was Bao's authorization to kill twenty goats all at the same time.

After five days in the sun, the skins seemed to Nabo to be dry enough. He repaired the drums and gave them to three of the sentries. But the first test of the alarm system almost turned into a disaster.

It happened about ten days after the attack, when the messengers were coming back. The first drummer who spotted them decided to announce their arrival. Hearing his drum the Aradas panicked and fled into the forest. It took several hours for Bao and a few others who hadn't reacted in terror to gather everyone back together. Nabo realized that something was missing from his system. The drums didn't have a language.

Later that day, when Bambolo came down from his sentry station, he found Ganiloa waiting for him at the foot of the mountain.

"The messengers have returned," she told him.

"What did the king decide?"

"Nothing."

"Nothing?"

"He said he was coming to Kalame."

"That's good," Bambolo said, thinking aloud. "He wants us to stay here. Otherwise he would have ordered us to move immediately.".

"Will you stay?"

"Yes."

This took Ganiloa by surprise. Bambolo had made it clear that he wanted to move away from Kalame. Several times he had asked her to go to Weewa with him whenever his duty as a sentry would end. What could have changed his mind?

Walking behind him on the path leading to the village, she couldn't help thinking how much he had changed. Gone were the ready smiles. Gone was his tireless energy to find something amusing to do, a new game to play. That she could understand, since it was the same for her. The tragedy that had fallen on their village had placed responsibilities on their shoulders that were far beyond their years and experience.

What she couldn't understand was that he had become so distant at the very time she needed him most. Many times she had shared with him her fear of another attack. Every time someone in her care died in the main hut, she ran to meet him at the base of the mountain to talk about her feelings of inadequacy and despair. But he listened inattentively and more than once interrupted her with questions that seemed irrelevant, such as, 'How do you mend a broken leg'? Or, 'Do you think our medicine can work on a pink man?'

She also wanted to know what was happening on the mountain, and how he felt being there alone with their ancestors' souls—not out of curiosity, but from concern for him facing the forces and mysteries roaming the Aradas' sacred place and because of her own fear. What would she do if he didn't come back one day? Would she survive the loss of her last friend? But more basically, she wondered whether he even was still a friend. In her thirteen-year-old mind, all these feelings, all these questions were arising without answers. She only knew that she felt calmer and safer with him, but her presence didn't seem to have the same effect on him.

"Bambolo," she asked feebly, "why aren't you my friend any more?"

"I *am* your friend. I will *always* be your friend!"

"But you don't talk to me anymore."

He stopped walking so abruptly that she almost bumped into him. They had reached the first huts of the village. A few seconds passed and then he started walking again, as if he had changed his mind about something he was going to say.

"Why did you stop?" she asked.

"No reason." And as if to change the subject, he added, "I wonder how long it takes to learn another tongue?"

In the village, people were talking about the panic that had occurred earlier. Some were laughing at Nabo's idea, but Bao thought it was a good one. The new chief authorized the killing of the goats, provided that it wouldn't be all at once. He ordered a group of young men to go with Nabo into the forest to cut the trees he needed for the drums. But he also asked the old man to find a way to make a distinction between friends and enemies.

As he did at the end of every day, Bambolo went to the main hut to hang the sacred drum on its post. Nabo was waiting for him.

"Come with me," the old man said, "and bring the drum with you."

Behind the singer's hut, a group was waiting for them. Bambolo recognized some as the young men who had volunteered as sentries.

Nabo sat down, put the drum between his legs and said, "You saw what happened today: Someone beat the drum and everyone ran away. It's because the drum has only one word: danger. I'm going to teach you all the rhythms I know, and then we'll give a meaning to each of them. It will take some time to train you and the others who are keeping watch now. But when I'm finished, you'll be able to talk to the village from wherever you are. As you know, the king is coming soon. What would he think if we all ran away instead of greeting him?"

From that day on, from the time the first shadows started licking away at the sun's anger, to the time they finally pushed it over the mountain range, the drums of Kalame filled the air. Every day new words were added to their vocabulary: man, group of men, Aradas, stranger, pink men, woman. It was as if Kalame was having a celebration every day. But it was quite the opposite. The Aradas were putting up their first line of defense.

Many full moons passed and the king still hadn't come.

"If he had ordered us to stay," Bao said, "all the huts would have been repaired by now."

"I don't think he cares," Nabo added.

But Bambolo had a different opinion. Even if the king had forgotten about Kalame, he was sure that Gaouno hadn't, and he wouldn't let his father forget. Actually, Bambolo was glad the king was taking his time in coming, since the delay was working in favor of his plan. He had decided to keep his awful secret from his fellow villagers. Remembering that Bao had said the Aradas wouldn't understand the pink men's tongue, he was sure that if the young chief knew, he would order the death of his captive.

But if he could talk to the king, he could explain why the pink man should be kept alive. There were so many things the

Aradas could learn from him. Bambolo knew he was taking a terrible risk. The Aradas might see him as a traitor and banish him forever. His only chance was to show to the king, in front of everyone, that he had already learned a few words of the pink man's language.

Finally the king arrived. Bambolo was sitting facing the pink man with Nguele's spear within reach. The young Arada wasn't afraid, for his hostage posed no threat to him. Although his wounds were healing and the broken leg was wrapped in a crude cast made of branches secured with a rope, the pink man was in no condition even to think of a fight. Yet Bambolo, convinced that this stranger belonged to a species as powerful as evil, considered no precaution excessive. That's why he had taken away and hidden the long knife.

Suddenly the boy stood up and listened intently. The breeze was carrying the pattern of a drumbeat. He repeated the same combination of rhythms on the sacred drum, and at the foot of the mountain another sentry relayed it to the village: armed men... large group... Aradas... king.

Bambolo had no one with whom to share his excitement and fear. He might be severely punished for having kept an enemy alive for so long. But his greater fear was that, no later than tonight, the king might order his prisoner's death. Then he would never know what had become of Nguele.

His only hope was to impress the king with the few dozen words he had learned of the pink man's tongue. It was so little that at the moment he couldn't even communicate to his prisoner the danger that was hanging over both their heads. He looked at his captive with great sadness, not because of any feelings of sympathy for the stranger, but only from concern for Nguele's fate.

A seemingly endless few hours later, Bambolo could see from his vantage point a long column of men armed with shields and spears walking towards the village. Near the end of the column, four men were carrying some kind of platform on which someone was lying.

"The king!" Bambolo said to himself. Turning to the stranger, he said, *"Émile, regarde!"* (Emile, look!)

With the help of a long staff, the pink man made a valiant effort to stand up on his good leg. He looked at the column for a while and then let himself fall heavily to the ground. Bambolo couldn't resist a faint smile. The pink man had gotten his message: No escape was possible.

When he returned to the village late that afternoon, he was surprised not to find Ganiloa waiting for him. He went to the main hut expecting to find a large gathering listening to the king, but the whole area was quiet. The people he met seemed to be going about their occupations peacefully. He hung the sacred drum in its place and proceeded towards Nabo's hut. Four men armed with spears and shields were guarding the dwelling.

"Who are you, and what do you want here?"

"I am Bambolo. I live here," he replied. Indeed, since the tragedy, Nabo had taken in both Bambolo and Ganiloa.

"Enter," a guard said. "You're expected."

"Who is expect...?"

"The son of the king."

"Gaouno!" Bambolo cried as he rushed into the hut. Sitting on the floor mat with Nabo were Gaouno and Adegba, the griot of the tribe. They both rose. Bambolo bowed in front of the old storyteller, but instead of touching the top of his head, Adegba took it in his hands and bent over until their foreheads touched in a sign of shared sorrow.

"Your pain is my pain," he whispered.

Repeating the same gesture, Gaouno also said, "Your sorrow is my sorrow," and added, "your anger is my anger." Then he took Bambolo's hand and made him sit down on the mat. For a while no one seemed to know how to start a conversation. But Bambolo sensed that something important was going to be said. Adegba and Nabo were visibly searching for words.

The uneasy silence was broken when Ganiloa entered from the back and asked, "Would you honor me by eating the food I've prepared?"

The girl placed on the mat between the men two large wooden bowls containing goat meat and sweet yams cooked in milk.

"Would you honor us by eating with us?" Gaouno asked Ganiloa. She sat and they ate silently for what seemed to be a long time.

Finally Bambolo asked, "Where is the king?"

"My father is with the defenders. They're camping outside the village."

"I have to speak to him."

"I'll tell him." Gaouno continued, "When I learned about the attack, my first thoughts were for you and Nguele. The messengers told me you were safe, but they didn't remember having seen Nguele. Now I know he's been captured. I also know that your parents have been killed."

"Nguele's parents were killed too."

"Nguele's parents? Weren't you brothers?"

"No, we were both only sons. That's why we became friends. Ganiloa also is an only child."

"And her parents?"

"Captured."

"They will all be avenged!" Gaouno declared.

It was clear to Bambolo that hundreds of armed men hadn't come from Weewa for nothing. But whom were they going to fight?

As if he had heard the thought inside the boy's head, Adegba added, "Of course, we are not strong enough to punish the pink men. But the tribe that helped them should be taught a lesson."

"Do you know which tribe it is?" Nabo asked.

"No. There are many tribes living between us and the great salty water: the Mandingos, the Ibos, the Kaplaous, the Bakas, the Congos and the Fons. The king doesn't want to strike at innocent people, so I'm here to learn which tribe was the guilty one."

"How are you going to find out?"

"By talking to people. I want to know how the attackers were dressed, how they wore their hair, whether they painted their bodies and if so, what color, what design, and whether they had a war cry."

"And we thought," added Gaouno, "since Bambolo was the first to see them on the forbidden mountain…"

"I was already punished for that!" Bambolo interrupted. "I told the chief as I promised you, and he sent me away…"

The griot put his hand on the boy's mouth.

"Quiet," he said softly.

"No one is here to punish you. I know the whole story from Gaouno and Bao. It's true that you violated sacred ground, but you have also seen the intruders. You were sent away for one night, the very night of the attack. Otherwise, you could have been killed or captured. I say that the gods have their eyes on you. You are chosen."

"Me? Chosen? To do what?"

The griot shook his head. "No one knows. Maybe they will teach you the languages of animals or how to interpret signs in the sky or on the ground. Maybe they will give you healing powers. The gods will tell you in due time."

"Do you mean that they'll speak to me?" Bambolo asked apprehensively.

"Not as I speak to you. Don't be frightened. If you are chosen, as I think you are, it's because the gods like you. They've already forgiven you a trespass for which they have punished others."

Gaouno was listening, but he had come to talk about something else. He knew from experience that Adegba could speak about the gods until the next sunrise. He respectfully stopped the griot by suggesting that he ask about the two men Bambolo saw on Gaou-Guinou's Mountain.

"Yes, describe them to me."

"I was hiding," Bambolo began, "so I didn't have a good look, but I could tell that they were tall. Each one carried two or three very thin spears."

"And their clothing?"

"It covered them from the neck to the knee, it was loose and was the color of the red earth around the water hole… And yes, their hair was the same color and braided. It looked as if they were carrying big red spiders on their heads."

"Do you recall any word from their tongue?"

"No."

"What about you, young woman, what can you tell me?"

Ganiloa was startled. She had been completely ignored up to that moment, and this was fine with her. Not knowing how to behave in front of such important people, she would have preferred to eat silently and to listen.

"Well," she said shyly, "I don't want to contradict Bambolo, but the people who burned the village were wearing only loin cloths. However, their hair was as he described it."

"Anything else?"

"No. But some were killed in the attack. The Aradas who buried them should be able to tell you more."

"I'll talk to them in the morning," Adegba said. "Now it's time for me to rest." Then turning back to Ganiloa, he added, "You're a very good cook. You are also very pleasing to look at."

"You are easy to please," she answered, embarrassed but flattered.

Gaouno decided to speak longer with Bambolo. He directed the four armed men to take the griot back to the king's camp. They formed a seat with their spears and helped Adegba climb onto it.

Before being carried away the old man instructed Bambolo, "Ask the gods to send you a sign."

"What is a sign?" the boy asked.

"It can be anything, anything unusual."

"If I see one, I'll tell you so you can interpret it."

"Young man, if the gods give you a sign, it's because they want *you* to be the interpreter, not me."

The moon was absent among the stars. From time to time the distant roar of a lion or the laugh of a hyena tore the silence. It was the dangerous hour when the flesh-eaters were feeding.

Gaouno and Bambolo didn't feel sleepy, so they decided to walk through the silent village.

"Do you believe I'm chosen?" the boy asked.

Without hesitating, Gaouno answered that he believed so.

When they reached the edge of the village, they could see camp fires at a short distance on the plain. The presence of the defenders gave Bambolo a sense of security he hadn't felt for a long time.

"Would you kill a man?" he asked Gaouno.

"If I have to."

"Aren't you scared?"

"Yes, I'm scared of killing and I'm scared of dying. But I have the greater fear that we may be attacked again. Today it's Kalame; tomorrow it could be Kilou, after that Weewa. Our only chance is to destroy those who led our enemies here. We can't kill them all, but they'll learn to fear us more than they fear the pink men."

"How long will it take to know who they are?"

"Not long. What will take time is to know where they are, how many they are and if they have pink men living in their villages. We have to know these things before we move from here. My father has sent spies in all directions, and we're waiting for their return."

"But," Bambolo asked, "suppose they're better fighters than we are?"

"They probably are. But even a cornered zebra will fight a lion. We've trained the defenders as well as we could. And we'll surprise our enemies as they surprised us. That's why we have to know every obstacle from here to their village."

Long after the king's son had gone back to his camp, Bambolo stood looking at Gaou-Guinou's Mountain. Someone there knew all the answers. The success or failure of the whole project might depend on getting them out of him.

"What are you doing alone in the dark?" Ganiloa took his hand. "Come," she said, "there's a soft mat waiting for you."

"What about you? Did Nabo's snoring keep you awake?"

"No. I want to talk to you about the griot."

"Do you believe what he said about me?"

"Yes. But I want to tell you what he said *before* you came into the hut. He said you will become a great griot. He feels he's too old to go back to Weewa. He's planning to stay in Kalame until his death to teach you."

After each sentence, Ganiloa paused, waiting for a reaction from her friend, but he said nothing. His dream of becoming a storyteller was still alive but buried so deep under new worries and pressing responsibilities that the last time he had thought of it was when he was lying in a tree the night of the attack. Seeing that Bambolo didn't react, Ganiloa changed the conversation.

"Do you think you are chosen?" she asked.

"I hope so."

"Have you seen some signs?"

"I think so. But don't ask me to tell you. I must tell the king first."

Entering the hut they could hear Nabo's heavy breathing. They searched for their places in the dark on either side of the sound and lay down.

Not to wake up the old man, Ganiloa whispered, "I like the griot. He's very wise, but he also makes people laugh. He arrived on a platform, carried by four men…"

"I saw him from the mountain, but I thought it was the king."

"A lot of us thought so. We went and knelt around the platform. Adegba was so surprised, he tried to stand up, lost his balance and fell, taking the four men with him. We rushed to help them up, but Adegba was struggling, pushing us back and exclaiming, 'I am not the king! I am not the king!' When he finally got up with dirt in his hair, he pointed the king out to us, saying, 'This is Gaoube, King of the Aradas.' "

"What did the king do?"

"He was laughing."

Remembering these two illustrious individuals trying desperately to regain some composure, Ganiloa started to giggle. She tried to stifle it but the laughter escaped through her nose and between her fingers. Infected by the contagious sound, Bambolo couldn't help giggling too. Soon Nabo was awake and upset, telling them to leave and not to return until they were finished making noise.

The two youngsters ran out laughing, followed by Nabo's grumbling something about respect for an elder's sleep. Outside, they still had trouble controlling their silliness. The giggling would subside and start anew again and again. They were no longer laughing at the griot; they were enjoying a familiar sound they hadn't heard for so long. It was the sound of friendship, of happiness, the signature of the mischievous children they used to be, that they still might be deep inside. Suddenly, for no apparent reason, they both stopped at once. Maybe they were ashamed to be laughing at a time like this. Maybe they felt that a voice was missing. They sat against the hut looking away silently. When Nabo's breathing signaled that it was safe to go back, they tiptoed in and lay down on both sides of the sleeper.

"Bambolo," Ganiloa whispered in the darkness, "am I really pleasing to look at?"

"Yes."

Bambolo had decided to keep his secret a little longer. If he could get enough information from Emile, he was sure he could easily convince the king to keep the pink man alive. He knew that communication would be difficult but far from impossible. His vocabulary in Emile's language was at first centered around his hostage's needs: food, hunger, thirst, water, pain and everything they could see, feel or hear, such as village, tree or wind. Moreover, using gestures and drawings on the ground, they had advanced far beyond that basic level.

Bambolo knew that sooner or later his prisoner would try to escape, and to do that, he would have to go back the same way he had come. Thus, the information Bambolo was seeking was precisely Emile's escape route. Believing that this strange creature was too smart to reveal such an important part of his plan, Bambolo proceeded indirectly and slowly. Impatience could compromise everything.

It's true that Emile was thinking of his escape, but it was just that—a thought. Too many elements were missing, too many questions unanswered for him to formulate a plan. It was clear that the little savage could have killed him but did not. He could have let him starve but did not. He could have watched him die of his wounds but did not. Why? That no other member of the tribe had come near his refuge seemed to indicate that the boy was taking care of him in secret. Again, why? Emile also realized that his broken leg would leave him with a serious limp. Escaping without help was out of the question even after it healed. Without weapons, without a good understanding of the environment, he wouldn't even know what to eat, or how to avoid being eaten himself.

How easily could he recruit Bambolo as a helper? For him, the boy represented a form of life just a few steps above the small monkeys frolicking in the canopy over his head. Many times he had heard stories about natives mistaking strangers for gods. Bambolo could well be fascinated by his hair, his beard and the color of his skin. As did any member of a conquering group, he saw respect and even love in the vanquished's fear and behavior to ensure survival. But also he believed that a native was by definition a savage. Maybe he was being fattened for some ritual feast. His only way to find out was to improve the boy's communication skills.

Conversations came to occupy the better part of the time they spent together, each one trying to lead the talking toward what he wanted to know. In this fencing with words, Bambolo clearly had the advantage. Not given any credit for intelligence, he could use any new word he learned to extract information without raising Emile's suspicion. In practicing the word *river*, for instance, he would ask the pink man how many he had crossed to get to Kalame, giving the impression that he wanted a practical application for the numbers he had learned a few days before. After one full month of this exercise, Bambolo was ready to face the king.

Gaouno came to Nabo's hut late the same night, woke up the singer and Bambolo, and brought them to his father's encampment. The king was sitting with an imposing group of dignitaries: Adegba, Bao, Kalame's elders and some people from Weewa. The supreme chief of the Aradas had accepted to see the boy only at the insistence of his son. In fact, among King Gaoube and his councilors, the debate was so intense that the presence of Gaouno and his friends wasn't even noticed.

One of the king's advisors was saying, "If we encounter pink men, we're doomed. We don't know if our weapons will have any effect on them."

"They will!" Bambolo stated as loudly as he could.

Gaouno put his hand over Bambolo's mouth and whispered, "Let me speak." Approaching the king, he said, "Father, this is my friend who wants to speak to you."

"Young man, come forth."

Bambolo had imagined the king as fat as Gaou-Guinou had been described to him, or as old as the griot. He was wrong on both counts. Although the king's body was partially covered with an ample white robe, it was obviously slender and muscular. He had piercing eyes tempered by an expression of kindness, and a readiness to smile hovered at the corners of his lips. He was visibly amused by this young man who had sought to address him. Bambolo was so nervous he couldn't move from where he stood. The king got up, came to him and put his hand on the boy's head. Only then did Bambolo realize he hadn't bowed. He regained some composure when he heard the griot say,

"My King, this is the chosen one."

"Oh? My son has told me a lot about you. What do you want to tell me?"

"My King," Bambolo began in initiation of Adegba, "the tribe of the Kaplaous was the one that helped the pink men attack us. They live in a place called Bakou where the earth is red. They walked eleven days to get here, and they came from the direction of the sunset. To reach Kalame they crossed three rivers. The second one is the biggest and is full of hippopotamuses and crocodiles."

The king took a circular look at his aides as to see if anyone else were as surprised as he was.

"Is there really a place called Bakou?" he asked. No one answered. Turning back to Bambolo he asked, "How do you know?"

This was the question the boy was waiting for. His answer was going to determine Emile's fate and his own.

"Wait!" It was Adegba's voice. "Did this information come to you in a dream?"

"No."

"Did it come to you on the forbidden mountain?"

"Yes."

"My King, he cannot tell you how the information was revealed to him. The mountain is taboo. No Arada should know what is happening there. This young man has been chosen. He can go on the mountain and no harm will come to him. But if he tells anyone what he has seen there, he would violate the taboo."

"Of course, you're right," the king agreed. Then turning back to the boy, he asked, "Anything else?"

"Yes. There are five pink men living near Bakou, on a small hill overlooking the village."

"We will be massacred!" said a voice in the assembly.

"We *have* been massacred," Bao answered, "and we will be again, unless we do something. The Kaplaous must be punished, but it is more important to kill these five pink men to prove to the Kaplaous that these men are not invincible."

"And suppose they are?"

"If they were, they would have attacked us at any time. But they attacked us in our sleep. This means they were not sure of winning if we were awake. Besides, the chosen one just said that our weapons can kill them."

Bao sat down and a silence fell on the assembly. Everyone was looking at the king, who was pacing while he considered everything that had been said.

"I don't want to doubt the words of the chosen one," he said finally. "It would be an insult to the gods. But I cannot base my decision on that alone. It's premature to speak of the Kaplaous as if they were the attackers. Let's wait for the spies to come back, and we'll see if their findings confirm what we've heard here. That's all."

A few days later, the spies started to return. From time to time, and coming from different directions, Bambolo heard the same message: two men… Aradas. On the new drum Nabo had made especially for him in order to keep the sacred drum in its place, he transmitted the message to the village. He was growing apprehensive. Would the spies confirm the information he had given to the king? Could Emile have lied to him? Bambolo realized how shameful this would be for him, but also for Adegba and even Bao and the king, who had publicly referred to him as the chosen one.

There was no conversation with Emile that day. Bambolo was too busy reviewing in his mind the events of the last few days. He sat alone, lost in his thoughts, interrupted only by the drum signals he had to relay to Kalame. He would have preferred to tell everything to the king and let him decide what to do with his hostage. Now it was too late. The responsibility was his, and his alone. How long could he carry the weight of this secret?

"The gods have chosen me, and they will help me," he said to himself.

Noticing that Bambolo was not in a talkative mood, Emile kept quiet all day long, but the boy's silence, as well as the sporadic drumming, worried him. He knew the drums were announcing something, but what? Could the drums be talking about him?

At nightfall, when Bambolo was ready to leave, Emile put on a brave face with a smile that was barely visible under his facial hair and said cheerfully, *"Bonsoir, mon ami."*

"Bonsoir, Émile," the boy answered absently, leaving the pink man to sleep on his anxiety.

When he reached Nabo's hut, the old singer was waiting to take him to Gaoube, who had sent for the boy. They rushed to the king's shelter and found the same group of dignitaries sitting around. Nabo took Bambolo's arm and approached Gaoube.

"My son," the king said, "I'm glad I didn't doubt your word. We know for sure now that we were attacked by the Kaplaous from the village of Bakou. Everything you told us was confirmed: the distance, the rivers, the red clay, the pink men—everything. But there is one question I must ask. Do you really believe that our weapons can harm them?"

"Yes," the boy answered firmly. "They can be wounded, they can bleed, they can be killed by our weapons, just like us."

"Then we march at dawn," Gaoube decided.

Bambolo turned to Gaouno, who was sitting beside his father.

"Are you going with them?" he asked.

"Yes, I'm one of the commanders," Gaouno said proudly. "I'm the one who will give the signal for the attack."

"If you die in battle, it will be like the day Nguele didn't come back."

"I'll be back. And our war cry is *Nguele!*"

Chapter Five

The Centaur

Nguele was already awake when the first rays of sunshine filtered through the cracks in the door. As happened every morning, it was the loud galloping outside his hut that woke him As he did every morning, he went to the small window to watch the old man play on that stripeless zebra. They would go in all directions on the empty field that extended from the group of small huts with their straw roofs to the big house where the pink people lived.

Nothing in this place made sense to Nguele. All the animals he had seen so far, even some birds, seemed to be obedient to humans. He couldn't understand why this old man was running back and forth on this beast, going nowhere. But there was something he understood very well, and it was that the old man and all the others living in the huts, including himself, belonged to the pink people, just as goats belonged to the Aradas.

In the few months that he had been living in this place, the old man had come to his hut every day after his morning ride, bringing food, nurturing him back to health and patiently teaching him the pink people's language. Thus the boy had learned the little he knew about his new environment.

Nguele's body was recovering well. His left ankle, where the chain had cut into his flesh, was almost completely healed and walking had now become painless.

His stomach had relearned how to retain food and he no longer looked like a skeleton. His strength had been restored, but from time to time he could still feel the rolling of the floating village.

He was vaguely aware that the old man had saved his life, but he wasn't feeling any gratitude. Not because he knew that he was brought back to health just to endure more suffering. Not because he was angry and rebellious. Not even because he was so sad. But because there was no room in his mind for anything but fear. The faintest noise startled him and his sleep was crowded with nightmares.

Two recurring dreams haunted him. Some nights he would see himself running desperately in the savannah, looking for a tree to escape from a pride of lions closing in on him. Other nights, a crocodile would grab him by his left ankle while he was attempting to cross a river.

His days were no better. Whenever he called on his memory to bring him the sound of Bambolo's laughter or the image of Ganiloa's smile, he only got back the horror of the last few months, from his capture up to the day he had landed in this place. Everything he saw or heard or smelled evoked the vivid images of one or another episode of his ordeal.

Now the dawn was setting the horizon on fire, profiling the mountains against an orange sky. It looked like the first morning of his captivity, the day after the attack on Kalame.

With five other Aradas, he had spent the night in a net hoisted by a rope up to a tree branch. Pressed against each other, twisted in painful positions, they hadn't even been able to sleep, much less escape. In the morning, a beautiful morning like this one, with the grass and foliage shining with dew that the sun had not yet licked away, the net was brutally dropped to the ground. Then the Aradas were taken one by one to have their hands tied behind their backs, and they were joined together by a long rope that looped around their necks. Dozens of such groups were held hostage throughout Kalame.

Nguele remembered looking around to find a familiar face. Of course, he knew everyone in the village, but he had thought that the sight of a close friend or a family member would bring him a ray of hope. Not far from where he was, the attackers were untying a man from a big tree. It was Eladjo. Bao's companion had spent the night on his feet, his back against the tree and his arms tied backwards around it. When the rope was cut, he fell helplessly on his face. Nguele turned away; he didn't want Eladjo to know that he had seen his humiliation. It was then that he realized how hopeless their situation was.

This daytime nightmare was suddenly interrupted by the sound of a loud gong. People started coming out of the huts. Men, women and children of both sexes silently assembled in a long single file. A dozen men, two of them pink, came and led everyone away. Soon they all disappeared into the surrounding fields.

Nguele knew that someday before long, the gong would call him to get in line. He would then join the others, go wherever it was that they went, do whatever they did all day and come back at sundown as exhausted as they looked every night. How long did they have to walk? However far, it couldn't be as long and as painful as the march the Aradas endured from Kalame to the big salty water. His mind again started to wander.

It had been several days into the journey. The long column of Aradas and their captors had reached a wide river. Since it was late in the afternoon, they were ordered to stop for the night. The children were untied and given gourds so they could fetch water for everyone. After serving those with whom he shared the same rope, Nguele took advantage of that brief freedom of movement to look for Eladjo. He filled the gourd a second time and headed towards the front of the column where he expected to find his mentor, but he looked in vain. On the way back to his place, he heard his name whispered.

"Nguele!"

It was Ganiloa's father. The boy approached and lifted the gourd of water to the man's lips, but he had already drunk.

"Have you seen my wife?" he asked.

"No."

"Look for her and bring her water every chance you get. She is with child."

"If I can, I will."

"Have you seen Ganiloa?"

"Ganiloa isn't here. She wasn't captured."

"Are you sure?"

"I helped her escape!"

Gazing at the boy, the man was unable to stop the tears from streaming down his dusty face. Nguele walked away not knowing if he had caused more pain or given some relief. He had taken only a few steps when he heard his name again.

"Nguele, tell that to my wife if you find her. The gods will reward you."

"Ta gueule!" a pink man roared.

The Aradas had heard this expression many times since their capture. Every time they spoke to one another, every time a child cried, a pink man would scream, *'Ta gueule!'*. They had to conclude that it meant to keep quiet.

That night, as they did every night during their long trek, the Aradas slept on the ground with their hands tied behind their backs and a rope around their necks.

The door of the hut squeaked open and the old man appeared on the threshold. As usual, he was bringing food, the same yellow mush mixed with little bits of salty fish. Setting the bowl on the ground, he complemented his words with exaggerated gestures to help Nguele understand what he wanted.

"Show me that ankle," he indicated to the boy. Then gently he massaged the boy's calf and leg, asking from time to time, "Hurt?" He had Nguele walk and jump, and was visibly satisfied with the examination.

It was about noon when he came back with some clothes. After helping Nguele into these unfamiliar garments, he motioned for the boy to follow him. They crossed the empty field where the old man had been riding earlier. When they had gone around to the back of the big house, Nguele noticed many other smaller houses that he'd been unable to see from his hut. The old man took him to one that was long and narrow. Inside were many of the same kind of beasts he rode every morning. The man picked up a brush and gently started to stroke one of the animals. Then he gave the brush to the boy and indicated to him to imitate what he had done. In the course of the afternoon, the boy learned what and how to feed the beasts, how to give them water and how to clean them. By then it was clear to him that this would be his chore.

That evening when Nguele was about to fall asleep, he heard voices outside his window, hundreds of voices. He got up to look. The field was filled with people. Soon many campfires were lit and the smell of food filled the air. It looked like a joyous occasion because some people were singing to the rhythms of drums. The pink people came out of their house and sat on the grass to listen.

His eyes searched the crowd for the only person he knew—the old man—but he couldn't see him. His mind drifted again to the recent past. He remembered another crowd in which he was desperately looking for someone.

When the Aradas and their captors reached the great salty water, they were herded into a vast enclosure surrounded by armed guards. At the entrance the bodies of two dead men lay in the dirt wet with their blood. The message was clear: No disobedience or rebellion would be tolerated. Pushed by the pink men and their helpers, the Aradas were quickly scattered among the thousands who were already there.

Nguele hadn't been able to find Eladjo since they'd left Kalame, but he knew he was there. Now that his hands were free and he wasn't tied to anyone, he set out to search for his friend. Finding an Arada in the crowd was hard enough; finding a specific one was almost impossible.

When he did see a familiar face, he asked, "Have you seen Eladjo?"

Some responded that they had seen him walking here or there, while others didn't even know he'd been captured. Finally the boy bumped into Ganiloa's mother, who was herself looking for her husband. Together they continued their search, but at the end of the day, tired and discouraged, they gave up.

The next morning they resumed looking and finally found Ganiloa's father, but the three were together for just a few hours. When the pink men started loading people in floating villages, Nguele watched helplessly as his friend's parents were taken to two different villages. Soon it was his turn. At the top of the wooden ramp extending from the shore to the floor of the village, he turned to look at the land one last time. To his relief he saw Eladjo climbing the same ramp. But before he could say anything, he was pushed on board and down a few steps, forced to lie on his back and then chained by the feet. In this position, the only thing he could see in the dark was that opening through which the human cargo was being loaded. When the operation was finished, the pink people climbed out and closed the hatch. Nguele opened his eyes as wide as he could but couldn't see his hand in front of his face. He started shaking so forcefully that the chain rattled.

"Eladjo!" he called in the dark.

"Who said my name?"

"It's me, Nguele!... I am frightened... I am frightened..."

That fright never left him all through the voyage. The constant motion wouldn't let him forget where he was. At times the rolling was so violent that salt water poured in on the captives through holes in the sides or cracks in the deck above.

At times, if the day were calm, the captives were taken outside one small group at a time. Then they were directed by gestures to walk and jump. The first time Nguele went up he saw that everything was blue, both the flat water and the curved sky. Seized by dizziness, he fell to the deck. From that day on, he threw up every time he ate. As the vomiting became increasingly painful, he ate less and sometimes not at all.

Nguele had another problem. The chain had cut into his flesh and the resulting infection caused his left ankle to swell to twice its normal size. It became more and more excruciating to stand up, let alone walk and jump.

One day the hatch opened, some pink men entered and proceeded to unchain the captives. Nguele noticed something different. Usually they would unshackle just one small group at a time, and only when that group was brought back and securely chained would the next one be freed. But this time, row after row of the captives were led up the steps. This could only mean one thing: Wherever it was, they had arrived.

As soon as the chain fell from his ankle, Nguele tried but couldn't stand.

"Eladjo, I can't walk!" he cried.

"I'll carry you, little brother." And before the pink men could react, Eladjo wiggled his way through two rows of captives, bent down and gently picked up Nguele in his arms. The boy was burning with fever.

They came out into a day that was in its last hour. But after so long a time in almost complete darkness, even a setting sun can be blinding. Nguele closed his eyes and pressed himself against Eladjo's chest until he was lowered to the ground. Opening his eyes, he saw that the captives had again been herded into a large enclosure guarded by armed men. Night came, and the unfortunate crowd, with few exceptions, lay down on the ground and fell asleep.

Awakening in the morning light, Nguele took a sweeping look at his surroundings. The enclosure was near the big salty water, and in the other direction was a village, an immense village many times the size of Kalame. The dwellings were huge and lined up in rows. The spaces between the dwellings gradually became filled with people coming and going in all directions.

There was also a crowd gathering outside the enclosure. They were looking at the captives with obvious interest, pointing a finger at one, laughing at another. From time to time, some pink men would come inside the fence, grab someone and take him or her out of the pen. Nguele shook Eladjo, who was still sleeping. The man woke up and observed the scene for a while. Two tears silently rolled down his cheeks.

"Why are you crying?" the boy asked with alarm.

"Because we're going to be separated and it pains me to leave you. You're hot with fever, and you can't even stand up. Who is going to help you? I feel like I'm leaving my companion to be eaten by wild beasts."

They sat on the ground waiting for the fateful moment. From time to time the boy took a long look at his friend's face as if to engrave it in his memory. The moment came around noon.

Two pink men spotted Eladjo and entered the fenced area to take a closer look. They made him stand up, studied him from all sides and felt his muscles. One of them parted his lips and peered into his mouth, pushed up his lids to inspect his eyes and, obviously satisfied, they escorted him out of the enclosure.

Sitting in the dirt, Nguele wiped away his tears so he could have a final look at the last person who knew his name. Then, overcome with grief, hunger, fever and pain, he lost consciousness.

He woke up in this hut with a bandage around his ankle, his fever gone and the face of that old man leaning over him. He didn't know how long he'd been there.

Bayon de Libertad never bought slaves. It was against his policy and the policy of his father before him. Together they had run the Bréda plantation for more than fifty years. Bayon had taken over fifteen years ago at the death of his father.

They were not the plantation's owners. The property belonged to a French aristocrat who never set foot in the colony. Apart from sending part of the profits to the count, Bayon managed the place as he pleased.

He was considered a good master by his slaves. No corporal punishment, no torture ever took place on the plantation. Unlike the other slave owners, he allowed two hours of recess during the day and one day of rest every week. This policy was not based on humanitarian concerns, but for practical reasons.

Bréda was a huge plantation with hundreds of slaves. The young would mature, bear children and provide Monsieur de Libertad with a steady supply of laborers. He was convinced that the Creole Negro, born in the colony, was a better investment than the 'Bossale' Negro freshly arrived from Africa. Born in captivity, the Creole would learn the ways of the white man, his language and the plantation's works as he grew up. On the contrary, the Bossale had everything to learn. Added to that, he was unpredictable and sometimes rebellious.

In 1788, the French colony of Saint-Domingue was peaceful and unbelievably prosperous. The "great planters" belonged to the high society that ruled the colony, and their life was simple and easy. They dressed in the latest French fashion, which for the men included wigs, embroidered overcoats, silk shirts, high heeled shoes with bows and, of course, their most prized possession, the sword. The colonial assembly was exclusively composed of members of their class.

Monsieur de Libertad was contented with his life. Contrary to some impoverished noblemen who came to Saint-Domingue to amass a quick fortune and return to France with a refurbished coat of arms, Bayon was exactly where he wanted to be. He had no desire to be seen in noble company in Paris or to be received by the king. The governor of Saint-Domingue was good enough for him.

This explained in part his leniency towards his slaves. He had no need to work them to death as was done on other plantations where the productive life of the average African didn't extend beyond seven years. Again, it wasn't a matter of principle, for he maintained friendly relations with planters who practiced torture and he wouldn't dream of bringing the issue before the colonial assembly. As a matter of fact, this particular Sunday he had invited his peers for a picnic and entertainment.

It was a lazy December afternoon. Nature seemed to have taken a breather as the sun had already spent its heat for the day, the clouds had retired beyond the horizon, not a breeze danced with the palm trees, not a bird provided the music. Only a chicken hawk was slowly cruising in circles high above in the sky. The busiest place at Breda was the big house's kitchen where an army of servants were preparing for the gathering under the watchful eyes of Placide and Isaac, two young house slaves in their early twenties who served as the butlers of the de Libertad mansion.

The guests started arriving at around three-thirty. Some came on horseback and others in ornately decorated horse-drawn carriages. A flight of domestics went to meet them and secure the animals. The host and his wife, Hortense; his son, Michel; and his daughter, Gaële, were waiting for them on the front lawn where several large blankets were spread. Between the blankets were low tables loaded with chicken, guinea fowl, pork and beef; mangoes, papayas, melons and pineapples. There was no shortage of drinks, either, from the finest French wine to the crudest white rum distilled right on the premises. The conversation was lively and idle.

"Monsieur de Libertad," one of the guests inquired, "I heard that you bought yourself a Bossale?"

"And a half-dead one, too!" Hortense de Libertad commented.

"Calm down, calm down! I didn't buy him, my coachman did."

"How so?"

"Well, I was in town on business," de Libertad started to say while getting to his feet, which seemed to indicate a predilection for public speaking. He was a fairly large man approaching forty, who could have been called fat if he were not so tall. His hair was the color of ripe oranges and, with the help of the white rum, a reddish glow was creeping up his face.

"What business was that?" his wife asked. A few suppressed giggles were heard among the guests. Rumor had it that he was keeping a mistress in Cap-Français, the most important city of the colony.

"Don't interrupt, woman," he said with a condescending smile. "As I was saying, I was in town on business. My coachman took me to Seashore Street to see if the ships I needed had arrived. I had two boatloads of sugar and one of mahogany to send to Bordeaux. While I was talking to the port master, my coachman wandered into the nearby slave market. A few hours earlier, a slave ship had dumped a load of Negroes who were quickly sold except for half a dozen rejects. Among them was a boy lying motionless, his nose in the dirt. My coachman ran back to ask me to buy him. I refused, saying that I had nothing to do with Bossales."

"But you bought him anyway."

"No, let me finish. He asked me for permission to buy him."

"What? A slave buying a slave?"

"I freed him a few months ago. So I asked him if he knew how much a slave costs. He answered that this one couldn't cost very much, since he was going to be thrown into the sea. I went to help him bargain with the auctioneer, and he got the Bossale for the price of three chickens."

A roar of laughter greeted the end of the story.

As the company continued eating and drinking, the manager of a neighboring plantation asked, "Hey, Bayon, what do you have for entertainment?"

The host made a sign to Placide, who rang a large bell hanging in front of the mansion. Imitating Monsieur de Libertad, every head turned towards the empty field between the mansion and the slaves' huts. They had also come out to watch, and maybe to dream that they were as well fed as the family dogs.

What was it going to be? First Isaac stepped forth and recited a few of La Fontaine's fables. The whites were amused to hear a Negro narrate them by heart and with perfect French diction. It was for them the sign of a superior intelligence... in a Negro, of course.

Following that, Gaële sang three songs very popular in Paris the year before. Then at a gesture of his master, Placide rang the bell again. What now? A silence fell on the audience. A buzz of approval arose when a black horseman, mounted on a black horse, entered the field.

"The centaur! The centaur!"

The horseman hurled his mount at full gallop towards the big house. At a mere ten paces from the group he pulled on the reins. The horse stopped sharply and rose on its hind legs almost to a vertical position, then slowly made a complete about-face. When its front legs touched the ground, it broke into a trot until it reached the center of the field. There a series of pirouettes dazzled the onlookers. Next the rider took a few mangoes and ears of corn from a sack hanging from the saddle and tossed them into the air one by one. Using zig-zag maneuvers, he caught most of them before they fell to the ground. Those he missed, he picked up afterwards hanging from the side of his horse galloping at full speed. At the end of the spectacle, the rider rode up to the audience, dismounted and bowed in response to the applause.

"It's your coachman, isn't it?" one of the guests asked.

"Yes, it is!"

"Isn't he rather old for this kind of exercise?"

"Not at all. I keep my slaves longer than you do, remember?"

"Is he the slave who bought a slave?" a woman asked.

"He's the one, but let me remind you that I freed him a few months ago."

"Why?"

"Why? Because he can't go anywhere. What do you think the old fool can do outside of this plantation? His two sons, Isaac and Placide, are here. They're house servants and I'm not about to free them. So he'll stay in Breda, taking care of my horses, my cows and my donkeys. The only difference is that now I give him some money from time to time."

This was casually said in front of the horseman and his two sons. But they appeared to have heard nothing. The old man continued to wear the same smile he had when he had accepted the spectators' applause. Only Gaële de Libertad seemed to have been embarrassed by the remarks. She lowered her eyes and her face reddened.

Noticing that the old man was still standing at attention holding the horse's bridle, Bayon de Libertad waved him away. The horseman had only gone a short distance when his master called him back.

"Toussaint!"

"Yes, Monsieur."

"How is the young Bossale doing?"

"He has completely recovered, Master. He's helping me in the stable until you find something else for him to do."

"Oh, no!" Monsieur de Libertad said, shaking his head from side to side. "He's your responsibility."

"Can we see him?" a young woman asked.

"Yes, Toussaint, go get him!"

"If it pleases you," the old man answered, and left, pulling the horse behind him.

"You train your slaves well," a sharp-featured man said, approaching the host. "But there is something about this Toussaint that disturbs me."

"Really? What's that?"

"When he's on the ground, he's the image of the perfect slave. He's polite, obedient and humble. He speaks only when asked and keeps his eyes down as he should. But when he's on that horse, he's a completely different man. He looks bigger than usual. His posture is haughty, his back straight, the expression on his face is hard. He controls the animal with a dexterity, a firmness that a French cavalry general would envy. What do you think he's dreaming about when he is riding?"

"How would I know? Why should I care? Obviously, Toussaint knows he is a superb horseman and is proud of it, but when he dismounts, freed or not, he knows he's a Negro."

"And the ugliest one in the whole northern plain," someone else added, to the amusement of the company. But Isaac, Placide and Gaële weren't laughing, and neither was the gentleman who had brought up the subject.

"Have you forgotten," he insisted, "that slave revolts have occurred in British Guyana and Jamaica? How can you forget the fear on our parents' faces thirty years ago when Mackandal was roaming the countryside, poisoning people and animals?"

"No, Monsieur de Hauteville, I haven't forgotten. But I fail to see the connection between the slave revolts, Mackandal and my coachman."

"The connection is, Monsieur de Libertad, that a slave revolt cannot take place without a leader, and your Toussaint may be dreaming of being one."

Bayon de Libertad loved these discussions where he could display what he thought was his oratory skill. He stood up and paced back and forth for a moment.

"Monsieur de Hauteville," he began, "Toussaint was born on this plantation some forty-five years ago. He has served my father and me all his life. Thanks to him, I have the best stable in the northern plain, maybe in all of Saint-Domingue. The Governor, the Superintendant of Finance buy their horses from me. He learned to ride only to present my animals to potential buyers. If you want to make him the leader of some hypothetical revolt, tell me, whom is he going to lead?"

Pointing to the slaves gathered on the other side of the field, he continued, "Those poor souls? They know no leader but the white man. We feed them, we clothe them, we give them shelter. Not all of them love us, but they all fear us. Of course they may dream of being free, but only individually. That's why I freed Toussaint. You talk of Mackandal, but you don't remember that he had few followers and it was his own people who delivered him to the authorities. My friend, slave revolts will occur as they have in the past, but there is no instance in history of a successful one. Even white slaves couldn't succeed. Remember this: Even Spartacus was a failure."

This speech seemed to have quickly appeased the apprehension created by de Hauteville's remarks. A burst of applause greeted the orator, not so much for his eloquence, but for the relief brought about by his words. De Hauteville was preparing to answer, but the guests' attention turned to Toussaint and his protégé who had arrived unnoticed during the discussion.

"Ah," de Libertad said, "here's the young Bossale. Bring him closer, Toussaint."

The whole company surrounded the boy, feeling his muscles, inspecting his teeth. He turned abruptly toward whoever touched him, and at the same time shrank back defensively. Not knowing why he was there and what these people wanted with him, the young African was shaking from head to toe and panting like a young antelope isolated from the herd by a pack of wild dogs. Its only chance not to be eaten alive was if its mother could muster the courage to jump amid the dogs, kicking with all four hooves and being lucky enough to open an escape route for her and her offspring to rejoin the herd. For the young African, there was no mother, no herd. But instinctively he scanned the crowd for possible help. His eyes locked on Placide's face, and on wobbly legs, he walked to Toussaint's son and stood beside him as if to place himself under his protection. Without any apparent emotion, Placide gently put his arm around the boy's shoulders and slowly walked him back to his father.

"Oh, he likes Placide," a woman said.

"But he's still wild," a man added. "I can tame him in a matter of hours."

"I know," de Libertad replied. "But our methods are different at Bréda."

Turning to his coachman he said, "Toussaint, take him to be baptized as soon as possible."

"Yes, Monsieur!"

"What name will you give him?" de Hauteville asked.

This was a trap. Toussaint was aware that some big planters were feuding because one had given to a slave the name of someone in the other's family. This was the gravest insult to a white man in the colony. If the family member were a woman, a duel might ensue.

"It's not for me to name him, Monsieur," Toussaint answered.

Seeing that his coachman had avoided the trap, de Libertad smiled and said, "Give him a Roman name; it's less risky that way. Tell the priest to baptize him Marcus. "

"It will be done next Sunday, Monsieur."

The following Sunday, Toussaint took his protégé to the chapel in Haut-du-Cap, a small village a few kilometers from Cap-Français and at walking distance from the Bréda compound. Two Masses were celebrated in this little church on Sundays: one for the slaves at four o'clock in the morning and the other at eight for the whites. Following the slaves' Mass, the boy was christened by the priest in a ceremony that lasted barely one minute. The new involuntary Christian was given the name Marcus Bréda, with Toussaint as his godfather.

After helping the other slaves clean the chapel to erase all trace of their presence before their masters came in, the old man and the instant Catholic headed back to the plantation. Toussaint was amused by the difficulty the boy had pronouncing his own name.

"Makis?"

"No. *Marcus.*"

But his smile quickly disappeared and his face returned to its neutral expression. Up ahead, a man on horseback blocked the path.

"Bonjour, Monsieur de Hauteville," Toussaint said, trying to get by.

"Stop right here, old man!" the planter ordered. "What is that book you're carrying?"

"It's a prayer book, sir."

"Can you read it?"

"No, sir."

"Why are you carrying it then?"

"It is the Word of God, sir. I carry it for protection."

"Protection from whom? From what?"

"From temptation and sin, sir."

"Let's see if it can protect you from me!" De Hauteville lifted his cane and struck the old man violently on the head. Blood gushed from Toussaint's scalp and soaked the front of the yellow vest he wore on special occasions.

"Monsieur de Hauteville," he said calmly, "if you tell me what I did to offend you so, I promise not to do it again."

"You think you're clever!" de Hauteville raged, "but I'll catch you and, by God, I'll kill you!"

"Yes, sir."

"And from now on, I forbid you to ride a horse in my presence!"

When they arrived at Bréda, Toussaint went to the stables and harnessed two horses to the carriage in which he took the de Libertad family to church every Sunday. He brought the carriage to the front of the house and waited. Gaële was the first one out. At the sight of the bloody vest, she let out a scream. The rest of the family rushed out.

"What happened to you?" Bayon de Libertad asked Toussaint.

"I met Monsieur de Hauteville and he was angry at me for some reason. He hit me with his cane."

"I'll talk to him. The books coming from Paris are getting to him. Go take care of that wound. Isaac will drive us to church."

Toussaint waited for Isaac to take his place on the coachman's seat before getting down. After the carriage had left the yard, Placide, who was watching the scene from a second floor window, came down to walk his father to his hut.

"Is it serious?"

"What?"

"Your wound!"

"It's nothing. Don't think twice about it."

When they reached the middle of the large empty field, Placide looked around to make sure they were alone.

"Father," he said, "it's getting harder to contain my anger!"

"You must, my son. If you vent your anger, you'll be removed from the house and I need you there. You might even be killed, and your mother would die of sorrow. Your first duty is to survive."

"I could kill Monsieur de Hauteville!"

"On the contrary, the next time you see him, tell him how sorry I am for having displeased him."

"Why?"

"Because he's a dangerous man. He can poison Monsieur de Libertad's mind against me. How is your brother?"

"I'm worried about him. He trusts Monsieur Michel and Mademoiselle Gaële too much. Because they treat us like human beings, he believes they're on our side."

"It doesn't matter. He can't tell them what he doesn't know."

The other huts were clustered together, but Toussaint's dwelling stood alone in a small banana plot. It had two rooms, one for Toussaint and his wife, Suzanne, and the other for his father, who was almost blind. The hut was obviously new, having been built only a few months before when Toussaint was given his freedom. The inside was as clean as a dirt floor could be kept. When Toussaint and Placide arrived, they were welcome by a familiar fresh scent. As she did every Sunday morning, Suzanne had sprinkled the floor with water perfumed with crushed basil leaves.

Unlike the typical slave dwelling devoid of any furniture, this one had a table, two chairs and a rocker. A partially burnt candle stuck on a saucer sat on the table. In each room there was a thick floor mat made of the soft bark of banana trees.

Suzanne had already heard from a slave about Toussaint's injury. She came to her husband with a washbowl of water and some clean rags to wipe away the blood that was now drying on his forehead and left cheek.

"I'll take that," Toussaint told her. "Go spend some time with your son. He has to return to the house before the masters do."

"Good morning, Papa Bréda," Placide said to his grandfather who was sitting in the rocking chair.

"Who is that?"

"Me, Placide."

"Come closer, my child. I can't see at that distance."

The young man came and planted a noisy kiss on his grandfather's shiny bald head.

"Why didn't Isaac come with you?"

"He drove the masters to church."

Placide took his mother's hand and made her sit on one of the chairs. He then knelt in front of her and put his head on her lap. While caressing her son's head, Suzanne eyes were following her husband's every move. He took off the yellow vest and his shirt, both stained with blood, and hung them on a nail.

"Soak them in water," Suzanne said. "Tomorrow I'll wash them in the river."

"You'll do no such thing," Toussaint replied. Taking the washbowl and rags, he went outside to clean himself up. When he returned a few minutes later, the rags were red with blood.

"Can I clean them?" Suzanne asked.

"These, yes," Toussaint agreed, "but the vest and the shirt will remain as they are and where they are."

"Why?"

"I don't know."

"Toussaint, let me warn you, if you keep these bloody clothes here, they will feed your anger and it will take you longer to forgive."

"Maybe I'm tired of forgiving."

"Bite your tongue, my son," Papa Bréda said. "Forgiveness is the greatest of all virtues—that's what the prayer says. It erases bitterness from your heart and allows you to sleep in peace. Forget this minor incident. Remember that you are free and so is your wife. You have two sons living in the servants' quarters in the big house. They wear good clothes and are treated very well. You could have been born on another plantation where the slaves are tortured. You know how lucky you are. Why spoil your happiness by harboring resentment in your heart? Look at me. I've been blessed with a long life because I always knew my duty and my place."

"Wouldn't you like to be free, Grandfather?" Placide asked.

"But I am free, my child. I was given my freedom the day Isaac was born."

"I'm not talking about this freedom. I mean free to go where you please, to read and to learn without having to hide what you're doing, to see your family whenever you want, not when it is allowed, free to speak without having to look over your shoulder to see who's listening, free to have no master. You're a freed slave, Papa Bréda, not a free man."

"Banish these thoughts from your mind, my child. They will bring death to you, and disaster to the family. As for you Suzanne, I want you either to wash those bloody clothes, or better, burn them."

"I'll do no such thing," Suzanne answered calmly.

Discussions about slavery had been recurring in Toussaint's household since the day Placide declared that he would not die a slave. Suzanne and Toussaint had run out of the hut to be sure no one had heard, and Papa Bréda had stopped rocking in the chair. They all had tried to convince the young man that his views were dangerous. But despite all the stories they told him of tortures and executions, every time he sneaked out of the big house to visit his family, he had another surprise for them. Once he told them he knew how to read and write. Another time he confessed that Monsieur Michel and Mademoiselle Gaële had been reading books critical of slavery and even of the king of France, and that he, Placide, had secretly read them, too. The family had always presented a united front against what they saw as Placide's irresponsibility, not to say blasphemies. But this time it was different. Placide perceived a breach in the front. So did Papa Bréda.

"Jesus asked us to forgive," the grandfather said.

"But we've been forgiving for generations, and we're still slaves," Placide countered. "Why is forgiveness the virtue only of the oppressed?"

"Placide, it's time to return to the house," Toussaint warned. "The Mass will be over soon."

"Yes, Father."

After saying good-bye to each family member, Placide was about to leave when a form filled the doorway.

"Good morning everyone."

"Good morning Uncle Paul," Placide replied.

"Toussaint, I have to talk to you."

The man could barely hide his agitation. Toussaint and Placide came out of the hut.

"What is it, Paul?"

Paul hesitated. His eyes went from Toussaint to Placide as if to ask whether he could talk in front of the young man.

"You can speak. He's with us."

"Early this morning," Paul whispered, "we found someone unconscious in the cane field. He'd been savagely whipped and has lost a lot of blood."

"A runaway? A maroon?"

"I can't say. He must have followed the river to hide his scent from the dogs. His pants were soaking wet."

"This is what you do," Toussaint said without hesitation. "Bring him food and a lot of water. Leave no trace of your passage and don't move him from where he is. If no one comes looking for him by sunset, put him with the young Bossale tonight. Post people to watch and listen to the overseers all day and report to me if they hear anything about this. I can't take care of him before knowing that it's safe for us. Placide?"

"Yes, Father."

"Go back to the house, and if there's any mention of a runaway from the surrounding plantations, let me know as soon as you can. Not a word to Isaac, you hear?"

"Yes, Father."

Placide was filled with pride. He now realized that not only was something brewing under this apparent servility, but also that his father trusted him. It was all the more significant because Toussaint was not his real father. Having been born of Suzanne's previous union with a mulatto who had since died, Placide had been adopted when his mother and the coachman were married. As much as slavery would permit, he was treated by his adoptive father, and the entire family for that matter, with the same love and affection they bestowed upon Isaac.

From an early age, Placide had felt boundless admiration for Toussaint. According to the family's history as told to him by his uncle Paul, his stepfather's life was nothing less than amazing.

Born prematurely, Toussaint had not been expected to survive. In his adolescence, he had been so thin and sickly that he was called Trash-on-A-Stick. But his sister Elise had taken great care of him and his health had improved. When he was in his early twenties, Elise had been sold and Toussaint never saw her again. To cope with the situation, Papa Bréda told the family to consider Elise dead and ordered that her name never be mentioned again. The separation affected Toussaint more than anyone else, but he chose a different method to try to forget.

He immersed himself in his work with the horses, learning to ride them, to treat them when sick, and little by little, becoming a skilled veterinarian. Toussaint became so important for the plantation that his family was given special privileges. His father was freed, his sons were taken to the big house, and his brother Paul was made a commander, a team leader in the cane fields, answering only to the white overseers. Moreover, the family was given Bréda as a last name. For Papa Bréda, this was the highest honor, but Paul was not impressed.

"If we must have a family name," he said, "it should be Guinou, because our great-grandfather was the son of an Arada chief called Gaou-Guinou."

Toussaint had learned to read and write from his godfather, Baptiste. Monsieur de Libertad, Bayon's father, hadn't objected, believing that his slave's interest in reading couldn't go beyond the prayer book.

Placide now understood that his father was using his skills to help slaves. The runaway found in the cane field could not have been the first, for Toussaint knew too well what to do in this situation. The young man also realized with great pride that the slaves of Bréda must be organized since Paul was to assign them to spy on the overseers, of whom there were eight. Now he understood why the Negroes treated him with so much affection in spite of his obvious privileges: He was their leader's son.

Later that evening, when he was sure that no one had mentioned a runaway, Toussaint went to the young Bossale's hut to take care of the wounded escapee. He found him lying on his stomach so as not to put pressure on the lacerations on his back. Trying to be useful, the boy was fanning the man's injuries with a banana leaf.

While cleaning the wounds with water, Toussaint asked, "What happened to you?"

"I ran away and I was caught. They tied me to a tree and whipped me until I passed out. When I came to in the night, an old black man with a knife was there and asked if I wanted him to kill me to escape what was awaiting me. They were going to cut my leg off in the morning. I asked him to cut me loose instead. He made me promise to be far away by sunrise. That was two days ago."

"So you're not from around here?"

"No, I came from the Cormier plantation near the village of Great River."

"That's pretty far," Toussaint said. "That's why the news hasn't reached us yet. I can't keep you here for more than a few days. After that you'll have to move on, but we'll guide you to the next place where you can be sheltered."

"A few days, that's all I need," the stranger said.

"If you want anything, wait for me to return. This boy is African and won't understand you," Toussaint said while applying ointment to his patient's wounds.

On his way out, he asked, "What's your name?"

"Dessalines."

Chapter Six

The Education of Bambolo

Messengers brought to Kalame the anxiously awaited word that the attack on Bakou had been successful. Three days later, when the sentries' drums told the villagers that the king was returning, they began preparing for a great celebration. Kalame was decorated with palm branches, the elders put on their ceremonial white robes and everyone waited at the side of the village where the victorious warriors would appear.

People usually don't have gods they don't use. Since the Aradas had never been in a conflict before, they didn't have a god for war. As a result, Nabo didn't know an appropriate drumbeat to give thanks to the deity who had protected his people. So he went to consult Adegba.

"A war is like a hunting expedition," the griot advised. "We should honor Ogoun, the spirit of the hunt, he who blows our smell away from the prey, he who allows us to approach it in silence and guides our spears to its heart."

Nabo agreed and started beating the drum as soon as the head of the defenders' column came into view. But when the king entered Kalame, he ordered the old singer to stop.

"There will be no rejoicing," Gaoube said. "We did what we had to do, and I hope that the Kaplaous have learned their lesson. We've lived in peace with them for generations, and I'm not happy that we had to kill some of them."

The people of Kalame had no choice but to obey, but they didn't like it. They wanted to celebrate the defeat of the enemies who had destroyed their homes, killed their parents and taken away their sons and daughters. They wanted to honor their avengers with songs and dances of joy. But the king remained firm: no celebration.

Adegba's concern was different. He had to find members of the expedition to tell him the details. The griot had been training Bambolo every day in how to select what to remember in a story and how to memorize. Now he had the opportunity to teach the boy how to collect facts.

After the defenders had eaten, the griot took Bambolo on a tour. They visited Gaouno and Bao, and they also talked to some defenders whom Adegba picked at random. By the time they rejoined Nabo and Ganiloa at the old singer's hut, they could tell the story of the attack on Bakou.

It had taken the Aradas seven days to reach the second river that Bambolo had mentioned. Up to that point they had walked by day and slept by night. But after this crossing, Gaoube decided to reverse the tactic. The Aradas would hide and rest during the day and advance under the cover of darkness. Some scouts were sent ahead with the order to spot sentries if there were any, and to use any means to prevent them from alerting their village. Others had to report to the king about the size and layout of Bakou, as well as the position of the pink men's dwelling.

Gaoube didn't just want to win a battle. He wanted to prove that the pink men could be killed and that the Aradas had the courage and ability to retaliate against anyone who dared to attack them. But more than anything, he wanted the Kaplaous to know that the Aradas wanted to live in peace. The king's objectives could be achieved only by a complete victory followed by some magnanimous gesture.

After listening carefully to the scouts' reports, Gaoube made his plan. He divided his men into three groups. The first, led by Gaouno, would surprise the pink men in their sleep. The second group, under Bao's command, would circle around Bakou and attack from the other side. The king himself would lead the third in a frontal assault of the village. The attack on the pink men would be first, followed almost immediately by the general assault.

The pink men's compound was located on a small hill overlooking the village. The enclosure was formed by a palisade of logs planted in the ground and tied together with ropes. It was as tall as a man standing on another's shoulders, which seemed to indicate that there was no trust between the pink men and the Kaplaous. The log gate was barred from the inside.

Gaouno and his men waited until they felt certain that the pink men were asleep.

Quickly and silently, the Aradas climbed the log wall and lowered themselves inside. Within the enclosed area, they saw that there was only one dwelling, almost as big as Kalame's communal hut. The Aradas approached cautiously, and at Gaouno's signal, they rushed in. The five pink men were dead in less than a minute. In the dark and confusion, three Kaplaou women who were inside also were killed.

Gaouno opened the gate, took a deep breath and yelled as loud as he could, "Nguele!"

At this signal for the general assault, the Aradas poured into Bakou. The surprise was complete, giving the Kaplaous no time to rally in defense. The village was burned to the ground and more than thirty people were killed, with scores more wounded.

The Aradas herded the survivors out of the village, made them sit on the ground and waited for daybreak. At the first light of dawn, the king ordered that the bodies of the five pink men be brought before the crowd. He called on two Aradas who could speak a few words of the Kaplaou tongue.

"Tell them," he directed the interpreters, "that I am Gaoube, King of the Aradas."

After waiting patiently for the message, accompanied by hand gestures, to be transmitted, he continued.

"You have destroyed one of our villages, killed our people and taken many more away. You have erased the peace that had existed between our tribes for generations. You have listened to these men," he said, pointing to the five bodies, "to attack the Aradas who were not your enemies. We were hoping to find our people here and to bring them back to their families. But they aren't here. You gave them to the pink men who took them away. What reason can you give me not to kill all of you?"

Then Gaoube sat down, indicating that he had finished speaking and was waiting for an answer. The interpreters continued for a while longer and when they assumed that the king's thoughts had been conveyed to the defeated, they also sat down.

The Kaplaous looked at each other, wondering who was going to answer. Finally a man stood and indicated that he wanted to speak. He was tall and slender, with skin was so black he seemed to be carved out of ebony wood. Gaoube ordered his men to allow him to approach. The Kaplaou stepped carefully between the survivors and planted himself proudly in front of the Arada king.

"I am Mioc," he said, using the same combination of words and gestures he had seen the interpreters use. "My father was the chief of Bakou before he was killed by these men you call pink. They arrived here seven or eight full moons ago. With the help of another tribe called Congo, they attacked us and took many Kaplaous away. They killed my father, his advisers and the sorcerer. I would have been killed, too, if they had known whose son I was. But my people saved me by hiding my identity."

Mioc continued, "A group of these men stayed here and we've been living in fear ever since. They made us build their shelter and cook their food. They took our women without our consent and hit our children. Everything had to be done for them. They didn't fish in the river or work the land. They didn't tend the herds or pick fruits. They only liked to hunt with their terrible weapons. They killed everything they saw—lions, zebras, people, giraffes—not for food, but for pleasure. We understand your anger, but we had no choice but to help the white men attack you. Now if you want more blood to satisfy your vengeance, kill me, but spare my people. They have suffered enough." Having spoken, Mioc went back and sat among his people.

The king's decision had already been made, but only his council knew that. He took his time to announce it, leaving the Kaplaous apprehensive about their fate. Finally, he rose and asked, "Why do you call these men white?"

"That's what they call themselves," Mioc answered through an interpreter.

"Well," Gaoube said, "they are dead now and our vengeance is satisfied. They were the real enemies responsible for the blood spilled in Kalame and here in Bakou. If you help them again, we will come back with the same anger. But if you don't, we will let time heal our sorrow. Now, if it is not against your customs, we will help you bury your dead."

"You are the victors. You may do as you please," Mioc said, "but we would prefer to bury them ourselves."

"So be it!" the king agreed. "By this time tomorrow, we will leave. But I have a last question. Where do these white men take the people they capture, and what do they do with them?"

"They take them across a great salty river and make them work for them, just as they did with us."

With the first rays of the morning sun, the Aradas departed from the Kaplaous' village.

This was the story of the attack on Bakou as told by Bambolo to Nabo and Ganiloa, while Adegba, his eyes closed, listened to his pupil. The boy waited anxiously for his teacher's reaction.

The old griot cleared his throat and said, "It was a wise decision for me to leave Weewa and come here. I had students there, and some had ability. But what they really liked was to listen to the stories I told them. They found them as amusing as hunting or dancing, but not more so. They didn't want to make the effort to memorize and to repeat them without changing anything. My last group of students preferred to be defenders. I feared that the story of the tribe would be buried with me. Then I thought of you, who sat at my feet in the sacred savannah, and I decided to come here. When the messengers came to tell the king what happened to Kalame, I was worried about you, but Gaouno told me that you had survived. I saw that as a sign that the gods had spared you for a purpose, and I was right. Nevertheless, you have missed three details in the attack on Bakou. Let's find them together."

"May I say something?" Ganiloa asked.

"Of course. What is it?"

"Bambolo didn't say if we lost anyone."

"You're right," Bambolo concurred. "No Arada was killed, but six were wounded."

"That's one!" Adegba said. "The second detail concerns the pink men. Remember?"

"Yes," Bambolo answered after some hesitation. "Mioc, the Kaplaou, pretended that there were six pink men and that one didn't come back from the attack on Kalame."

"Why did you say that he pretended? Do you have any reason not to put that in the story?"

"No!" Bambolo answered quickly, visibly troubled by the question.

"I think I know what happened to that pink man," Ganiloa interrupted.

"You know what happened to the pink man?" Bambolo asked.

"I think so. I told you how Nguele helped me escape. He threw his spear at the pink man who was running after me along the edge of the ravine. The spear must have hit him, since I heard a scream."

"But where is the body?" Nabo asked

"Later on," Ganiloa continued, "some people went to the ravine. They probably took the body away."

"That makes sense to me," Adegba said. "They picked up the body and buried it somewhere between here and Bakou. This is good news. I must report it to the king. He was worried about that sixth pink man."

Once again, the opportunity had presented itself for Bambolo to reveal his secret. And once again, an apparently logical explanation had been found to stop him from speaking. Moreover, the chain of events had convinced the boy that the gods had saved him for a purpose. He hadn't yet discerned what that mission would be. But how else could he explain that he had escaped capture and perhaps death by being sent away from the village, that he had become the sentry posted atop the sacred mountain, that he had found a pink man too incapacitated to cause him any harm, and that he had been able to give to the king the information that was so instrumental for the Aradas' victory over the Kaplaous?

"Bambolo."

"Yes," the boy answered, coming out of his thoughts.

"Do you remember the third detail?"

"Yes, it's about the quarrel between Gaouno and his father."

"What?" Nabo exclaimed. "Gaouno had a quarrel with the king?"

"Not exactly," the griot said. "It was more of a misunderstanding. Tell them, Bambolo."

"Just before the attack, King Gaoube talked to the chief defenders, Gaouno and Bao. He told them that his purpose was not to kill every single Kaplaou but to inspire in them the same fear they had of the pink men. He ordered that women and children be spared, as well as men who were not actively engaged in fighting. But he insisted that all the pink men be killed to prove that they were not invulnerable.

"Gaouno disagreed with his father and voiced the opinion that all the Kaplaous should be exterminated as the only way to inspire fear. The king replied that the dead had nothing more to fear and ended the discussion by ordering Gaouno to follow his plan exactly. After the attack, Gaoube learned that three Kaplaou women had been killed in the pink men's dwelling. When Gaouno proudly came to present to his father a long knife he had taken from the pink men's hut, the king asked him why the women's lives hadn't been spared.

"It was dark," his son answered. "We realized that Kaplaou women were in there only after we lit torches." Gaoube didn't seem convinced, and Gaouno was so saddened by his father's doubt that he asked to remain in Kalame, which may indicate that he no longer considers him self the king's first heir."

"Good," a satisfied Adegba said, "the story is now complete. At another time I'll talk to you about a god the Aradas used to serve when we lived near the great salty water. Then you'll understand another reason King Gaou-Guinou decided to move far inland and why we don't serve that god anymore."

"How many gods are there?" Bambolo asked.

"No one knows," the griot answered, "since there is a god for everything. But we give our thanks only to those who favor us. I must retire now."

After the excitement of the Arada victory and his training in storytelling, Bambolo wasn't sleepy. He accompanied Adegba to the main hut where the griot spent his nights and then went looking for Gaouno. He found the king's son with a group of men eating around a campfire.

"What brought you here, little brother?" Gaouno asked. "Shouldn't you be sleeping?"

"I have no sleep in my eyes," Bambolo answered. "May I talk to you?"

"Let's go for a walk."

Out of hearing of the other warriors, Gaouno asked, "What's troubling you? Is it my misunderstanding with the king?"

"Yes."

"This was bound to happen sooner or later. As you know, the king can have as many wives as he wants, and from my father's five wives I have six brothers and three sisters. His favorite wife would like her son to be the next king, although I am the firstborn. She and the healer, her father, are poisoning the king's mind against me. Because my mother died giving birth to me, they have convinced my father that I am a born killer and that I'll bring disaster to the tribe if I am king."

"You shouldn't have suggested killing all the Kaplaous."

"The king asked for my opinion and I said what was in my mind. But he should have known that I'd never disobey his order. When I was younger, my father was like a companion to me. He took me along with his hunting parties, taught me how to make and use a spear and sat me on his lap at meetings with the council of elders. When I realized that he would have to die for me to be king, I wished he would live forever. I thought he knew that I'd be always devoted to him."

"What are you going to do now?"

"I'm staying here with Adegba. He's a friend and an adviser to me. Then I'll send for Maïle to join me. If Bao agrees, I'll help train Kalame's defenders. I'll be happy here, away from the slander of my father's wife."

"So you'll not be king."

"It doesn't seem like it."

The two friends continued on to Gaouno's shelter, a simple structure of a few posts holding up a roof of leafy branches. It was enough to keep out the sun but not enough to fool the rain. Such temporary shelters were built in the dry season when a hunting party spent a night away from the village.

The gods had herded the stars to graze in their blue savannah. Bambolo could see beside Gaouno's sleeping mat a long, shiny object that he recognized at once. He picked it up but said nothing.

"This is a long knife," Gaouno explained. "I wanted to give it to the king, but he was more concerned about the three Kaplaou women who were killed."

"Do you still think he was wrong?"

"Yes. Many Kaplaous who took part in the attack against Kalame are still alive. Sooner or later they will have a chief who will think of avenging their defeat. If the pink men come back, that tribe can be used against us again, and they already know the way here. Who knows how many villages they have and how many men they can gather for an attack?"

"Wouldn't they be angrier if we had killed all the people in Bakou?"

"Maybe, but other pink men would know we are merciless, and they would have to start all over to find Kalame again."

"Are you sure they'll attack again?" Bambolo asked.

"They may, they may not. But we'd better be ready. That's why I want to help Bao organize the defense of Kalame. I prefer to die fighting than to cross their salty river."

"But that's the only way to see Nguele again."

"Do you think of him a lot?"

"Every day."

"Little brother," Gaouno said, putting his arm around the boy's shoulder, "we have to accept that we'll never see our friend again. I've heard that the salty water is so wide that both banks cannot be seen at the same time, and sometimes not even one can be seen. How could we follow tracks on water?"

"I know," Bambolo admitted, "but for Ganiloa and me, he's still here. We talk about him often, and sometimes we even pretend to talk to him. Every few days one of us dreams of him."

"And what do you want to do? Let yourself be captured? Nguele was your friend, but he is just one person. The whole tribe needs you now. Thanks to you, the gods seem to favor us. The information you gave to the king brought us victory. You were as useful to us as those who fought in Bakou. Go now, my friend, and let a peaceful sleep come to you."

When Bambolo reached Nabo's hut, he found Ganiloa outside waiting for him.

"Where were you?" she asked.

"I was with Gaouno."

"You should be resting now. Come!"

But before they could enter the hut, Gaouno came running towards them.

"Wait! I forgot to give you this," he said.

"The long knife? Why?"

"Except for the king, you deserve it more than any one else."

Emile Berthier had been in the slave trade for a long time. He had faced its dangers and shared in its profits. In almost three decades of roaming the sea, he had survived many battles against British, Spanish and Portuguese slave traders. During his turbulent life, he had acquired a well deserved reputation as an expert marksman and a feared swordsman. He had escaped capture, hanging, shipwreck and starvation countless times.

But if a truce were to occur among the European powers and a policy of "trade and let trade" were put into effect, still the sea itself would always remain an unwilling partner, ready to transform the sweetest breeze into the most vicious cyclone.

Upon reaching his forties a few years previously, Emile had settled on the safest aspect of the human chattel business—the capture and sale of slaves. With a dozen other Frenchmen, he had formed an outfit that employed a method that was simple but highly effective. They would choose an isolated village and place themselves in two or three vantage points around it. With a small cannon, they would blast the biggest hut because, more often than not, it was the residence of the village chief.

Next they would shoot at the people running in all directions but particularly at those who tried to flee the village. This operation was usually conducted in broad daylight. Soon the Africans would realize that they were trapped. Emile and his men would then enter the village.

Their first order of business would be to identify anyone of importance among the terrified crowd. An elaborate headgear, an ornate robe or an amulet would indicate either a chief, a healer or an elder. The wearer of these signs would be summarily put to death, depriving the natives of anyone of authority who could rally them for a last attempt at resistance.

If a residue of unrest were still noticed among the Africans, one would be chosen at random and tied to the mouth of the cannon, which was then fired so his guts and blood would splatter all over the crowd. After this gruesome demonstration of their power and cruelty, the invaders would appoint a new chief. Only a few inhabitants of this village might be sold into slavery. Instead the majority would become the unwilling allies of the traders. It was from such a terrorized population that the Frenchmen would recruit the scouts and troops necessary to start capturing slaves. The subsequent raids would take place at night as had happened in Kalame.

Everything had been going Emile's way before that last attack. The business was running smoothly, although some dissension had started to appear. Usually only half the outfit, led by Emile himself, was involved in the capture of Africans. The other half was responsible for herding the blacks to the coast, selling them and collecting payment.

As they ventured further inland, the marches to and from the sea became longer. The herders suggested limiting the theater of operation but Emile disagreed, arguing that many coastal tribes had moved inland and therefore the pickings were better away from the sea. Emile's opinions carried much weight for two very good reasons. When the money was collected at the slave market on the coast, it was brought back to wherever the group had its temporary base of operation. There it was counted in the presence of all the members and saved in an iron box whose key hung on a chain around Emile's neck. The second reason explained the first. The fear of Emile's mighty sword was unanimous.

The money had very little usefulness in Africa. Besides ammunition for their firearms and a copious supply of rum and tobacco from the Antilles, the slavers had no need to buy anything. Everything else they needed or wanted was given from fear or taken by force: food, women and shelter.

After years of accumulation, the iron box was practically bulging with gold and silver coins, as well as what could well be precious stones taken from the natives. Some men wanted to take their share of the loot and return to their cities or villages in France to retire. Such was also Emile's dream, but he wanted a few more successful raids before returning to his native Bordeaux. It was there that he had caught the adventure fever while unloading ships coming from the colonies.

To convince the others to stay longer, Emile argued that before any equitable sharing could be done, the stones would have to be evaluated by someone who knew their worth. In the meantime, he cajoled, why not capture a few more shiploads of blacks? Reluctantly everyone agreed, and the attack on Kalame was carefully planned and carried out.

The raid was well executed. The Aradas were completely taken by surprise. When the Frenchmen entered the village and started killing people wearing distinctive signs, Emile noticed a girl just the way he liked them: young, no older than fifteen and probably a virgin. Seeing that she was petrified with fear, he sneaked up behind her and grabbed her arm. This contact woke her up, allowing her to shake him off and run from him. Emile was pleased. She was going to be a lively one. Laughing, he took off after her.

What happened next was still fuzzy in his memory. A boy had come out of nowhere, bent slowly backward and sprang up. A sharp pain engulfed Emile's entire left side as the spear pierced his chest. He lost consciousness even before hitting the ground.

When he regained his senses, he was lying on his back at the bottom of a ravine with the spear in his chest pointing to the sky. He pulled it out with great pain and only then did he become aware of another pang. His right leg was broken. With the dawn stretching across the sky, Emile realized he had been unconscious for hours. He wanted to cry out for help, but the silence worried him. Where was he? Where was everyone else? How long had the raid been over? Surely his men must have noticed his absence. According to the plan he had drawn up himself, his men and their prisoners should have left the area by now. Who or what would answer his call? A white man? An African? Or a hyena?

He decided to crawl out of this hole. After what seemed to be hours of excruciating effort, he managed to haul himself out of the ravine on the far side from the village. Some huts were still smoldering and he saw no signs of life. The pain was agonizing and blood from his wound was still trickling down his left arm. Attempting to tear off his left sleeve to make a bandage, he discovered that the chain around his neck and the key were missing. His men had abandoned him to die.

The story of his life passed before Emile's eyes. It had been a story of danger, violence, cruelty and resilience. Now, here he was, disabled by a boy, a little savage, and held hostage by another—or was it the same one? He couldn't tell; they all looked alike anyway.

In fact, Emile wasn't the boy's prisoner. There were no bars on his cell. He was alone every night, and free to leave his mountain refuge. But beyond his tree home and tiny clearing there was Africa with its immensity, its wild beasts, its unforgiving sun, its abundant rains and dangerous rivers.

There were also the countless tribes he had plundered. How could a lone and crippled white man, without his instruments of terror, cross the territories he had violated? His prison was the whole continent he had raped.

Two meager tears ran from his eyes and disappeared into his beard. They weren't tears of regret or remorse. They were instead an expression of his silent and powerless rage, his frustrated desire to have the traitors at the point of his sword, the fading dream of finishing his life comfortably in his native Bordeaux. Except for his physical existence, which was quickly ebbing, he was already dead to his world.

All he had left was a trickle of conversation in his own language with that little savage. This bit of communication had become so important to Emile that he couldn't wait for each morning. He had discovered a side of himself he'd never suspected: He enjoyed teaching. He loved the challenge of increasing the boy's vocabulary and was amazed by his own patience in explaining concepts that were completely foreign to Bambolo's way of life, such as money, slavery and ownership of land.

Something else was coming back to Emile—religion. Lost in a hostile continent, he remembered the God of his childhood. But his knowledge in the matter was limited at best. Like so many conventional religious people, he perceived of God as a powerful being who, just by hearing his name uttered in prayers, could rescue a distressed person from any impossible situation.

The problem for Emile was that even the Lord's Prayer had defected from his memory. This was a serious handicap for someone who believed that God couldn't be reached without the recitation of some prescribed words.

Emile searched his memory until he found a tune to which, as a child, he used to sing the prayer. Then, putting syllables to notes, he finally reconstructed the whole text. From that moment on, he recited the Lord's Prayer not once, but hundreds of times, so as to fill the void left by decades of absence from religious practices.

He vaguely knew that he had led a sinful life. Now that he had time to think, he started to doubt the argument he had heard so many times in taverns on both sides of the ocean that God allowed the enslavement of people of another race. Yet this awareness wasn't entirely new. Emile had always been convinced that the killing and raping wouldn't be forgiven without some serious *mea culpas*. However, he had been postponing his repentance and a life of virtue until, his youth spent and his table well supplied, he could retire in his hometown. Now everything was upside down! His youth was gone, the money was out of reach, and Emile was forced to rush his reconciliation with his God.

The morning after Bambolo received the long knife from Gaouno, he took it with him to show to Emile. He wanted to prove to the pink man that no rescue should be expected from Bakou because the five pink men who lived there had been killed. At first Emile showed no emotion, thinking that Bambolo was returning his own weapon which had been previously hidden by the boy. But he realized soon enough that he was mistaken. A swordsman will pick out his own rapier among a hundred. His eyebrows arched in interrogation.

"Where did you get that?" he asked.

"Pink men, five, in Bakou, killed," Bambolo answered in his hesitant French. To remove all doubt from Emile's mind, he went into the bushes and reappeared a few minutes later with two swords, one in each hand. A little chuckle escaped from Emile's throat and increased in volume until it became a raucous and uncontrolled laughter. Startled by the commotion, a flock of guinea fowl in the underbrush took off noisily in all directions and disappeared from view.

"Why you happy?" Bambolo asked when Emile regained his composure.

"They abandoned me to die, but I'm still alive and they're all dead! This is a punishment from God."

"What god?"

"God! There's only one!"

"I know you have two: one good, one evil."

"No! I have only one God, and he is good."

"Why *you* evil?"

"I am not..." Emile stopped in mid-sentence and limped away. Although his life hadn't been saintly, he didn't like a little savage passing judgment on him. What right did that subhuman have to condemn the profession he had chosen to earn a better life? That was between himself and God. But Bambolo wasn't about to absolve him.

"You evil," the boy said again as he followed Emile. "You kill, you burn, you take Aradas away, you take Kaplaous away. You evil, your god evil."

"If I am so evil," Emile answered, "why didn't I kill you?"

"Emile can't kill Bambolo. Bambolo protected by gods—Arada gods, not pink men gods." The boy threw both swords at Emile's feet with the challenge, "Try kill Bambolo."

This was said without arrogance or bravado. Bambolo was sure that on this mountain inhabited by the spirits of his gods and his ancestors, everything was going according to a plan. Being the chosen one, he had a unique role to play in this plan, although what it was, he didn't yet know. But for whatever he had to accomplish, he had to be alive, and so he was confident that his life could not be taken from him.

The Frenchman's first reaction was one of surprise. Someone had dared to defy him while giving him his favorite weapon.

This had never happened before. A gesture like that would have been fatal for every man he had known. Did this young blasphemous savage know the danger to which he was exposing himself? Was he even aware of the art of fencing?

But Emile had to acknowledge that Bambolo was right. Crippled as he was, he had no chance of cornering the agile boy. Besides, he had no intention of harming the youngster, not out of respect for any primitive pagan god but for his own survival. Bambolo was his lifeline. So far, with his crudely mended leg, he hadn't even been able to explore beyond a few meters around his shelter, the hollow trunk of a huge baobab tree. Emile walked away from the two swords to indicate that he had no hostile intentions.

"I can't kill you," he said. "We're friends."

"You, friend of no one," Bambolo retorted.

To his own surprise, this statement disturbed Emile. He knew it to be true that he had never cultivated any special relationships in his life, neither with his siblings nor with his co-workers on the docks of Bordeaux. His contacts with women had been limited to brief encounters by rape or for pay. He had also kept a safe distance from his colleagues, preferring to be feared than to be liked.

Actually, his relationship with Bambolo was the closest he'd ever had. When he had said, 'We're friends', he wasn't lying, but mistaken. He had taken for friendship the sentiment he was developing towards Bambolo, a feeling similar to what humans feel for their pets. He had also mistaken the attention the boy paid to whatever he said for admiration. That simple sentence, 'You, friend of no one', made him realize how wrong he had been.

"Why haven't you killed me then?" Emile asked.

"Tell Bambolo where pink men take Nguele, where take Aradas. Tell everything."

"What can you do?"

"Gods tell Bambolo what to do."

"What's in it for me?"

"Don't understand."

"What Bambolo do for Emile?" the pink man asked, mimicking the boy's broken French. "Can you get me to the sea?"

"No!"

"And if I refuse to tell you?"

"Bambolo not come here. Emile die."

The time had come for King Gaoube to return to Weewa. In a last meeting with Bao and Kalame's council of elders, it was decided that the village should be rebuilt, but not at the same site. A wooded area was chosen. The idea was to hide the huts under the trees so they wouldn't be easily spotted by a potential enemy. It was also decided to leave the ruins untouched to give the impression that the Aradas had moved away from the area. Half the defenders from the other villages would stay a while longer to help build the new Kalame.

The meeting had taken place in the damaged main hut where Adegba slept, so the old griot had to wait outside. Gaouno and Bambolo sat with him. When the king came out, he went to them and helped Adegba to his feet.

"My old friend," he said, "I agree with your decision to remain here, but I'm going to miss you. From now on, I'll be at the ceremony of the pledge every year so I can consult with you."

"Your son is also staying. Won't you miss him?"

"Of course I will, but I think it's good that he remain in Kalame."

The king greeted the two young men by putting his hands on their heads.

"May the gods reward you," he said.

"Father," Gaouno asked, "may I have your approval to take Maïle into my hut?"

"You have my permission. I'll send her to you as soon as I get to Weewa."

Happy for his friend, Bambolo hurriedly bowed to the king and ran inside to tell Adegba the good news. He found the griot deep in thought.

"The king agreed," the boy announced.

"I heard."

"Why are you sad?"

"Call Gaouno and I'll tell you both."

When the young man had entered and seated himself beside Bambolo, the old man began, "The other day I promised to tell you another reason why King Gaou-Guinou moved the tribe inland. No griot before me ever mentioned that part of the story at the ceremony of the pledge. Maybe it's just a legend that I heard when I was very young. But the more I think of it, the more it worries me."

"What's the story?" Bambolo asked.

"Well, they say that King Gaou-Guinou had a favorite wife. One day she went out in a canoe looking for fish in the salty water and never came back. For many days, the king made offerings to the salty water god, asking him not to kill his wife and to return her safely. The king's prayers remained unanswered. So he gathered the whole tribe and together they vowed never to serve that god again. This was a big mistake, because the pink men's attack occurred soon after. The surviving elders begged the king to appease the god's anger, but he refused, deciding instead to move away from the god's domain."

"What could the king have done to appease the god?"

"The story says that Gaou-Guinou should have sent a large group of young people in a big canoe far out on the salty water. Then they would throw away their oars to be completely at the mercy of the god. They would wait as long as it took for the god to choose either to capsize the canoe or to push it back to the dry land. If the canoe returned with even one survivor, it would mean that the debt was paid."

"And in case there were no survivors?" Gaouno asked.

"The king would have to send another canoe."

"And another, until the god's anger was appeased?"

"Yes. But Gaou-Guinou refused."

"Good! Now what are you worried about?"

"If the story is true, the pink men are the instrument of the god's vengeance. They have attacked us twice, taking large numbers of young people across the salty water. No Arada has returned yet. The debt is still not paid and our people have been found."

"As far as I'm concerned," Gaouno said, "this is just a legend."

"And if it isn't?"

"If it isn't, the spell has been broken. We have killed the pink men."

Chapter Seven
And The Sky Caved In

It was August, it was hot. Monsieur de Libertad was sitting in his rocking chair on the veranda. Although his wife and children were seated around him, each of them avoided looking at the others. The sun was setting gloriously over the western mountains but no one seemed to notice. There was no real conversation between them, although from time to time someone would come up with a sentence.

"I tried to prevent it. I asked the governor not to go on with the executions, but he wouldn't listen."

Bayon de Libertad was referring to two mulattoes who had led an armed rebellion a few months before, after the governor, Monsieur de Blanchelande, had refused to publish a decree from the French revolutionary assembly proclaiming the equality of all free men in the colony, regardless of their color. Instead, he had sent the colonial troops after the little group.

The rebels were massacred except for their two leaders, Ogé and Chavannes, who were brought back to Cap-Français. A special court sentenced them to be tortured on the wheel. Facing a blinding sun, they were tied to two horizontal wheels that were turned while the executioner broke their limbs with an iron bar. In spite of the excruciating pain, they bled to death without uttering a word.

"The law is the law," de Libertad continued. "If the law says they are our equals, so be it. How bad can that be? Except for a few freed Negroes, they are the sons and daughters of whites anyway."

"Your father must have a mulatto child somewhere," Hortense de Libertad quipped, pretending to speak to Gaële. No one reacted.

"What did he expect?" Bayon went on, ignoring his wife's remark. "To scare them? We aren't dealing with pure Negroes here; they're half white. I knew it wouldn't work. Some of them were sent to France by their white fathers to study. They came back with their heads full of stupid ideas. Public executions aren't going to stop them. They're fanatics like the early Christians. This execution has given them their martyrs and now they've won the first battle."

"But it was a small battle," Michel said.

"It would have been small in Europe. But when you lose a hundred white soldiers here, it's a serious defeat."

"Where did the battle take place?" Gaële asked.

"A few days ago near Port-au-Prince, in a place called Pernier. A group of about three hundred armed mulattoes were ambushed by a whole regiment of white soldiers hidden in a sugarcane field. How stupid can one get? During the fight the fields were set on fire by a bunch of slaves. The soldiers who weren't burned to death came out to be picked like ripe fruit. I've told the governor a hundred times, the mulattoes have two choices—either make an alliance with the white man, his father, or with the Negro woman, his mother."

"Bayon," Madame de Libertad interrupted, "I am asking you directly now: Do you have a mulatto child?"

"No, I don't!" de Libertad shouted. "And let me tell you, Hortense, your obsessions are the least of my worries! Don't you realize what can happen here?"

"Can the mulattoes really win, Father?" Gaële asked.

"Of course not! But they can disrupt the commerce of the colony. The new government in Paris is on their side. We should ally ourselves with the mulattoes to prevent an alliance between them and the Negroes. They were helped by slaves in the battle. That's not a good sign."

The silence that followed was interrupted only by the creaking of the rocking chair on the wooden floor of the veranda. Night came on slowly. Like two living lamp posts, Isaac and Placide, each holding a candelabrum, came out and stood on either side of the large front door.

Breaking the silence, Gaële said, "The ideals of the revolution are not going to stop at the borders of France. Today the mulattoes are claiming them for their own. Tomorrow the Negroes will talk about liberty, equality and fraternity. The two groups will then become natural allies."

"The mulattoes aren't fighting for the ideals of the revolution," Michel said. "They only want equal rights with the whites. They'll never accept the blacks as equals. Why, some of them have slaves themselves. An alliance between the freed and the slaves is not about to take place."

"Two years ago, I would have agreed with you, Michel," his father said, "but today, I'm not so sure. Sooner or later, the mulattoes will realize they cannot win, and then they'll think of the half million Negroes we have here. They'll try to corrupt them. I know that the Negroes are naturally passive, but who knows?"

Gaële turned to look at the two servants flanking the door—two black statues dressed in white except for their black shoes and vests. They didn't seem to be listening, but she knew better. She had known them all her life. When she was a child, Isaac and Placide were the de Libertad children's favorite playmates. Gaële and Isaac were about the same age; Michel and Placide, a few years older.

Because Hortense de Libertad considered such a friendship against nature, she had convinced her husband to send their children to France for their education. When Michel and Gaële returned five years later, they found Isaac and Placide distant and proper. Trying to revive the old friendship, Gaële taught them to read and write, and Michel talked about the winds of change blowing over their motherland. But the innocence of the earlier relationship was forever lost. Only in secret could they be friends. In public they were slaves and masters.

Her father's remark made Gaële uncomfortable. She waited a few minutes to regain her composure, then with the calmest voice she could manage, asked, "If the Negroes are so passive, why is there such an increase in the number of runaways?"

"Where did you learn that?"

"Here, in the *Colonial Monitor*," Michel replied, handing the paper to his father.

"Laziness, that's why!" Bayon answered dismissively without even looking at the paper. "Two-thirds of the slave population are Bossales. They don't have any work habits. In Africa they were roaming the savannah half naked, doing nothing. Here, they are asked to do an honest day's work, but it's too much for them. They prefer to hide in the mountains so they can sleep all day."

"Why are you so afraid of an alliance then?"

"If the mulattoes seduce a few thousand of them, the colony will be destroyed before we can prevail."

"How many mulattoes and how many whites do we have in Saint-Domingue?" Michel inquired.

"About forty-five to fifty thousand of each."

"The Negroes have five times that combined number. If they wanted to rebel, they wouldn't need any alliance."

"As far as the numbers are concerned, no. But when it comes to intelligence, they would need more than an alliance. They'd need a miracle."

Monsieur de Libertad stood up, stretched and let out a loud yawn.

"What a year!" he said. "I'm going to bed. Lead the way, Placide."

To everyone's surprise, the order didn't activate the young slave as usual. He remained motionless, his mouth open, staring at a point far in the distance. All heads turned in that direction. To the east, a large hill was profiled against the night sky by a red glow so intense it could have been mistaken for the dawn, except for a column of black smoke reaching for the clouds.

"It's a fire!" Hortense cried.

"A huge fire!" Bayon added. "It must be on the Noé plantation. We have to help out. Placide, get all the overseers! Tell them to gather every able bodied slave! Go quickly!"

Placide set down his candelabrum and disappeared into the dark. But instead of heading for the overseers' compound, he went straight to his father's hut. He was stopped at the door by Marcus.

"I'm sorry Placide, but you'll have to wait here."

"How is it going? Tell me!" Placide demanded impatiently.

"According to plan. We have reports from the closest plantations. Trême, Turpin, Flaville, Noé, Clément are burning."

"I have to see my father! I must know what to do!"

"I'll announce you."

Marcus entered the hut and emerged a few minutes later motioning for Placide to go in. Toussaint's son found his father sitting with a group of Negroes he had never seen before.

"This is my son," Toussaint said. "He is the one who will carry out what has been decided about the big house."

"What should I do?" Placide asked.

"Eight days ago, at a meeting in the Caiman Forest, it was agreed that some plantations would be spared to provide us with food, and some whites designated by their own slaves wouldn't be killed. Bréda has been made a sanctuary. No one should be killed here, and no fire lit. Go now and take over the big house! Prevent the de Libertads from leaving the plantation. We can't protect them outside of here."

"The overseers?"

"Prisoners! They're well guarded by Paul and his group. Go!"

Coming out of the hut, Placide saw that besides the first fire, there were now half a dozen more. Some were close enough for him to hear the crackling of burning wood.

Against the flickering red light, he saw in silhouette Marcus, standing on one leg and on its knee resting the foot of the other, as he leaned on a spear. Placide remembered having seen in a book a drawing of this classical pose of African men.

There was no light in the big house, no one on the veranda. The de Libertads had barricaded themselves inside. They had seen the fires and realized that something terrible was happening, but what? They were anxiously waiting for the overseers.

When Placide stepped onto the veranda, a voice from inside shouted, "Who is it?"

"It's me, Placide."

"Where are the overseers?"

"Let me in. I'll explain."

"No! Go back and tell them to come here with their weapons!"

"There's no need for that."

Bayon de Libertad opened the door a little and pulled Placide inside.

"What do you mean, there's no need for that? Where are the overseers? What in the name of God is going on?"

"It's a general revolt of the slaves."

"It's not the mulattoes?"

"No, just us—but all of us."

As if to underline Placide's announcement, the wailing of a couch shell exploded nearby.

"Too late," de Libertad despaired. "We're trapped like rats."

"It's not too late for you," Placide said calmly. "But you have to listen to me."

"What should we do?" Gaële asked.

"Nothing. Stay here and you won't be harmed. This plantation and anyone on it will be spared because you never allowed cruelty here."

"What guarantee do we have?"

"My father's word."

"Toussaint is involved in this?"

"Yes. And so am I."

This conversation was taking place in complete darkness. Placide couldn't see the expression on anyone's face. He didn't even know who was in the room except for those who had spoken.

"Isaac," he asked, "are you here?"

"Yes."

"Would you please light some candles?"

In the dim light, Placide saw that furniture had been pushed against the doors and windows. Bayon and Michel de Libertad were fully armed with rifles and swords. Hortense and Gaële were sitting on the same chair, holding on to each other.

"Put down those weapons," Placide said. "They won't be necessary."

"This is wrong!" Isaac exclaimed. "I don't want any part of it! I'm not against the freedom of my people, but they're spoiling everything. There's a revolution going on in France, and sooner or later it will free everybody. Why couldn't they wait?"

"Maybe you could have waited," Placide answered, "and so could I. But those who were going to be tortured tomorrow, those whose children were to be sold off tomorrow, have decided that tonight should be the night. They probably think that too many ears, hands and legs could be cut off while waiting for the French Revolution to save them from the French."

"To think that we have nurtured this serpent in our breast!" Madame de Libertad raged. "If I were a man, I'd kill you right where you stand!"

"Mother, please! Don't make matters worse!" Gaële pleaded.

"Shut up, you Jacobin! Isaac, go get the house servants—the cooks, the maids, all of them! You, Michel! Get me the overseers!"

Isaac, sitting with his elbows on his knees and his head in his hands, didn't move from the chair.

"When Monsieur ordered me to put out all the lights," he said, "I went through the house and found no one."

Michel stood and said to Placide, "You know that I am for the abolition of slavery, but I have to defend my family."

"You will find the overseers tied up and well guarded. I would advise you to go unarmed, because if you kill anyone, this house will cease to be a sanctuary."

After a few seconds of hesitation, Michel decided to keep his weapons. He opened the door and another surprise awaited the de Libertad family. In the heat of their discussion behind closed doors, no one had been aware of what was happening outside, the house being some three hundred meters away from the main road to Cap-Français. But now through the open door, a clamor invaded the de Libertad's residence. It drew them out onto the veranda, where they could see thousands of torches moving across the countryside, casting the shadows of a crowd whose number couldn't even be estimated. From time to time, above the general rumbling a scream would rise, piercing and barely human, like the cry of an animal being slaughtered.

Bayon de Libertad pushed his family back inside.

"Good God!" he cried. "It's a general revolt of the slaves!"

The incredulous look on his face reflected a generation that believed in the inherent inferiority of the African race, a race created to serve and be led. But there was no hatred in his racism. Contrary to those who thought that the Negroes should be tamed by force, Bayon de Libertad thought they should be trained to the extent of their limited intelligence. If he could play with his dog and pat his horse, why not his Negro? He firmly believed that the blacks could be taught to obey and to be loyal, although some concepts like dignity, honor and pride were frankly beyond their grasp. To him the Negro's idea of liberty was limited to doing nothing, as opposed to the white man's concept of freedom as doing whatever he chose to do. Therefore this revolt made no sense to him. It wasn't even supposed to be possible.

"Placide," he said in a condescending tone, "I know what the mulattoes want: equality with the whites. What do your people want?"

"The abolition of slavery!"

"Do you plan to achieve that by killing all the whites?"

"No. You and your family are alive, aren't you? But tonight is the night of anger and vengeance."

"It's easy to kill poorly armed farmers, but what will you do against the colonial army and the reinforcement that will come from France?"

"I don't know," Placide acknowledged. "Maybe we'll get weapons and learn from them how to fight."

Since the family had come back inside, Gaële had fallen on her knees and was praying. She was a fervent Catholic and had threatened to embrace religious life each time her mother tried to marry her off to some impoverished nobleman.

One by one, the other members of the family came to join her, even Michel, whose religious conviction was doubtful at best, and the prayer became a collective humming with Gaële leading the chorus. Isaac also felt the need to commend his soul to God, but as a model slave who knew his place, he knelt in another corner of the room, away from the family group.

"Come, pray with us," Gaële invited him.

Visibly flattered, Isaac came closer and the group opened up to make room for him in their midst.

"You too, Placide."

"No, thank you. We wouldn't be praying for the same thing and God would be totally confused."

"This is not the time for blasphemy, Placide," Gaële admonished. "This is like Passover night in Egypt, when the children of Israel put lamb's blood on their doorposts so the exterminating angel could identify and spare their households. This is a time for prayer."

"Mademoiselle Gaële, my father is the lamb's blood on your doorpost. Without his word, no amount of prayer can save you."

From time to time a gunshot interrupted their prayer or conversation. Everyone would fall silent, trying to guess what was happening outside.

The night crawled toward dawn, sleepless, hot and endless. But the morning held no promise of relief. On what scene of apocalypse would the sun rise? Soon after two o'clock rang on the grandfather clock, there was a knock at the door.

"Who is it?" everyone called out in unison.

"Me, Toussaint."

The huge sofa blocking the door was dragged aside and Toussaint entered the room. He went straight to Placide.

"Is everything under control here?"

"Yes, Father!"

Toussaint's walk, the way he carried his head, everything about him seemed different, at least to Bayon de Libertad, whose lips were burning with dozens of questions. But he didn't know how to address his slave—or better said, his former slave.

As soon as Toussaint had come into the room, he had sensed that Bayon wanted to speak. He also had understood that the Frenchman didn't want to say anything that would jeopardize his family's already precarious situation. So Toussaint decided to speak first.

This had never happened before. Usually, even when his master had sent for him, the coachman would stand in front of Monsieur de Libertad, his head lowered and eyes to the ground, waiting patiently to be addressed. Now he stood straight, looking squarely into Bayon's eyes.

"Have you any questions?" he asked.

"Yes! We seem to be relatively safe here, but how long will this sanctuary last?"

"There is no limit to it. But at the first opportunity, we'll take you and your family to the gate of Cap-Français. You'll feel safer in the city."

"If some white people take refuge here, would they benefit from the sanctuary?"

"No. Only their own slaves can give them protection."

"My overseers, are they safe?"

"Not all of them. Some have been accused of raping black women in front of their families. Monsieur Leduc, for instance, is accused of raping a fourteen-year-old girl while dozens of slaves watched. I don't see what can save him."

"But he's my foreman! How am I going to run this place without him?"

"Haven't you realized that you may never run this place again?"

"Yes, he will!" Madame de Libertad yelled. "The colonial army will come after you and those who are lucky to survive will beg to come back to the plantations. As for you…"

"Shut up, Hortense!" Bayon snapped. "Why weren't these things reported to me?"

Placide replied, "I did mention this incident to Madame Hortense. She asked me if I wanted Leduc to marry the girl."

"Madame de Libertad," Toussaint said, "you are alive, not on your own merits but because of your children. As for me, I will never be a slave again. I'll die first."

As he turned to leave, Gaële asked hesitantly, "Toussaint, is Monsieur Dubreuil... well?"

"There are three overseers who will be taken to the city with you. Gaston Dubreuil is one of them."

"What about the others?" Michel inquired.

"Except for Leduc, they will be asked to leave the plantation."

"But that's worse than a death sentence!"

"We don't care if they reach Cap-Français or not."

It was a strange situation. Toussaint had come and left unarmed. His two sons carried no weapons, while the de Libertad men were wearing their swords and had their rifles within reach. But no one doubted who was in control of the situation, except for Hortense de Libertad, who was incapable of admitting that her world was falling apart.

"Leave us!" she ordered Isaac and Placide.

Instinctively Isaac stood, ready to leave the room, but Placide remained seated.

"I said leave us!" Hortense repeated. "I want to talk to my family."

"I'm here to prevent any of you from doing something foolish like leaving the plantation," Placide answered. "I'm not moving. Besides, you've always talked freely in front of me. There's nothing about you that I don't already know."

Toussaint's son was right. The two young butlers had heard and seen everything about their masters, witnessed their most private moments and listened to their most intimate conversations. If it's true that the eyes are the windows of the soul, they had managed to draw before theirs a curtain so opaque that Hortense had concluded there were no souls within. But now that the curtain had been withdrawn, she felt as naked as Eve in the garden of Eden after eating the fruit from the tree of knowledge.

"I don't want to talk in front of them," she whispered to her husband. "Make them leave, Bayon."

But Bayon was exhausted and completely disinterested in whatever his wife had to say.

"You'll have to wait until we get to the city," he answered wearily.

Hortense de Libertad, however, had never been good at holding a thought. Once an idea was conceived in her mind, she had to express it immediately, if not before. It was no concern of hers if the notion was out of place or out of context, as long as it had something to do with embarrassing someone.

"No, I will not wait! Gaële, are you still seeing Monsieur Dubreuil?"

"No, Mother!"

"Are you still interested in him?"

"Yes, Mother!"

"I remember having told you to sever that relationship. Isn't that right?"

"I haven't talked to Monsieur Dubreuil since, but I haven't stopped loving him. Now this night has also liberated me. It is telling me that I was wrong to obey you. If I survive, I will take charge of my life, and if I decide to get married, it will be to a man of my own choosing!"

After gasping for air, Hortense turned to her husband and said, "Bayon, talk to your daughter! I wash my hands of her!"

Monsieur de Libertad was following this conversation with an expression of disbelief on his face.

"Leduc may be killed tonight, if he's not dead already, » he said. Four of my men are going to be kicked out of Breda to fend for themselves through hordes of savages. We don't know if or when we ourselves will reach the safety of the city, and she is asking me to reprimand my daughter for something that is now completely irrelevant! Gaële, follow your mother's example! Marry the man you want to make miserable!"

The subject of this controversy, Gaston Dubreuil, had been sitting on the floor of the overseers' dormitory with his hands tied behind his back. The seven other overseers were also in the same position. Gagged, they couldn't communicate to one another their surprise and their terror. But these feelings were apparent in their eyes and by the perspiration running abundantly from their brows and soaking their shirts.

Gaston must have been in this uncomfortable position for two hours when a group of slaves led by Paul entered the dormitory. The Frenchman was lifted with two others and carried outside. To their surprise, the three were ungagged and untied.

"You're free," Paul told them, "but don't leave the plantation. As you can see, there are fires everywhere. You'll leave Bréda at your own risk."

"Would you please tell us what is happening?" Gaston asked.

Paul walked away without answering. Left alone, the three Frenchmen looked at each other, their eyes filled with unanswered questions.

The overseers were never together during the workday but stationed throughout the plantation supervising the work in the cane fields, the mill, the corn field and the mahogany forest. Almost at the end of the day's work, they had been seized by their own men in broad daylight and disarmed without one having had time to alert the others. They knew it was a revolt, but they had no idea of its magnitude, since they shared the upper class certainty that slaves were incapable of planning a takeover in which not a gun was fired, not a drop of blood spilled.

"Gaston," one of them now asked, "why do you think they've separated us from the others?"

"I don't know... I have an idea but I wouldn't want to give you false hope."

That was exactly what the other two were asking for—a ray of hope.

"Tell us! Tell us!" they urged.

"How do you treat the slaves working under you?"

"Very humanely," Didier replied. "You see, Antoine and I agree with the principles of the revolution. We're for the abolition of all privileges, so we're against slavery. We treat our workers as well as we can under the circumstances."

"We should say, under Monsieur Leduc," Antoine added. "Once he caught me eating with my men and threatened to fire me if I ever did that again. Since the ideas of the revolution aren't very popular in the colony, Didier and I never talked about this with anybody before now."

"I was right then," Gaston concluded. "I also treat my men well. I grew up in a religious family, and I was raised believing that I should treat others the way I want to be treated. I think the Negroes noticed and decided to spare our lives. That's probably what Paul meant when he said that we're free."

"In that case," Antoine observed, "Leduc is a dead man." This was said without pity or regret, and the others agreed in the same matter-of-fact way.

They decided that they should take turns standing guard to avoid any unpleasant surprises. But hours later, although they had kept silent, no one had fallen asleep. Gaston was leaning at the open window looking at the big house fifty meters away. Fires were burning at a distance in all directions. From time to time a group of insurgents going down the main road could be heard blowing conch shells and beating drums. Danger was everywhere, but he was not thinking of his own safety; he had Gaële's in mind.

It had been six months since they talked last. Without an explanation, she had put a sudden end to their long walks along the cane fields and their horseback rides in the woods. There had been no talk of love between them, only pleasure in being together, an ease in speaking about anything and a readiness to laugh. He was saddened but not surprised that the relationship had ended. The gap between them was too wide. In Saint-Domingue, he was a "little white" like other penniless Frenchmen—laborers, artisans, even doctors and teachers—as opposed to "big whites" like Monsieur de Libertad.

"Look!" Gaston cried suddenly, interrupting his daydreaming. "Someone is crossing the yard toward the big house."

Didier and Antoine jumped to their feet and joined Gaston at the window.

"It's old Toussaint," Antoine said.

"Poor man, his whole life has been destroyed."

"Yes, he's worked so hard to reach a position of some importance on the plantation and now this."

Their eyes followed the old slave until he entered the big house.

Gaston Dubreuil, Didier Godart and Antoine Poussin each had similar histories. They had left France to seek a better life in the new world. But having no money to pay for the passage, the three of them had followed the common practice of selling themselves to a ship captain for three years.

During that time, they had become skilled sailors, and because the ships were places of bondage, they had also developed an intense longing for freedom. A captain had the right of life and death over his crew and the officers demanded blind obedience. The slightest negligence was severely punished. The sailors were often put in irons or flogged. In cases of disobedience, they were simply hanged.

When each of the Frenchmen had completed his three years of service, he had asked to be left in Saint-Domingue, the richest French colony. From odd job to odd job, they had all ended up on the Bréda plantation.

Each had actively sought employment there while waiting patiently for an opening. They had heard of Monsieur de Libertad's leniency towards his slaves and thought it was the place where they'd most like to work. They had never met before, but soon Didier and Antoine started developing a timid friendship closely watched by Leduc, the day-to-day manager of the plantation.

Leduc believed strongly in keeping people separated: the de Libertad family from the overseers, the overseers among themselves and away from the slaves. Next to the masters, he had absolute power over Bréda. He could have the white overseers not only fired, but deported from the colony. As for the blacks, he couldn't torture them, but other types of abuses were overlooked by the master. And Leduc could sell them to other plantations where corporal punishments were commonplace. With these threats hanging over them, all who worked at Breda kept to themselves, and even among the whites a conversation would rarely go beyond routine greetings. It was Leduc who had put an end to the budding friendship between Gaston and Gaële by reporting it to Madame de Libertad.

Less than fifteen minutes after he had gone in, Toussaint emerged from the big house.

"Do you think we can talk to him?" Antoine asked.

"I have to," Gaston said. "Hey, Toussaint, come here!"

The three Frenchmen were on the second floor. Toussaint came and stood under the window.

"How are your masters?" Gaston asked.

"You mean my former masters," Toussaint replied. "They are well. We've decided to spare their lives."

"What about us?" Didier inquired.

"No harm will come to you. You have my word."

A collective sigh of relief was exhaled from three chests.

Gaston felt encouraged enough to ask, "Is Gaële all right?"

"Yes. She asked me the same question about you."

"She still cares, she still cares!" Gaston thought.

He turned towards his friends with a broad smile on his face, but they weren't smiling back. Staring at each other, they shared an expression of complete disbelief.

'What? What?" Gaston demanded.

"Toussaint!"

"What about him?"

"He's in the revolt!"

Not all the slaves at Bréda remained on the plantation that night. Some, like Paul, wanted to participate more actively in the revolt—in other words, in the killing of whites. After ejecting the four overseers and hanging Leduc, they left to vent the anger and hatred that had accumulated for generations. From this group, only a few returned in the morning to give a detailed account of events to those who stayed. But the violence still hadn't subsided when the sun came up.

Completely taken by surprise, the French succeeded in organizing only a few pockets of resistance in isolated towns and villages. The countryside, however, belonged to the insurgents. The besieged villages were fast running out of ammunition and in danger of being overrun. The colonists were victims of their own racism. They believed that one of them with a whip could control a hundred Negroes. Many lost their lives trying to do just that.

Paul made an enthusiastic report to Toussaint about the devastation and the killings he had seen.

"We'll soon be free!" he exulted.

"There's no freedom without peace," Toussaint replied, "and we've just started to fight. The army is going to move against us. We must leave Bréda before they arrive."

"What will we do with the whites we still have here?"

"I want them escorted to the outskirts of Cap-Français this morning. You, Isaac, Placide and Marcus will accompany them. Go get everyone ready."

Less than an hour later, the de Libertads and the three overseers were in two loaded horse-drawn carriages and Toussaint came to say goodbye. As he was speaking to them, a horseman entered the plantation's gate at full speed. It was Monsieur de Hauteville, chased by a large group of insurgents armed with hoes and machetes. The blacks stopped at the gate, but their threats and insults followed the Frenchman up to the front of the big house.

"Poor man," Bayon de Libertad observed. "He's running from the rain and he's going to fall into the river."

De Hauteville jumped from his horse.

"Quickly!" he shouted. "Let's get into the house and barricade ourselves!"

Seeing that no one moved, de Hauteville took a sweeping look around. What he saw made no sense to him. Bréda was not burning, everything was peaceful, his pursuers didn't enter the plantation.

"What's going on here? Where are you going?"

"To Cap-Français."

"How in hell do you think you're going to reach the city? I spent the whole night hiding in the bushes, walking in rivers and running for my life! Between here and Cap, there are bands of Negroes killing men, women and children, and you think you're going to reach the city in broad daylight? You're crazy!"

"They're under my father's protection," Placide said. "We'll reach Cap-Français without incidents."

"Your father? Where is he?"

But Toussaint was nowhere to be seen. He had left as soon as he had seen de Hauteville charging in.

"What protection can anyone give against those dogs?" de Hauteville demanded, pointing to the crowd visibly growing at the gate. "Have you any idea of what they've done? My wife is dead, my overseers are hanging from trees! No one is in control of those bloodsuckers!"

"In that case, Monsieur de Hauteville, how do you explain that they didn't set foot on the Bréda plantation?" Placide asked.

De Hauteville turned slowly towards Placide.

"Toussaint!" he exploded. "Where is he?"

"There," Placide answered, pointing to a horseman coming at them across the empty field. An expectant silence fell on everyone, including the blacks at the gate. Only the hoofbeats of the approaching horse could be heard. When Toussaint stopped in front of de Hauteville, he was wearing the shirt and yellow vest stained with his blood.

"Monsieur de Hauteville," he said, "I am riding a horse against your direct order. Aren't you going to kill me?"

"I am unarmed."

"Do you remember this shirt and vest? Three years ago you soaked them with my blood. Do you remember?"

"I am unarmed," de Hauteville repeated. "You're not going to attack an unarmed man, are you?"

"God forbid!" Toussaint exclaimed. "Placide, take this weapon to Monsieur de Hauteville."

From his vest pocket, he pulled a little black book.

"It's my prayer book, the only weapon I had when you attacked me. Let's see if it can protect you."

De Hauteville didn't wait for Placide. He took off toward the house, leaped on the veranda and reached the door. It was locked. He turned, looking for an escape route, but Marcus' spear found him first and nailed him to the door.

When the young African man started to retrieve his weapon, Toussaint stopped him.

"Leave it where it is," the old man said. "From now on you and I are going to treat the wounded and mend broken limbs. You will kill no more."

A few minutes later, the crowd at the gate parted to let the two carriages pass. Placide was driving the second one with Marcus sitting on his right.

They rode in silence for a while, everyone reflecting on the momentous changes that had occurred in the past twenty-four hours. Placide broke the quiet by asking Marcus, "The circle on your cheek, does it mean anything?"

"Yes, but it's a long story. I'll tell you some other time."

"What's your name?" Placide asked with a bit of tenderness in his voice.

"I am Marcus. You know my name."

"No, I mean the name you received at birth, the name your mother called you, your African name."

"Nguele."

"Nguele," Placide repeated. "That's what I'll call you from now on."

"No, don't. I'm afraid I'll never be Nguele again."

The early success of the revolt was due to the slaves' overwhelming numbers and the complete surprise by which the

French were taken. The revolution occurring in their own country should have taught the Europeans that when the humanity of a people is denied for too long, they might choose the worst way to reaffirm it. After all, violence is as human as charity. But in the colony of Saint-Domingue, the French were blinded by their own arrogance.

Nevertheless, the colonial army succeeded in fighting the slaves to a standstill. The cities, the towns and villages were the military strongholds of the colonizers, while the insurgents were firmly entrenched in the mountains. The battlefields were the fertile plains in between. By day they belonged to the whites but by night, to the blacks.

When a French brigade finally entered Bréda, they found the plantation intact and empty. They found no trace of burning, no evidence of violence, except for a bloodstain on the mansion's front door.

Chapter Eight

The New Kalame

This rainy season had started like any other. Day after day the clouds had gathered over the savannah, closing ranks and leaving no cracks for sunlight to pass, but the heat was oppressive. People, animals, trees and grass—all were begging for water.

Then thunder rumbled as if some giant were rolling a huge boulder on top of the clouds, creating flickering sparks. Suddenly lightning tore the sky apart and the rain descended in sheets twisting in the wind. But something was different this time. Never in the Aradas' memory had they seen so much rain. The ravine was filled almost to the top with a fast flowing-stream that had already drowned dozens of domestic animals. The water hole increased to many times its normal size and flooded the surrounding plain. Every hut was surrounded by a curtain of water running from the roof to the ground like strings of beads.

From his refuge in the trunk of the baobab tree, Emile was looking sadly at the downpour. Rainy seasons were difficult times for him. He had already faced two of them and this one could well be the worst yet. In the two previous years, the mornings had generally been sunny. That had allowed him to go for a short walk, to stretch, and more importantly, to spend a few hours with Bambolo. His pupil, now a young man, had remained his main food supplier, although Emile had attempted to gather a few roots, leaves and some fruit on his own. This was somewhat risky since some of the plants were poisonous. After a few severe stomachaches, Emile realized that he was not about to be self-sufficient.

What further complicated his situation was that he had fallen sick at the end of the last dry season. His eyes and skin had taken on a yellow tone. The burning of a low-grade fever had exhausted his energy and the swelling in his bad leg had made it impossible to practice his favorite exercise of fencing with Bambolo.

It had taken the Frenchman some time to make a worthy opponent out of the young African. Many times he had pinned Bambolo against the baobab with the tip of his blade at the youngster's throat. Bambolo was fascinated by this new game, and in time he had managed to match the pink man's skill with his youth and agility.

Now the rain hadn't stopped for eight days and during that time Bambolo hadn't come. Emile was well sheltered, but his food supply was disappearing fast in spite of his lack of appetite. The fever hadn't left him, and the humidity had awakened every ache in his body. Despite his misery, the thought of escaping had long ago deserted his mind.

From Gaouno's hut in the new Kalame, Bambolo was staring in the direction of the mountain—a useless effort, since it was shrouded in fog. Visibility was so limited that if he had thrown a spear through the rain, he wouldn't have seen where it landed.

"Is something calling you to the mountain?" Gaouno asked, placing his hand on Bambolo's shoulder.

"Yes, maybe for the last time."

"Why?"

"I can't see the new village from the mountain. We no longer need a sentry there."

Bambolo was right. The new Kalame was built on a wooded hill downstream from the water hole. From his vantage point, he could see the village's approach from the direction of the sunrise. But an enemy coming from the opposite direction would be hidden from view by the forest that stretched all the way to the savannah. Only the sentries on the ground would be able to detect the danger.

"Do you mean you won't go to the mountain anymore?" Gaouno asked.

"I'll go, but not every day and not as a sentry."

Since Nabo's death Bambolo had been living with Gaouno, his wife Maïle, and their twin babies, and Ganiloa had moved in with Bao and his new wife, Sako. The burial of a sacred singer was an elaborate ceremony conducted by the local healer with the assistance of healers and singers from all over the Aradas' territory. This was far beyond Ganiloa's experience. She turned the responsibility over to Mboko, a healer from the village of Kilou who had come to Kalame for the occasion with his son, Bakao, who was himself a sacred singer.

After Nabo's burial, father and son were asked to remain a while longer in Kalame. Bao had always thought that Ganiloa was too young to look after the villagers' health and, of course, someone had to take over Nabo's duties. It was time to train another singer.

Nabo and his two adopted children had just moved into a hut in the new Kalame when the old singer died. Bao decided to give the hut to the two newcomers from Kilou, with the result that Bambolo and Ganiloa found themselves separated.

The young woman didn't like the arrangement. She wanted to be left alone with Bambolo so they could reminisce about their mentor whom they had called The Coconut because, like the fruit, Nabo had a hard shell hiding a good swallow of fresh and tasty milk.

There was also another reason that Ganiloa couldn't explain, even to herself. Her feelings towards Bambolo had changed, or rather, had evolved from the camaraderie of their childhood to a mixture of pleasure and pain, happiness and sorrow which she couldn't understand, let alone control. She spent her days waiting for Bambolo to come down from the mountain and was jealous of any time he spent with Adegba, Bao or anyone else, as if they were stealing from her own time with him. The slightest touch of his hand brought her so much physical pleasure that her first gesture when they met was to take his arm and put it around her own shoulders, but somehow this wasn't enough.

During the few nights between Nabo's death and his burial, when she had slept in the hut alone with Bambolo, she had crawled onto his mat and lain close to him to feel his skin against hers.

Confused by these strange emotions developing in her mind and body, she confided in Maïle, with whom she had developed a strong friendship. Amid tears and giggles they finally concluded that Ganiloa wanted Bambolo as her man.

On the other hand, Bambolo was sometimes embarrassed by Ganiloa's open display of affection and Maïle's smiles of complicity that followed them wherever they went. It was Bambolo who had first suggested to Bao giving Nabo's hut to Mboko and Bakao. But soon he regretted his offer because, in spite of his reserve and shyness, he was harboring toward Ganiloa the same feelings she had for him. However, for reasons known only to himself, he had chosen to discourage her and to repress his own emotions.

Life hadn't stopped in Kalame because of the rain. People moved about when needed, sharing food, dry wood and even fire that they transported quickly under overturned utensils. The children were having the time of their life running naked between the huts. A group of them ran past Gaouno's hut screaming and carrying on. Bambolo couldn't help thinking that he would have been one of them a few years back. The image of Nguele crossed his mind.

"Gaouno," he asked, "why don't you have a companion?"

"The sons of the king don't have companions."

"Why not?"

"They don't have chores to do because they're always surrounded by people to serve them. Besides, they are considered above any other Arada. Why did you ask?"

"I must have a companion for the coming ceremony of the pledge, and I don't know whom to choose. Because I've been living on the mountain for the past three dry seasons, my closest friends are Adegba, Ganiloa and you."

"And also," Gaouno added, "because you want to remain faithful to Nguele."

"I've asked the gods to erase this circle on my cheek if they wanted me to have a new companion. You can see that the circle is still there. I believe Nguele is still alive."

"I believe so too, but he isn't here. I wish I had a friend as faithful as you."

"Bao is your friend, and so am I."

"You're right, Bao is my friend. And you are more than that; you're my little brother."

From the other side of the hut where she had been cooking, Maïle called to Bambolo.

"The food is ready. Would you like to bring some to Adegba?"

"Yes. Put in enough for two so I can eat with him."

Minutes later, Bambolo was running through the rain carrying a wooden bowl covered with large green leaves. The old griot received him with a broad smile.

"You're the third person to bring me food today," he said.

"Too bad you've already eaten," Bambolo said, bowing to the elder. "This was prepared by a woman from your village."

"I always have room for Maïle's cooking. Besides, I haven't touched anything because I hate to eat alone."

"May I eat with you, then? I have something to ask."

"Certainly! Dry yourself and come sit with me."

Bambolo did what Adegba asked and silently they started to eat. The old man waited patiently for the young man to say what was on his mind, but Bambolo was obviously having trouble finding a way to start.

Finally, as if he were speaking to himself, he said, "I remember things that others seem to forget."

"Me too," Adegba added, encouraging his pupil to continue.

"I mean," Bambolo continued, "we've built a new village, husbands have replaced wives and wives have replaced husbands who were taken away, children have found new families. We're talking less and less about the people we've lost. Even Ganiloa hasn't mentioned the name of Nguele for many moons. Have they forgotten?"

"They haven't," Adegba answered. "But the grass will grow again after a savannah fire, and the gazelle that has lost a fawn to a lion will give birth again next season. That's why there will always be grass for gazelles to eat, and gazelles to eat the grass. The Aradas are not different. We have cried over our dead and avenged them, as well as those who have been taken away. We haven't forgotten, but it's time to go on living in the present."

"I understand all that, but Ganiloa…"

"Have you looked at her lately?" the old man interrupted. "Her hips are larger, her breasts are fuller. She is no longer a child, but a young woman ready to carry new life. If you haven't noticed, you must be the only one. She still thinks of her childhood friend from time to time, but her attention now is elsewhere. It is for us to remember. We are the custodians of the past, we are the memory of the Aradas."

An easy silence lay between the two friends as they continued eating with their hands from the bowl. Adegba sensed that Bambolo still had something to ask, but he didn't want to rush his student. When they finished their meal, Bambolo took the bowl out to wash it in the rain and realized that what was falling was finer than it had been for the last few days.

"We'll see the sun before long," he said.

Painfully the old man stood up and came to look.

"Yes," he agreed. "The ceremony of the pledge will take place on time."

"I wanted to talk to you about that," Bambolo said. "It's time for me to choose a companion and I don't want to. I took a pledge with Nguele. Although I know it didn't count, I consider myself his companion. If I take a new companion, I'll betray him, and if I don't, I won't pass from a boy to a man."

"The ceremony doesn't make you a man; it acknowledges that you have become one," Adegba explained. "Besides, you cannot have a partner. You are the chosen one, you are the only one who can step on the sacred mountain."

"I thought that only the king's sons didn't have companions."

"Yes, but sometimes someone is born under the protection of the gods and needs no other protection. When I was your age, there was a man in the village of Kilou to whom the gods had given the secrets of the leaves and herbs. He found cures that the old healers didn't have. Before he was old enough to take the pledge, he saved the life of the king, Gaouno's grandfather. He was called the chosen one, like you, and never had a companion."

"So I don't have to betray Nguele."

"Even if Nguele were here, he couldn't follow you to the mountain. You are the companion of the gods."

Custodian of the past, memory of the Aradas, companion of the gods. These responsibilities that might have crushed anyone else didn't frighten Bambolo. He was convinced that they were his lot. The reason for his destiny would be revealed to him in due time, but he was already convinced that there was a reason. He was also relieved not to have to choose a partner, for in his heart he would always be Nguele's companion.

He was about to leave when Mboko and Bakao entered the hut. After the usual greetings, Bambolo sensed that the two men from Kilou were seeking a private conversation with Adegba.

The griot sensed it too and said, "Go tell Maïle how much I enjoyed her cooking."

Bambolo understood and left. The rain had become so light that he could see the profile of Gaou-Guinou's Mountain in spite of the deepening darkness. He thought about Emile and wondered how the pink man had survived the downpour. His arrival at the hut seemed to interrupt a conversation among Gaouno, Maïle and Ganiloa, who had come to visit in his absence. He inquired about the sudden silence.

"Were you talking about me?" he asked jokingly. No one answered. He went to Ganiloa seated on a floor mat, and knelt in front of her. He noticed that her eyes were red from crying.

"What's wrong, little sister?" he asked.

"Mboko wants me to marry his son, Bakao."

"How do you know that?"

"I overheard them talking about it in the big hut. They were wondering whom to ask for me because my parents aren't here."

"I met them at Adegba's hut. That's probably what they came to ask."

"I will not be Bakao's wife!" Ganiloa said forcefully. "I would rather run to the sacred mountain and let the gods strike me down!"

The young woman's friends looked at her incredulously. In the Arada society the girl to be married had no say in the matter. It was an arrangement between parents.

When a young man reached adulthood, his parents would start looking for his future wife. She could be found within their own village or at the ceremony of the pledge. Then they would approach the girl's parents with gifts that could be accepted or refused. If the affair were concluded positively, the young people were informed of their approaching wedding.

Sometimes the future groom could initiate the process by pointing out to his parents the girl he would like to take into his hut. However, the girl had no choice but to obey her parents' decision. Only after the wedding was she forever free of her parents' authority.

"I don't understand. Why are you so much against this union?" Gaouno asked. "You've been working with them since Nabo's death. You told me yourself that you're learning a lot from Mboko. You also said that Bakao's voice is so clear and beautiful that the gods had to be listening."

"Why don't you understand?" Maïle asked her husband. "It's obvious that Ganiloa would prefer to be someone else's wife."

"But she has no choice!"

"Of course she does. If there is more than one young man acceptable to the parents, the girl may be asked to choose."

There were few rigid laws in the Aradas' culture, but rather only traditional ways of conducting themselves in normal circumstances. However, in unusual situations there was room for improvisation. In such cases they would ask a griot if he remembered a similar occurrence, and if so, his story would serve as a guide.

"But Ganiloa has no parents," Gaouno said.

"Because she is living with Bao and Sako," Maïle reasoned, "they are her parents now. Even Adegba cannot say otherwise."

"In that case, Mboko will present his gift to the chief and his wife. Their offer will be accepted unless…"

"Unless," Maïle continued, "Bao receives a gift from someone else at the same time."

"Yes, but from whom?"

"You and me."

Maïle, Bambolo and Ganiloa were following on Gaouno's face the progression of the idea. His first reaction was to smile, no doubt thinking that it would be a few years before he offered marriage gifts for his two boys, who were still babies. Then he looked at his wife and realized that, in spite of her smile, she was serious. Frowning, his eyes went from Bambolo to Ganiloa, and finally the idea registered.

"Bambolo?"

"He lives with us," Maïle said. "We're his parents now."

During this exchange, Bambolo hadn't said a word. Now he got up and walked out. Ganiloa followed him.

The rain had stopped completely. It was dark and silent.

"Don't you want to take me into your hut?" she asked.

"You belong to Nguele."

"What?"

"When the chief sent me away from the village on the night of the attack, did Nguele ask you to be his wife?"

"Yes."

"What did you answer?"

"He told me about your agreement and I said yes. I was very flattered."

"You belong to Nguele."

"We were children! We had no right to make that decision. His parents didn't offer, and mine didn't accept any gift. I liked you both, and I would have said yes to you, too."

"But he was the first one to see you."

"You're talking about Nguele as if he were here. My choice is not between him and you, but between you and Bakao. I know you believe that Nguele will return to Kalame. If I'm living with you, he'll find us both here. But if I'm living with Bakao, I won't be in Kalame when Nguele returns."

"Why not?" Bambolo asked with apprehension.

"Because Bakao's companion and his friends are in Kilou. He may choose to go back when his work here is done."

Bambolo hadn't thought of this possibility. The contact between the three villages was negligible at best. The first people he had ever seen from Kilou were those whom he had met at the sacred field. If Ganiloa moved to another village, he might never see her again. The thought was intolerable. He realized that a decision had to be made. Lost in his thoughts, Maïle's voice startled him.

"Gaouno has agreed."

Ganiloa was elated.

"We have to hurry," she urged, "and bring gifts to Bao."

"There's no need to rush," Maïle replied. "Mboko has no possessions here. His gift will have to come from Kilou."

Ganiloa released a sigh of relief.

"What about you?" she asked Maïle. "Have you thought of a present to bring to my parents?"

"Gaouno has a good idea," Maïle answered, "but it's up to Bambolo."

"Up to me? Why?"

"My husband thinks that Bao would be very happy to have the long knife Gaouno gave you when he returned from Bakou."

"The long knife is on the mountain," Bambolo said. "I'll bring it as soon as I can go there."

Ganiloa had to restrain herself from throwing her arms around Bambolo. Everything was perfect! Gaouno was Bao's best friend, Bambolo and herself were his protégées, and the gift was the best anyone could offer a chief. There was no way Bao could give his preference to Mboko and Bakao, two complete strangers.

Two days later Bambolo was climbing the slopes of the mountain. The rainy season was not yet over, but the steady downpour had stopped. It was the time of year when the mornings were clear, the afternoons cloudy and the nights misty and fresh, excellent for sleeping.

Halfway to the top, Bambolo sat down facing the plain below. He needed a few moments to prepare himself for whatever was waiting for him at the baobab tree. He didn't know in what shape he was going to find Emile. Maybe he was already dead.

The time he had spent with the Frenchman had been beneficial to him. He had gained knowledge that any other Arada had no way of knowing. Besides learning another language, Bambolo was now aware of faraway places where his friends could have been taken, places with names like Cuba, Jamaica, Virginia, Saint-Domingue and Martinique.

In spite of this, Emile's oncoming death hadn't filled him with sorrow, for he had never developed a feeling of friendship toward his captive. Emile was still his parents' killer and Nguele's kidnapper, a vulture with a broken wing, but a vulture nonetheless.

He was about to continue climbing when he noticed a small group leaving Kalame in the direction of the sacred field. From this distance, he couldn't recognize anyone but he knew who they were. Bakao and a few defenders from Kilou were going to their village to bring back the gift Mboko would present to Bao. Bambolo's eyes followed the group for a while. Then, thinking of the long knife he had to get to keep Ganiloa in Kalame, he decided it was time to be on his way.

Approaching the baobab tree, he noticed that Emile was not at his favorite place. On sunny mornings, the Frenchman liked to sit in a small clearing near his shelter where he could warm up. But today the clearing was empty.

Bambolo leaned into the hollow tree and called Emile's name. A grunt was his only answer. Emile was lying on his back, his mouth and eyes wide open like someone who couldn't believe what he was seeing. Instinctively Bambolo turned his head in the direction the pink man was looking, but there was nothing to be seen.

"I thought I was going to die without seeing you for a last time," he finally said.

"The rain stopped me from coming. Do you have any food left?"

"I haven't eaten for two days."

"I'll get something for you."

"I'm not hungry. Give me some water."

Emile's drinking gourd was empty. Bambolo went outside and filled it in the brook nearby. He lifted the man's head to help him drink. His lips were calloused and cracked into a dozen miniature ravines.

"Is there anything else you want?"

"Yes, I need to talk to you. I've been here for about three years. I've told you everything about me and taught you everything I know. Now you can speak my language. You know the name of my country. I've told you about slavery. I've drawn maps on the ground to show you where the slaves were taken. But you've told me very little about yourself. I know just a few words of your language. I know nothing about the history of your tribe, only the name of your village. I admit that in the beginning I didn't think you had a history or a language. But even when I recognized my error, you taught me nothing. You never trusted me. Why?"

"Because you are the lion cub."

"What does that mean?"

"Once there was a crippled lion cub that couldn't follow the pride, so it was left behind. A mother gazelle found it and took pity on it. She fed it side by side with her own baby. The lion cub grew stronger and stronger. All babies drink milk, but when they grow up they change to other food. The young gazelle started eating grass and the lion cub went hungry. One day, the mother gazelle found the cub eating her baby. "Why?" she asked. "Because," the young lion answered "a crippled lion cub is still a lion, and your flesh is my only food.""

"If I could have helped you reach the sea, you would have taken me captive, then you would have come back with your people and your weapons to kill and capture more Aradas. You had no other reason to be here."

"Bambolo," Emile said with a barely audible voice, "I need you to forgive me."

"Why?"

"I'm going to die and appear before God. If you can forgive me, He will too. If you don't, He will throw me in hell and I'll burn forever."

"I'll forgive you when Nguele returns."

"Listen to me. Your friend will never come back. Let me tell you again how the operation is conducted. When we attack a village, the first thing we do is to kill anybody in authority. We recognize them by the way they dress, by the way they act and how others react to them. This is to prevent any organized revolt between the village and the sea. Besides, the captives are tied together. If your friend escaped, he'd be dead by now; otherwise he'd be here already.

"When we reach the sea, all the tribes are mixed together. The slaves are sold to different buyers, loaded onto different boats, and taken to different places. I have more chance to reach the sea in the state I'm in now than your friend has to come back."

"If you want me to forgive you, why are you reminding me of all this?"

"You have to know what you're forgiving."

"The death of my parents too?"

"Yes."

"What will I gain from that?"

"God will forgive you as you forgive me."

"When I die, I will join my ancestors. I will not appear before either of your two gods."

"Bambolo," Emile said, "I gave up long ago trying to convince you that there is but one God. You can believe whatever you want. I'm only asking you to say that you forgive me. What do you have to lose?"

"All right, you can die in peace. I forgive you."

This pardon was given more to stop Emile's whining than anything else. But something in the pink man's belief intrigued the young Arada. The idea of a place where people would burn forever after death was amazing enough, but what really interested him was the ease with which one could escape punishment.

"Emile," Bambolo asked, "what about the others?"

"What others?"

"All the people you've killed and captured. Shouldn't they too forgive you before you die?"

"You know I can't find them all. I have to count on you and on my own repentance."

"Will that be enough?"

"That's what I was told."

"Then your people will always be killers."

"Why?"

"Your good god forgives too easily those who disobey him. And when he doesn't forgive, he sends them to the evil one for punishment. But why should the evil one punish those who have served him all their lives?"

"I don't know. Now let me die in peace."

Bambolo hadn't forgotten that his reason for coming to the mountain was to bring back the long knife that would be his engagement gift. He picked up the two swords lying side by side on the ground. When he went outside into the daylight to make sure to take the one from Bakou, he noticed that the clouds were gathering for the afternoon shower.

"I must go before the rain begins," he said.

He put the water gourd and some fruit within Emile's reach and left with the sword. The next day he came back and buried the Frenchman in the shade of the baobab tree.

"Adegba, are you awake?"

"I am now," the griot answered from inside his hut. "Come in."

Bao parted the curtain of stringed beads and entered.

Adegba was still lying on his sleeping mat, rubbing his eyes to prepare them for the light that had entered his abode in the company of the village chief.

"I'm sorry to have awakened you, " Bao apologized, "but I need advice. I didn't sleep at all last night."

"What was troubling you?"

"Yesterday morning, I received a beautiful gift from Mboko. He informed me that he wanted Ganiloa for his son, Bakao. I was going to agree, because I want them both to stay in Kalame. The father is a very able healer and the son, a gifted singer…"

"You said that you were *going* to agree," Adegba interrupted. "What stopped you? Didn't you like the gift?"

"I did. It's a beautiful carved amulet made of polished black wood hanging from a string of rare beads. Mboko told me it would protect me in any situation. What stopped me was another gift…"

"From?"

"Gaouno."

It didn't take long for the old man to figure out for whom the second gift had been presented.

"What did he bring?" he asked.

"The long knife he brought back from Bakou."

"And you came to ask me which gift to accept."

"That choice would have been hard enough, but it's more complicated. I would like to keep the healer here. If I reject his present, I'm afraid he'll leave Kalame. On the other hand, how could I reject the offer of the king's son? And the choice between the two young men is not easier. One is a sacred singer who has chosen to serve the gods, and the other has been chosen by the gods."

"My friend, you have no problem," Adegba said with a wise smile. "When the parents cannot decide, the girl is asked to choose."

"But I know what's going to happen," Bao answered. "Ganiloa will choose Bambolo, and Kalame will loose a talented healer."

The Arada Pledge

"And if she marries Bakao, how would you stop the two men from leaving for Kilou with their new daughter and wife? Kalame would lose two healers instead of one."

"Thunder on the savannah!" Bao exclaimed. "I hadn't seen that part."

"You still have no problem," Adegba explained. "Let the young woman choose. That will keep at least one healer in the village. Besides, I don't think Mboko will go anywhere. Bakao may feel angry and jealous and want to go back to Kilou. But Mboko will stay."

"What makes you think so?"

"In Kilou, Mboko was just one of many healers. But here in Kalame he's important as *the* healer."

"Very well. I'll let the girl choose and hope that the gods will guide her."

A few hours later, Bao and his wife received in their hut all the parties involved. The chief was sitting on a floor mat facing Gaouno, Maïle and Mboko. The young adults—Ganiloa, Bambolo and Bakao—were asked to wait outside.

"My friends," Bao said, "I've received your gifts with great surprise. I never thought it would be my responsibility to accept a husband for Ganiloa. I consulted Adegba who informed me that it is my duty since the girl is living under my roof. After my surprise came my embarrassment. I've been unable to determine which gift pleased me more, which proposal honored my family more, or which young man would be better for my adopted daughter. I was told that in cases like this, the girl is asked to choose. But before I call her, I want you to know what I fear. It would be a great loss for me if the family that is not chosen felt rejected and left the village. Kalame needs its chief healer as well as its chief defender."

"I won't move from here," Mboko assured him. "I'll accept her choice, no matter what it is. I feel honored that my proposal was considered as important as the one from the king's son."

Was it a last effort by the healer to sway the chief in his favor? Gaouno didn't know, but he was not about to leave Mboko's generosity unanswered.

"I will also abide by Ganiloa's choice," he said. "If my son isn't chosen, I'll still stay in Kalame. And you won't have to return my gift."

"Mine either," Mboko added.

"Thank you, thank you my friends," Bao said. "Maïle, ask Ganiloa to come in."

Ganiloa entered and was invited to sit between Bao and Sako. As Maïle had advised, she kept her gaze on the ground as a sign of submission, pretending not to know why she was there.

"Daughter," the chief said, "it's time for you to become a wife. If you had the right to choose between the two young men who are outside, what would your choice be?"

"You mean Bambolo and Bakao?"

"Yes."

"My choice would be Bambolo."

"Why?"

"Because I've known him longer. We've laughed and cried together since we were babies."

"Everyone here has agreed to accept your choice," the chief said. "Now go tell the young men to come in."

When Bakao heard from the chief what the decision was, he respectfully protested against the way the choice had been made. Being rejected by the parents would have been painful enough, but by the woman he wanted was unbearable.

"I'll leave Kalame when my work is done here," he said. "I'll go with you to the ceremony of the pledge, but there I'll join the people from Kilou and return to my village."

Turning towards Bambolo, he added, "I wish you many children."

The apparent generosity of the wish was not supported by the look Bakao threw at Bambolo. Jealousy and hatred flew from his eyes like spears, and everyone in the hut noticed it. Mboko, wanting to prevent an embarrassing situation, took his son's arm and tried to lead him out.

"We've accepted the decision," he said. "At the sacred field, we'll find a girl who wants to share a hut with you."

"Ganiloa also should find someone to share a hut with her," Bakao fumed, "someone who's not going to spend his days on the mountain doing nothing."

"My son," Mboko said, "don't let your sorrow turn into anger. What you've said was unfair."

"Unfair? Why? Does he tend the herd? Has he ever gone with a hunting party to help feed the village? Does he train with the defenders? No! He goes to the mountain every day at dawn and comes back at sundown."

"You're right," Bambolo said. "From now on, I'll stay in the village and do my chores like everyone else. I'm no longer needed on the mountain. As far as being a defender, I can assure you that I'm well trained."

"By whom? By the gods? Aren't you afraid you might have to prove it?"

These were not questions. They were a direct threat underlined by Bakao's sarcastic tone and an ugly smile twisting his face. Everyone in the hut understood, and while they were trying to find the words that would defuse the tension, Bambolo's voice rose with calm determination.

"I don't have to prove anything to anyone," he said. "But if I had to, I could surprise even you."

Since his arrival in Kalame, Bakao had been training with the defenders every day. He had the reputation of being one of the best fighting men in the village. He was taller, more solidly built, and a few years older than Bambolo. The outcome of a fight between the two left no doubt in anyone's mind. But to everyone's surprise, there was neither fear nor anger in the younger man's attitude.

The sacred field hadn't changed. Bambolo hadn't attended the ceremony of the pledge for the past two years, but the place was forever engraved in his memory. He remembered the trees, the tender green of the grass at this time when conditions were no longer wet but not yet dry. He had come from Kalame with a group of adults that included Bao and Adegba. Of course, the old griot couldn't walk the whole way. From time to time he was carried on a wooden platform by four strong men.

The group reached the sacred field at sundown, and Bambolo immediately circled the field, retracing the steps he had taken not so long ago with Nguele. He passed by the campfires of several groups from Kilou and Weewa and stopped at the tree that had served as a target for the spear throwing contest where he had met Gaouno for the first time. Back at his own camp, he found Bao sitting alone.

"Where is everyone?" he whispered to the chief.

"Adegba went to see the king, and the others have gone to visit the other Kalame camps. By the way, Ganiloa came looking for you."

Bao also was keeping his voice low, for by tradition, Aradas avoided making noise before the ceremony proper.

"And you?" the young man asked. "Why are you sitting here all by yourself?"

"I was thinking of Eladjo."

"That's what I thought. It must be sad for you to come back to this place."

"No, I'm not sad any longer when I think of Eladjo. I only remember the good times we had. As long as I thought he was alive, I wondered about his health and wept over his fate. I avoided the places we had been together while tending the herd. Then one day I noticed that the loss of my parents was less painful to me than the loss of my companion, because I saw my parents dead and I buried them. So I finally accepted that Eladjo was dead, since I'll never see him again."

"Do you suffer less now?"

"Yes. I was sitting here thinking of the last time we came to the ceremony. Eladjo and I went to wash up in the river before we entered the sacred field. A group of women arrived while we were leaving. They dropped their garments on the ground and stood naked on the river bank. Eladjo was walking towards the sacred field but looking back at the women. He left the path without noticing, hit his head on a low branch, and fell on his back. The women's laughter followed us all the way to the field. Now when I think of Eladjo, it's with a smile, not a tear."

"I wish I could do that, but I can't."

"You will. Soon you'll be married, you'll have children, and other concerns will occupy your mind. Nguele will always be in your memory, but you'll have many other things to think about."

This was rather confusing for Bambolo. Wasn't it treason to abandon your companion? At the same time, how could he consider Bao a traitor? But how could the chief consider Eladjo dead when there had been no body to bring for burial? He didn't want to follow this line of thought for fear of admitting that Bao's position was the wisest. He wasn't ready to consider Nguele dead, so he changed the topic.

"Aren't you hungry?" he asked. "I am."

"I am too, but Ganiloa offered to bring us food. Let's light a fire so she can find us."

Bambolo didn't want to talk about Ganiloa either, so he left silently to look for dead wood. When he returned, Bao wasn't there. He put the wood down and sat in the dark, waiting. His conversation with the chief kept slipping back into his mind, especially Bao saying, 'Now when I think of Eladjo, it's with a smile.'

Other words came back to him as well. Ganiloa had told him, "My choice is not between Nguele and you, but between you and Bakao." He also remembered Adegba saying, "The gazelle that lost a baby to a lion will give birth again next year." Even Emile, on the day before he died, had said, 'I have more chance of reaching the sea in the state I'm in, than your friend has to come back.'

A small but tenacious doubt was finding its way into Bambolo's belief as all these voices were leading him to the same conclusion: Nguele would never return.

More than any Arada, he knew how far they had taken his friend. His hope of seeing Nguele again was slowly fading, but he wasn't totally unhappy about that. How else could he enjoy a relationship with Ganiloa without remorse? Then the thought came to reproach him that he was an unfaithful companion to think this way. Now he had increased the problem he wanted to solve. He was relieved when Bao reappeared.

"I've brought the wood," Bambolo said. "Where is the fire?"

"We don't need fire," Bao replied. "I have the food and also the cook."

Bao stepped aside and Bambolo saw that the chief had been closely followed by Ganiloa.

"Bambolo," she said, "I have something important to tell you. Avoid Bakao as much as you can."

"Why?"

"He intends to prove in front of the whole tribe that you are not a chosen one."

"And how does he plan to do that?"

"I know," Bao said without hesitation. "He's a good fighter. If he challenges you in front of everyone, he's sure to win. He'll appear to be stronger and better than the chosen one. It would be wise to avoid him, as Ganiloa says. But no matter what happens, remember that the short spear is his favorite weapon."

The short spear was half the length of a regular one. It wasn't for throwing but for stabbing and hitting at close range. Usually the defenders carried a long shield on their left arm and in their left hand, behind the shield, they clenched three long spears. In battle they would run toward the enemy and, at a signal from their group leader, throw the spears one after the other. But then when they reached the enemy line, they would be left without an offensive weapon. So Gaouno had the idea of the short spear to equip the defenders for hand-to-hand combat at this stage of the fight.

The ceremony took place the next day, with everything happening as Bambolo remembered. Early in the morning, the smell of food being cooked filled the air. The elders started making their rounds tasting food from different campfires, and the young people broke the silence singing and dancing to the beat of the drums. But no one set foot yet on the sacred field. When Bambolo decided to go for a walk, Ganiloa realized that he had no intention of avoiding Bakao. She followed and soon caught up with him.

"Bambolo, are you looking for a fight with Bakao?" she asked.

"I'm not looking for a fight. I just refuse to hide from him."

"He's blind with jealousy. He may do anything."

"If you believe that I've been chosen by the gods, you must believe that I'm in no danger."

"Promise me that you won't provoke him."

"I promise, but if he provokes me, don't interfere."

"I promise."

They continued walking under the trees on the path worn around the sacred field by generations of Aradas until they reached a group of young men engaged in martial exercises.

Noticing Bakao among them, Bambolo went straight to him and bowed in a sign of respect. But Bakao didn't return the greeting by touching Bambolo's head.

Instead he turned to his friends and said, "In the village of Kalame, they call this man the chosen one, not by the gods but by a woman."

"He is called the chosen one by the king, the griot of the tribe and the village chief of Kalame," Ganiloa said. "You refuse to admit it because the woman you mentioned chose him over you."

"Ganiloa," Bambolo said, "you promised not to interfere."

"Why shouldn't she?" Bakao asked. "She's your only protection."

"Against what? Against whom?"

Bakao couldn't answer without revealing his jealousy, a feeling considered ignoble among Aradas. He chose to keep silent, but Bambolo decided not to let the insults pass.

"Tell me Bakao," he insisted, "tell everyone: Against what is Ganiloa supposed to protect me."

"An attack by the Kaplaous."

"There are no Kaplaous here. There were no Kaplaous in the chief's hut when you first accused me of being unable to defend myself."

"I've never seen you train with the defenders."

"In that case, pick up your favorite weapon and give me my first lesson."

Bakao had been dreaming of this moment, the moment when he could prove his superiority over his rival. But now here was Bambolo giving him this opportunity so willingly. What if he really were trained by the gods?

It was too late to back out. Bakao picked up a shield and a short spear. Bambolo had also armed himself with a spear, but he didn't take up a shield. Ganiloa brought him one but he refused it, saying simply, "I wasn't trained with that."

Bakao charged. He tried to strike Bambolo on the head, on the left, on the right, at the ankles, but Bambolo had an answer for every blow. He blocked, dodged and escaped each time Bakao thought he had him cornered. Finally Bambolo sent the short spear flying out of the singer's hand. It landed on the grass at Ganiloa's feet.

"Give it back to him," Bambolo said to his fiancée.

Bakao took the weapon and again tried to strike his rival. Again he was disarmed, but this time his spear landed on the sacred field where he couldn't retrieve it.

"You see," Bambolo said, "you had no reason to worry about me."

Bakao threw down his useless shield and walked away.

Later that same day, Bakao's pride suffered an even greater blow. Almost at the end of the story of the tribe, Adegba left the mound in the middle of the sacred field, went to King Gaoube and whispered in his ear. Gaoube answered by a visible sign of approval. Adegba returned to the mound and announced that, because of his age, he was unable to finish the story and that the king had given permission for someone else to do so. He called Bambolo to the mound and sat down among the young men who were about to take the pledge.

Bambolo started where Adegba had left off. He told the story of the attack on Kalame, the victory over the Kaplaous, the destruction of Bakou. He related the quarrel between the king and Gaouno because he thought it was going to affect the future of the Aradas. When he finished, he was going to join Adegba among the companions-to-be, but the old griot signaled for him to continue.

Bambolo directed the young men to kneel two-by-two facing each other and to repeat the pledge after him. They were about his age, and there he was, standing in the center of the sacred field, telling the story of his tribe and conducting the ceremony of the pledge that he himself had never taken. Such consecration had never been bestowed on any Arada before him.

He had realized his dream far sooner than he had expected. Was this what the gods wanted? Had he used all the knowledge and skills he had acquired on the sacred mountain? Something in his mind answered No. It all couldn't have been to simply to win a fight with Bakao.

As for the unhappy singer, he had left for his native village the moment Adegba called on Bambolo to finish the ceremony.

Chapter Nine

The Curse of the Pledge

The year was 1802. From his headquarters in Gonaïves, General Louverture was receiving messengers from all over the island—not only the colony of Saint-Domingue, but also the eastern part of the island that had formerly been a Spanish colony. He had occupied the latter the year before in the name of the Republic of France. The news wasn't good and the general, now also the powerful governor of the entire island, was worried.

A French expedition had successfully landed at different locations in the colony. This had been expected, and his plan was to face them with fierce resistance and then burn to the ground any place that couldn't be held by his men. The French forces would reach the mountainous interior completely exhausted and the indigenous army could then easily cut them to pieces.

Some of his generals had followed the plan to the letter. Christophe torched the city of Cap-Français and retreated beyond the northern range. Dessalines destroyed Saint-Marc and took his troops to the central plateau.

But the governor's own brother, Paul, surrendered Santo Domingo without firing a single shot. Another of his generals, Laplume, welcomed the French soldiers to the city of Cayes. And General Lamartinière tried but failed to burn down Port-au-Prince. From these cities that had fallen, three French divisions were converging on the interior without having suffered significant casualties. The original plan had failed.

The sun, slowly sinking into the bay, was coloring everything a rosy pink—sea, clouds and the arid hills around Gonaïves. Somberly the governor paced the floor of his office while he reviewed in his mind the worsening situation. Not an hour passed without a messenger coming to deliver more bad news. He was relieved when an aide announced the arrival of Colonel Arada.

Instead of saluting militarily when he entered the room, the colonel embraced the general as a son would his father.

"I came to tell you that your two sons are in Ennery. They arrived this morning."

"From where?"

"They rode from Cap-Français, where they landed with the French expeditionary forces. They're with a French citizen named Coisnon who seems to have been their teacher in France. Before leaving Paris for Saint-Domingue, they were received for dinner by the first consul, Bonaparte himself. They obviously have a lot to tell you."

Minutes later General Louverture and Colonel Arada were galloping toward Ennery, a village some thirty kilometers north of Gonaïves where the governor had a private home on a small plantation. They rode at a furious pace, and the colonel couldn't help thinking that the old general was still the best horseman he had ever seen. If they could have read each other's thoughts, they would have known that both of them were thinking of the almost eleven years following that night of terror when freedom from slavery had come to the Breda plantation.

Two hours later they reached Ennery. Without slowing down, they left the main road and followed a path that only a person familiar with it could detect. They entered Louverture's property by jumping over a laurel hedge.

"You're still the centaur," the colonel said.

Returning the compliment, the general replied, "You've been imitating me pretty well."

Many people who had known them wouldn't recognize old Toussaint and the African boy renamed Marcus. Toussaint was wearing the uniform of a general of the Republic of France, complete with epaulets, sword, and the red, white and blue sash of the revolution tied around his waist. The uniform worn by Marcus, as Doctor of the Army, was not as brilliant.

When they had left Breda more than ten years before, they went to join the insurgents in the mountains. They enlisted as a doctor and his assistant, because the only skill they could bring to the struggle was their ability to heal wounds and mend broken bones.

One day while Jean-François and Biassou, the two supreme leaders of the revolt, were out of the camp, a large group of French soldiers attacked. Toussaint quickly organized the defense. After resisting the French assaults for an entire day, at the end of the afternoon he succeeded in pushing them down the sides of the mountain, through the valley below, and all the way to the outskirts of the fortified town of Plaisance. For the first time the rebels realized there was a science to war.

The two leaders received the news of Toussaint's victory very differently. Jean-François asked Toussaint to become his secretary and personal representative; Biassou, on the contrary, was consumed with jealousy. From that day, Toussaint was involved in military affairs and Marcus replaced him as doctor.

Soon after, Spain and Britain formed an alliance against the French Revolution, and the war spilled over into the colonies. Saint-Domingue was invaded by two powerful armies, with the Spanish coming from Santo Domingo, the eastern part of the island, and the British attacking from Jamaica to the west. Jean-François and Biassou embraced the cause of the Spanish crown, and Toussaint followed his leaders.

In the Spanish camp, Toussaint received professional military training. He then carefully recruited three thousand blacks whom he molded into a modern army according to European standards of the time. With these troops well structured and disciplined, Toussaint not only cleared the countryside of French soldiers but even occupied a few towns of the northern province in the name of the king of Spain.

With two-thirds of the colony thus occupied by the Spanish and British forces, the French governor, General Lavaud, realized that the only way to save the colony for France was to persuade Toussaint to change his allegiance. To convince the black leader, Lavaud argued that revolutionary France with its ideal of equality was the only nation of the three that could favor the abolition of slavery.

In the summer of 1794, Toussaint summoned his staff and lieutenants and said, "I have been in contact with General Lavaud by letter for some time now. He has asked me to join forces with him against the British and the Spanish. What do you think I should do?"

"Tell him to go to hell!" Dessalines spat out.

"Why?"

"Why? Because they were the ones who enslaved us! Our revolt was staged against them and we've been fighting them for three years!"

"It's always good to know whom we are fighting against, but who can tell me what we're fighting for?"

"The abolition of slavery!"

"Voilà!" Toussaint exclaimed. "And who proclaimed the abolition of slavery? It was the French commissar of Saint-Domingue, Sonthonax," he said, answering his own question.

"He had no choice! We all know that the French royalists and republicans were killing each other in Cap-Français. He only gave us our freedom in exchange for our help,"

The discussion was moving in the direction Toussaint wanted.

"I'm very glad you mentioned the enmity between royalists and republicans. When we started our revolt, France was ruled by a king. After he was decapitated by revolutionaries, the same republicans abolished slavery here. You said that Sonthonax had no choice, and I agree. But what he did was more than England and Spain have ever done, because they are still ruled by kings. Clearing the colony of all sorts of royalists is precisely what General Lavaud has asked our help in doing."

"Did he also speak to Jean-François and Biassou?" Christophe asked.

"Yes, but they refused."

"Will we have to fight them?"

"Absolutely!"

"Wouldn't that be treason?"

Toussaint looked straight into Christophe's eyes and said slowly, so as to measure the effect of each word, "Let me tell you what treason is. You know that I'm Jean-François' secretary. I write all his letters and read the ones he receives because he's illiterate. Last week he dictated to me a letter to the Spanish governor of Santo Domingo, asking for permission to sell into slavery every young black who refuses to fight for Spain. The governor granted his request. I have these letters with me and I would like you to read them aloud for everyone."

Toussaint handed the letters to Christophe, his only lieutenant who could read and write.

After this revelation, Toussaint said to his amazed men, "*This* is treason, and I'll have no remorse fighting anyone who's selling black men into slavery. I know that our last battle will be against the French, but the time hasn't come yet."

Although that conversation had taken place eight years ago, Toussaint's last sentence was still ringing in Marcus' ears.

"Maybe the time has come to fight the French again," he thought. "If so, we've just started the last stage of the struggle."

Marcus didn't have the political mind to understand Toussaint's strategy. His only compass was the knowledge that his leader, in addition to being the one who had saved his life, was the descendant of an Arada king. It was therefore his duty as an Arada to follow him.

But now thoughts of war were put aside for an intensely emotional reunion. The door of Toussaint's house was thrown open and Isaac and Placide ran out to fall into their father's arms.

"My dear sons," the general asked, "how long has it been since I hugged you?"

"Four years," Placide said.

"Let me enjoy your presence first. Later I'll worry about why the French government returned you to me."

"I can tell you right away…"

"But I'm not interested now. Tell me about your travels, your stay in France, your studies."

Suzanne was surprised to see her husband in such a buoyant mood despite the gravity of the situation. After kissing her, Toussaint went upstairs and cautiously pushed open his father's door. Papa Breda was in his bed pretending to be asleep.

"Papa," Toussaint said affectionately, "stop this nonsense! I know you're awake."

The old man, now blind, rolled over to face his son.

"Oh!" he said, "What an honor to be visited in my bedroom by the governor and commander-in chief of the colonial army."

Toussaint was used to his father's sarcasm. Since they had left the plantation in 1791, his every move had been followed by his father's bitter criticism. According to Papa Breda, slaves had no business revolting. After all, the Bible had accepted slavery. It only recommended that the master be lenient to his servants. He was convinced that if God wanted blacks to be free, He would have sent them a prophet. To which Toussaint had answered that maybe he, Toussaint, was that prophet.

Papa Breda's reasoning was that he himself had led an exemplary life, always obedient to his master, hard working and polite, and as a reward he had been given his freedom. Gaining his liberty in any other way was unthinkable.

When the revolt had occurred, he was enjoying a peaceful retirement on the plantation as a freed slave. He had to be carried out of Breda in his rocking chair. Since then he had never ceased complaining that these rebellious Negroes had spoiled his old age. He had denounced every move of the rebels and complained about the hard life of the camps, the incessant movements, the unexpected attacks. When Toussaint changed his last name from Breda to Louverture, his father was so furious that he fainted three times in one afternoon.

This name change happened soon after Toussaint changed his allegiance from Spain to France. By that act, all the territory he had occupied in the name of the Spanish crown had become

French again. With his constantly growing and disciplined army, he had pushed his former leaders, Jean-François and Biassou, across the eastern border and also he'd retaken many towns and villages from the British forces. Learning about these victories, the French governor, General Lavaud exclaimed, "*Ce Toussaint, il fait ouverture partout.*" (This Toussaint, he makes openings everywhere.) The black man was so flattered that he changed his last name to Louverture. This new name was adopted by the whole family—his wife, sons, brother and sister-in-law, but of course, not by his father.

"It is for me to give you my name," he had said, "not the other way around."

Marcus added Arada to his name in memory of his African tribe.

Toussaint wouldn't have been worried about his father's opinions if Isaac were not so influenced by them. Not that the young man shared each of his grandfather's views, but basically he was convinced of the white race's superiority. To him it seemed impossible for the blacks to win a military confrontation with any European force. His father's victories over the armies of the French, British and Spanish empires hadn't changed his opinion in any way. Having been introduced to French literature by the de Libertad children, he had a naïve admiration for French culture and this, in his mind, superseded any wrongdoing that country could have committed against his own people.

Placide, on the other hand, realized that very few French authors had protested in their writings the enslavement of his race. He believed that the French revolution would be incomplete without the general emancipation of the slaves, and this new conflict that Napoleon had just started against his father had no other objective than to erase all the gains made by the former slaves of Saint-Domingue.

After a few minutes of verbal fencing with his father, Toussaint went back downstairs.

"Where is the Frenchman who came with you?" he asked, letting himself fall into a big armchair.

"He went out for a walk in the dark," Isaac answered.

"Good! I wanted to speak to you alone first."

"But Monsieur Coisnon has a letter for you from First Consul Bonaparte."

"I know almost everything that is in the letter."

"How could you know?"

"I understand what the first consul wants, and after talking to you two, I will also know how he plans to get it. Marcus told me that Napoleon invited you for dinner. Who else were at his table?"

"General Leclerc, his brother-in-law, and Monsieur Coisnon."

"What did he talk about?"

"About peace and order. He said that France is at peace with Europe now and it was time to take care of the colonies."

"Saint-Domingue is at peace. We have taken over the eastern part of the island from Spain, kicked out the British and destroyed the mulattoes' army. We've given a constitution to this colony and restored prosperity. In other words, we have accomplished here what he has achieved in Europe. What else does he want?"

"May I answer the question?" Coisnon asked, entering the room. "The first consul thinks that Saint-Domingue, being a colony of France, had no right to give itself a constitution, unless you intend to make it independent."

"That seems logical to me," Isaac remarked.

"Not to me," Placide answered. "Saint-Domingue is not France. We must have our own laws here. If the royal family regains power in France, something has to protect us from going back to slavery."

"Listen to me, Monsieur," Toussaint said to Coisnon. "Bonaparte is a soldier. He came to power by being a good general. War is the only way he knows to maintain himself in power. The peace you are talking about will not last. He has turned toward Saint-Domingue for resources that can help finance his future war efforts. For this colony to play that role, slavery has to be re-established. That's what explains the size of the forces he has sent against us and the commander-in-chief, his own brother-in-law."

"General Louverture," Coisnon answered, "this letter from the first consul will prove to you that your conclusions are erroneous."

"As I was telling my sons, I already know the contents of the letter. In essence it says, 'General Louverture, your country holds you in high esteem. You have saved Saint-Domingue for the Republic and your rank of division general is well deserved. However, as a French citizen you must understand the right of the Republic to have direct control over its colony. Therefore I am sending General Leclerc to be the general-in-chief of all the French possessions in the Antilles. He is coming with sufficiently large military forces to repress any movement of insurrection in the region. Give him all your support; otherwise we will be forced to consider you in rebellion against your homeland.' Now read it and tell me if I'm wrong."

Coisnon asked and received permission to open the letter. After reading it, he hesitated.

"Am I wrong?" Toussaint insisted.

"No, General. But there is one point you didn't foresee. General Leclerc has authorized me to tell you that if you accept his authority, you'll be his second in command."

"Too late. My generals have opposed the expedition's landing and have begun to resist. I'm already a rebel. If the first consul wanted to avoid a conflict, he would have sent the letter and waited for my answer before sending an armada here. Besides, why has he returned my sons? Is their education complete?"

"If you accept General Bonaparte's proposal, I was ordered to continue teaching them here."

"What you and your first consul don't understand is that here, it's for my sons to teach *you* and for me to teach *General Leclerc*. That's what I intend to do to the best of my ability. Now please leave us. I want to speak to my sons alone."

Toussaint turned toward Isaac and Placide while Suzanne led Coisnon to his room.

"What do you think of all this?" he asked. "Isaac first."

"I think that you should accept General Bonaparte's offer. Your choice is simple: either be second in command to the first consul's brother-in-law or face certain defeat. The French armies have dragged their victorious cannons throughout all of Europe. They will not be beaten here. As far as I'm concerned, I will not fight against France. It would be treason because I'm a French citizen."

"Now you, Placide."

"I'm a black man and a former slave. If I'm free today, it's thanks to the revolt of my people. Treason would be to turn against them. I consider you, my father, their legitimate leader. I will win or perish at your side. Anyway, I'm convinced that General Leclerc will never place you above the other French generals, not even above the mulatto leaders who've come with him."

"What mulatto leaders?" Toussaint asked, obviously alarmed.

"Those you defeated in the southern war of 1799."

"They've come back with the French expedition? How do you know?"

"There were three on the same ship with us. I heard them speaking Creole and I also know that one of them is named Pétion."

"This changes everything," Toussaint said. "I have to be alone to think."

The two young men went to their room at the top of the stairs, leaving their father sitting alone in the dark.

Toussaint was awakened at 4:30, not by the timid rays of the early sun, but by the smell of coffee brewing. From the armchair where he had spent the night, he could see Suzanne preparing his favorite breakfast of cassava bread, cottage cheese, a few slices of avocado and coffee.

Joining her in the kitchen, he said, "It seems that we had more time for ourselves when we were slaves."

"It seems," she answered. "But who's complaining?"

"I know you'd prefer that I stay home."

"Yes, but not as a slave."

"I promise to come back soon. I'm thinking of retiring."

Suzanne was going to ask for an explanation, but Isaac, Placide and Coisnon, following the aroma of the coffee, had entered the kitchen.

"Isaac," Toussaint said, "I was too preoccupied last night to answer you, but I was very disappointed to see to what extent they have succeeded in turning you against your own people. You are very smart and studious, and I had hoped that you would be our first historian, but you are too partial to France to tell the story of our people. The white men went to Africa, tore families apart, turned tribe against tribe, massacred entire populations and called us savages. They took us across the ocean, brought us to this island, made us work from sunup to sundown for almost three centuries. We created riches beyond their wildest dreams and they called us lazy. When we fought to regain our freedom, they called us barbarians."

"Marcus told me a proverb of his tribe. It says, *If the game could tell the story of the hunt, the heroes would be the animals themselves.* Who will tell our side of history? Who will explain the reasons for my different alliances? First I fought directly against the French masters, then I joined the Spanish to combat them. When the French were almost completely defeated, I rescued them and expelled the Spanish. Today I am facing the French again. Their historians will talk about me as a traitor. But who will present my reasons? Who will point out that through all these changes, I have remained faithful to one idea—the abolition of slavery. I regret only one thing: the war against the mulattoes."

"Father," Isaac said, "I understand your objectives. I only disagree with your methods."

"Yes, I know. You think that we should have begged for our freedom, found lawyers to defend our cause and waited for the master to admit the inhumanity of slavery. Tell me, my educated son, where and when in history has anyone abandoned his privileges in the name of justice or humanity? Tell me where and when liberty has ever been given?"

Then turning to Placide, Toussaint said, "Go get Marcus. I have a mission for him."

Less than half an hour later, Placide returned with Marcus, whose family lived nearby.

It was clear that Toussaint had a plan that included Marcus and Placide, but he wasn't ready to share it with them.

At seven o'clock in the morning, the three men arrived in Gonaïves. Already several messengers were waiting for the governor. From them he learned that the French divisions that had landed in the bay of Samana and in Santo Domingo had already reached the city of Santiago in the former Spanish colony. The southern peninsula all the way to Port-au-Prince was in French hands and the northern province had also surrendered. All Toussaint had left were the central plateau and the Artibonite valley.

"It seems that all is lost," Placide said.

"No," Toussaint said, "I'm just paying for my biggest mistake—the war against the mulattoes."

Four years before, the victory over the British and Spanish forces had been due to Toussaint's leadership and troops and also to the determined resistance of the mulattoes in the southern peninsula. Toussaint had been promoted to the rank of division general, while the leader of the mulattoes, Andre Rigaud, was made brigade general, a rank inferior to Toussaint's.

The two men conceived a profound distrust for each other. Rigaud hated the idea of having to obey a former slave, and Toussaint accused Rigaud of wanting a society modeled on that of the United States, where colonialism had been abolished but slavery maintained. Both men were wrong. Toussaint had proven beyond any doubt that he was deserving of his rank, and Rigaud, as well as his lieutenants, were strongly against slavery. But the personal ambitions of the two generals had made war between them inevitable.

On the pretext of insubordination and that Rigaud's men had killed blacks in the south, Toussaint moved his army against his rival. The conflict started in June 1799 and ended in July 1800 with the total defeat of Andre Rigaud. At that time, Toussaint considered that victory as his finest hour, but now that the mulatto leaders had come back with the French expedition he realized that it was indeed his greatest error.

"The mulattoes are going to be the eyes and ears of the whites," he explained to Placide. They know the terrain, they know the language and they still have thousands of supporters all over the country. We have to find a way to divide them from the French, or together they might be too much for us."

Toussaint gathered his messengers in the back yard and told them, "Return to your units and transmit this word to your commanding officers: The French have come to re-establish slavery. I want our forces to burn the ground under their feet, to poison the streams with dead animals, to retreat to the mountains and wait there for the rainy season. Tell them also that if they take mulatto prisoners to treat them with kindness, to talk to them not as traitors but as confused brothers. Now go."

"And what is our mission?" Marcus asked.

"Your mission is to find General Dessalines in the Cahos mountains and report to him my views on the present situation. The French are using the mulattoes only to fight us. Without us they wouldn't have any need for them. I've decided to surrender and to recognize Leclerc's authority. I have two reasons for doing this. First, if I'm out of the picture, the mulattoes will no longer be needed by the French, whose racism will come forth and they'll turn against them. Then we'll work on an alliance with our half-brothers. The second reason is that the mulattoes will never ally themselves with me. Their hatred is still too strong. They will more easily accept Dessalines."

"But General," Marcus objected, "it was your army that Dessalines led to victory in the south. Why would the mulattoes accept him any more than they would you?"

"He can claim he had no choice, that he was obeying my orders."

"And what will you do after the surrender?"

"I'll retire. The more important question is what will we do before we surrender? I want Dessalines to choose a highly defensible position in the mountains. We'll then let the French divisions converge on that place and give them a good measure of our resolve. After that battle, win or lose, Leclerc will be more than happy to accept my peace proposal. Then, in the middle of the rainy season, we'll rise up again and finish them off."

"Will you come out of retirement for that?" Placide asked

"Perhaps. I'm an old man. Whatever time I have left, I wouldn't mind spending with my wife. But if my country needs me, I'll still be more than happy to serve it."

"Can Dessalines replace you?"

"Militarily, yes. Politically, I don't know. Placide, I want you to stay with him and you, Marcus, to bring me his answer."

Marcus and Placide left Gonaïves at nightfall with an escort of five soldiers. After a few hours' ride, they decided to camp on the bank of the Estère River. One of the soldiers warned them that it wasn't safe to wander too close to the water because the river was full of caimans.

Marcus replied, "In my childhood I've seen crocodiles that could swallow three of these little caimans whole."

Placide had been fascinated by Africa, specifically the Arada tribe, since he had learned that his father was the descendant of an Arada king. Whenever his African friend mentioned his lost homeland, Placide never missed the opportunity to inquire further.

"Marcus" he asked, "what's the difference between the freedom you're enjoying now and the one you had in your native home?"

"Here, I'm aware of my freedom because I fought to gain it and I'm fighting to keep it. In Kalame, we never talked of freedom, the same way we don't speak of the air. We breathe it and assume that it will always be there. I had to be captured to realize how free I had been."

"You had no limits."

"Oh yes, we did! We couldn't roam the savannah and the forest as we pleased. There were poisonous plants, poisonous snakes and flesh-eating beasts. We had to share our freedom with them. We had to know them, their habitats and their ways in order to avoid dangerous confrontations."

"How did the children learn all that without schools?"

"We learned from our parents, from the whole village and especially from two adults who were our protectors whenever we had to go out of the village."

"Two companions—I remember your telling me. I always wanted to be your companion, but for some reason you've always refused."

"I can't."

"Give me a good reason why not. First you said I was not an Arada. When Papa Breda and Uncle Paul convinced you that we descended from an Arada king, you said you already had a companion."

"That's true."

"But he's in Africa and you are here. You'll never see him again."

"Listen to me, Placide. You know that I like you. But there is a curse in the pledge, at least for me. When we took the pledge, we weren't supposed to, because Bambolo and I were too young. A few days later I was captured and we were forever separated. I'm afraid that I'll be separated from you if we make the same mistake."

"Marcus, we're at war with the most powerful nation in the world, so our chances of being separated are very good. Curse or no curse, I'd be surprised if both of us survived this conflict. The curse of the Arada pledge is less dangerous than the flesh-eating expedition that just landed in our country."

"All right, we'll take the pledge since it's so important to you, but first we have to accomplish the mission assigned to us."

"I understand exactly what the governor wants and I agree with his strategy," General Jean-Jacques Dessalines said, "but my problem is this. If I take his place as leader of the movement, I'll be regarded as a traitor by some of the black generals. At the same time, if it becomes known that the governor has chosen me, the alliance with the mulattoes will be impossible.

"Other than that, I know exactly what to do. Tell General Louverture that I've found the location where the battle has to be fought. It's a fort called La Crête-à-Pierrot that was built by the mulattoes and reinforced by the British a few years later. I'll need fifteen days to rearm it, then with a garrison of two thousand men, I can give the French a good idea of our determination. There's another point where I disagree with the governor. I'd prefer to keep Marcus with me and send you, Placide, back to your father with my answer."

"But my father clearly said that I should stay here and that Marcus..."

"I know," Dessalines interrupted. "However, the governor will understand that I have all the soldiers I need, but I have no doctor."

This conversation among Dessalines, Placide and Marcus took place under the shade of a huge mapou tree where Dessalines had established his campaign headquarters. Once the general had made a decision, he acted on it immediately.

"I have things to do. When are you leaving, Placide?"

"General," Toussaint's son answered, "my father wanted me to stay with you to see what my conduct would be under fire. But I don't want to disobey you, either. Allow me to leave after the battle."

"Very well, but the governor must have my answer before the battle. He needs to know the place I've chosen and when I'll be ready. Since the roads between here and Gonaïves are still under our control, you can go and return within fifteen days."

Minutes later Dessalines was on horseback riding to La Crête-à-Pierrot to prepare his battle plan.

"Mission accomplished," Placide said to Marcus. "We should take the pledge now. What do I have to do?"

"Kneel in front of me, put your right hand on my left shoulder and repeat after me."

Marcus couldn't recall the exact words of the pledge but he remembered clearly their meaning.

I will never lie to you. If you die outside the village, I will bring your body to be buried so wild animals will not eat your flesh. If you die before me, I'll take care of your family.

When they stood up, Placide reminded him that they had to have an identical sign on their bodies, but they dropped the idea because they couldn't agree on the marking.

Preparing to leave to bring Dessalines' message to his father, Placide said, "Don't worry about my body, Marcus. I'll bring it back here alive."

Each coming from a different direction, the three French divisions entered the Artibonite Valley, then converged on the Cahos Mountains. They had been led there by a series of maneuvers executed by the indigenous army. Marches, retreats and fake defeats had convinced the French that they were pushing Toussaint's forces toward their final collapse.

They had another good reason to head for these mountains: a persistent rumor that a fortune in gold and silver coins was buried there, guarded by General Dessalines. Little did they know that the rumor had originated from Toussaint himself and had no foundation whatsoever.

Ten days after his departure, Placide returned and rode straight to La Crète-à-Pierrot to warn Dessalines that a French division led by General Debelle would reach the fort the next day. Dessalines elevated him to the rank of captain and ordered him to join a regiment whose job was to harass the French from the rear.

La Crète-à-Pierrot was already in ruins when Dessalines decided to make it the site of his last stand. It was built at the summit of a small elevation overlooking the east bank of the

Artibonite River. Dessalines enlarged it to accommodate his eighteen hundred soldiers. Since there was no time to build walls of brick, he made do with huge logs cut from the nearby forest. A large trench was dug around the outside perimeter.

When the French division, guided by mulatto scouts, came in view of the fort, General Debelle looked at it with disdain and couldn't understand why the revolutionary flag of France was floating over the ramparts. He thought that he could take the place with a simple bayonet charge.

Just taking long enough to put his soldiers in formation, he pulled out his sword, pointed it toward the fort and bellowed, "Charge!"

Every section commander repeated the order as loudly as they could, and the whole division, marching in step to the beat of their drums, started toward the ramparts.

It was the first week of March. The tropical sun peeked over the mountains to unveil vegetation in shades of light and dark green, punctuated by the red of a hundred Flamboyant trees, the scarlet flame tree of the Caribbean. Some of the French soldiers were asking themselves why people should kill and die in a country like this. Wouldn't it be better to rest, dream and be lazy?

They also had another problem. Not only were they marching against a French flag but from within the fort came the sound of a song they knew only too well: *La Marseillaise,* the French revolutionary anthem. How many times had they sung this same song defending their young republic against the crowned heads of Europe? Were they now the ferocious soldiers described in the lyrics? Were they those who had come to slaughter someone else's wives and daughters in their very arms? Weren't these words even more legitimate coming from a people fighting to ban slavery from their shores forever?

Other than the song, the fort showed no signs of life as they moved forward. When they came to within fifty meters of the walls, a salvo flattened their entire first row.

"*En avant, en avant!*" Debelle shouted, urging them forward.

The French kept advancing. A second salvo harvested another row. Debelle ordered a retreat to put his men out of range and to regroup. Suddenly the French heard a clamor from the fort. They turned to see Dessalines' men throwing planks over the trench, crossing it and running down the slope toward them. The Europeans hastily but methodically formed a defensive square and received the first charge with a volley of their own. The blacks seemed surprised to meet strong resistance. They hesitated and tried another charge. Two more bursts of gunfire convinced them to run back to the protection of the fort.

The French were no less surprised. How could a gang of savages imagine they could so easily rout a French division? Hadn't they heard of the battles of Arcole and Rivoli? Their surprise turned to anger when they saw how poorly equipped the enemy was: no boots, no uniforms, many half naked. The French attacked the retreating enemy with renewed vigor but when they thought they had their foe pinned against the walls of the fort, the blacks, by jumping in the trench, appeared to vanish into thin air, leaving the French exposed to the guns from within the fortification.

General Debelle realized then that it had been a tactic to bring his forces back into range, but it was too late to do anything about it. The French suffered an immense carnage. Hundreds of them lay dead or dying on the slope. The rest ran back to safety, carrying their wounded general.

Before they could catch their breath, they faced another complication. A cavalry appeared from nowhere, attacked their left flank and disappeared as fast as it had come. The following night, that same cavalry conducted three raids against the French, leaving them no time to sleep.

Two days later, the second French division entered the area. General Boudet was the commanding officer, but the commander-in-chief, Leclerc, also came with his honor guard. When they saw and heard an account of what had happened, their pride was wounded and they planned to avenge the Debelle division. They attacked the fort in exactly the same way and had exactly the same result. Even General Leclerc was slightly wounded.

Later that night he summoned the other generals, as well as the artillery commanders, to his tent. Two were mulattoes who had come from France with the expedition. One, General Andre Rigaud, had fought and lost the civil war against Toussaint Louverture. He was as light-skinned as a southern European. The second was Alexandre Pétion, Rigaud's trusted lieutenant. Tall, with wavy hair and darker than the average mulatto, he was the colonel-commander of the artillery for Boudet's division. Leclerc was adamant that they be present over the objection of some of the French generals.

"Gentlemen," the commander-in-chief said, "since we landed on this godforsaken island, we have advanced from victory to victory until we came to this place. You haven't followed my plan and we have paid a very high price. We've lost twelve to fifteen hundred men. We have been stopped here for more than a week by a small band of barbarians. What happened to you, Debelle?"

"I was wounded on the second assault…"

"I'm not interested in your wound!" Leclerc cut in sharply. "I want to know why you didn't wait for the other divisions as planned."

"General, when my scouts told me this was La Crête-à-Pierrot, I didn't believe it. I was expecting a sizable fort at the summit of a steep elevation. Instead I saw a small building sitting on a gentle slope and surrounded by a palisade of tree trunks. I thought it was a diversion, but I didn't think it was safe to leave it behind, so I attacked it."

"Why didn't you believe your scouts?"

"They're Negroes. I don't think we should trust these people. They're natural traitors."

"May I be excused, General?" an offended Rigaud asked, standing up to leave.

"General Rigaud, please remain seated," Leclerc ordered. "What about you, Boudet? Why did you make the same mistake?"

"You were there, General. You saw what happened. My men were furious to see a French division stopped by a bunch of savages. They launched the attack without my order. I had no choice but to lead them."

"That's a serious breach of discipline!"

"May I say something?" Pétion asked.

"Speak."

"The problem we have here is not really of a military nature. It's a problem of attitude. We speak of barbarians, traitors, savages—in other words, of people who are too stupid to master military arts. If this fort were manned by Italians, Austrians or Prussians, we would have laid siege to it, smashed it with artillery and attacked only when we were sure they had been softened up enough. Instead we led bayonet charges as if the blacks were going to run away at the sight of our uniforms. Your generals and soldiers have completely underestimated their ability to fight and their courage. You're the victims of your own prejudice."

"Let me add something else," Rigaud said. "All this sacrifice, all these deaths, all this war are useless. The blacks are fighting because they believe that you came to re-establish slavery. If you could dispel that rumor, they would put down their weapons and Toussaint would be isolated."

"Would he stop fighting?"

"For a while, yes. But every mistake you make would be a pretext for him to reappear with his idea that only the independence of the colony can guarantee that slavery will not return."

"And you? Are you against slavery?"

"Yes."

"Why aren't you with Toussaint?"

"This country is too small to be independent. Slavery would be brought back by the British or the Spanish. Our only guarantee is to be under the protection of the French Republic and the generous ideas of the Revolution."

The Arada Pledge

After looking at the French generals one after the other, Leclerc took a deep breath and said, "General Rigaud, what would be your reaction if I told you that my mission here is to re-establish slavery?"

Rigaud, who was known for his hot temper, rose and declared, "I would resign from the French army and fight you with any means at my disposal!"

Then he grew calmer and laughing, added, "General, you got me that time. This can only be a joke, right? Good night, gentlemen."

"Colonel Pétion," Leclerc said as the two mulatto officers were leaving, "tomorrow morning I want you to choose the sites where the batteries will be placed."

"I've already done that, General. My cannons will be ready by noon. Good night."

Walking to their tents, Pétion confided to Rigaud, "I don't think it was a joke."

"I agree. It's painful to admit it, but Toussaint is right."

The next day at noon, Colonel Pétion was inspecting the cannons he had positioned toward the fort.

"Tell General Boudet I'm ready to fire at his command," he ordered one of the three soldiers accompanying him.

But the man, gazing through a telescope, didn't seem to have heard.

"What is he doing there?" he wondered aloud.

"What is it?" Pétion asked.

"Look there, Colonel. There's a rebel on the slope. He seems to be searching for something on the ground."

After peering carefully, Pétion said with apparent indifference, "He's picking plants, probably for medicine. Maybe he's a doctor."

"I can drop him from here," another soldier offered.

"No," Pétion refused nonchalantly, "he's too far from us." And seeing that the soldier was still aiming at the rebel, he pushed the barrel of the rifle to the ground, warning, "If your shot starts the battle, I don't think General Leclerc would be pleased."

Back in his tent, Pétion mused, "Someone important must be sick in the fort; otherwise the chief doctor of Toussaint's army wouldn't be risking his life like that."

Before switching his allegiance to Rigaud during the Southern War, Pétion had served in Toussaint's army where he had had the opportunity to meet Dr. Marcus Arada.

Since early that morning, Dessalines had been watching every move of the French army in order to anticipate where and when the next attack would take place. From time to time, he would report his observations to his second-in-command, General Lamartinière, or his chief artillery officer, General Magny, who were following him everywhere.

Marcus also was following Dessalines, but his reason had nothing to do with military matters. The general had been running a fever since the night before and Marcus was insisting that he rest before the upcoming battle.

"I have no time for that," Dessalines retorted. "It's for you to find a way to bring down the fever."

This was what had brought Marcus outside the fort to search for herbs and leaves. Through his telescope, Dessalines witnessed the whole scene: the soldier spotting Marcus, the other aiming at him, Pétion pushing the rifle to the ground.

"Can you identify this officer?" he asked Lamartinière, who was also mulatto. Looking through the telescope, Lamartinière identified him as Alexandre Pétion.

"Hmm…" Dessalines said pensively, "Toussaint was right."

An artillery duel started that afternoon and lasted through the night. By morning, huge gaps had been opened in the fort's walls, but also many artillery positions established by Pétion the day before had been obliterated. Leclerc was still in his tent when a messenger announced the arrival of General Rochambeau's division.

After reviewing the situation, the two generals agreed that it had turned in favor of the French forces, that the fort was now wide open, and that it would fall to the next assault. The Rochambeau division was assigned the task of taking La Crète-à-Pierrot.

Napoleon Bonaparte customarily addressed his troops before a battle. Perhaps thinking that the secret of his military successes was in the speeches, many French generals had picked up the practice. So Rochambeau strode to the front of his division, signaling that he wanted to speak.

"Soldiers of eternal and immortal France," he intoned, "what would Europe say if they learned that three French divisions had been stopped by a group of subhumans who used to flee at the sight of a whip? We are going to storm this miserable fort and kill its last occupant so the story of our shame is buried under its rubble forever!"

In the fort, Dessalines also was making a speech. It was simple and to the point.

"Our choice is clear. Either we surrender and become slaves again, or we die free. For those who prefer slavery, this is your last chance to get out of here now."

"We'll die free," Lamartinière cried out with all his might. Other voices repeated the declaration until it became a chant cadenced by more than a thousand voices.

Storming up the slope, the Rochambeau division met the pledge rolling down the hill and realized that it would not be easy to defeat people who had already accepted death. Nevertheless, his men advanced farther than the other divisions. After pouring into the trench, some French soldiers even succeeded in entering the fort itself. But none came out alive.

Finally Leclerc ordered Rochambeau to retreat. The French had lost three hundred more men.

"We're going to lay siege to the fort!" the commander-in-chief declared. "I want it to be completely encircled and shelled night and day. None of these Negroes shall live to tell the story of La Crète-à-Pierrot."

The black generals were carefully monitoring the movements of the French. Realizing that they couldn't resist for long unless the attacks at the rear were reactivated, Dessalines decided to attempt to slip through enemy lines. He told Lamartinière that if he didn't succeed, he would send his ring as the signal to evacuate. Marcus insisted on accompanying him. The two rode out on two of only five remaining horses.

The following night, the encirclement of the fort was completed hours after Dessalines and Marcus had already passed through an opening in the French line. The shelling began at dawn. Around noon Leclerc ordered a cessation of hostility to conserve ammunition, which was in short supply. While he was assessing the situation with his generals, a soldier entered to announce that two black spies had been captured: a man who seemed to be in his early thirties and a woman old enough to be his mother. They had been caught crossing the French lines apparently unaware that they were wandering into a battlefield.

"Did you make them talk?" Leclerc asked.

"We've tried," the soldier replied. "The woman is completely incoherent and the man is an idiot. We hit him with rifle butts and pricked him with bayonets. The only sound he makes is a good imitation of a sheep."

"Bring them to me," Leclerc ordered, "and ask Colonel Pétion to join me."

A fleeting expression of amazement passed over Pétion's face when the idiot was put in front of him.

"Ask him for his name," Leclerc directed.

"Do you have a name?" Pétion asked in Creole.

"Baa!"

For his insolence, the idiot received a rifle butt in the forehead. He fell over straight as a log and stood up immediately without losing his expression of blissful stupidity. The woman started laughing softly.

"What should we do with them?" Leclerc asked Pétion.

"This is your decision, General, and yours alone."

Pétion wanted to spare their lives, but he also wanted the order to come from the commander-in-chief. Leclerc was not a cruel man, but he was criticized by some of his generals for being under the influence of Rochambeau, who had a morbid hatred of both blacks and mulattoes.

"Make them dig their own graves and bury them alive," Rochambeau advised. "They'll talk if they know how."

This was exactly what Pétion was hoping for. By telling the highest-ranking officer that the decision was his alone, he had made Leclerc feel compelled in front of his subordinates to disagree with Rochambeau.

"Let them go," he said, going back to his tent. To Pétion he added, "I don't want our mulatto friends to think that we're barbarians."

The two idiots were led to the Artibonite River and left on the bank. To everyone's surprise, they entered the water and started to cross with great difficulty. Some soldiers wanted to bet that they'd be carried downstream and drowned. To their amazement, the two reached the other bank, made some obscene gestures toward the French lines, and, with the agility of mountain goats, ran into the fort under a hail of bullets.

"I knew they were spies!" Rochambeau said triumphantly.

"Maybe," Leclerc answered, "but that doesn't change anything. The only thing they can report to the rebels is that they're surrounded by twelve thousand French troops. I want the shelling to start again at the first light of dawn. At nine in the morning, we'll launch a general assault. I want those spies brought to me dead or alive."

The couple was received in the fort with immense joy. But Lamartinière didn't participate in the general jubilation.

"Doctor Arada," he said, "your life is too valuable to be put at risk in this way."

"Someone had to bring you this ring."

"We'll leave tonight."

During the night a ferocious battle broke out at one point in the line held by the Rochambeau division. By the time the French could organize any kind of reinforcement, Lamartinière and his remaining six hundred soldiers had pierced the line and disappeared into the tropical night.

When Leclerc entered La Crête-à-Pierrot the next morning, he muttered, "There were no more than two thousand and they held three French divisions here for the best part of the month of March. Two more victories like this and the colony is lost to France."

The month of April would have been uneventful without the arrest and deportation of Rigaud. The minute he heard the news, Toussaint's mind was made up. He sent Isaac to Cap-Français with a letter to Leclerc proposing his submission. Leclerc immediately summoned his generals to obtain their opinion, but his decision was already made. He would not only accept Toussaint's submission but he'd also maintain the black and mulatto officers in their ranks.

"Why?" Rochambeau demanded. "We've completely disorganized his army and occupied his strongholds. What else can he do? He's finished!"

"He may be finished, but this war isn't over," Leclerc replied. "We've been fighting his regular army but not a general uprising. I know that, and so does he. The only reason for his submission is to buy time. And right now, as you know very well, we're dealing with an outbreak of yellow fever, with hundreds of our men jamming the hospitals. I intend to use Toussaint's generals to fight the revolt that's sure to come. That's the only way for us to gain time to rest and re-organize the colony."

"What make yon think his officers will fight against their own people for us?"

"Without Toussaint they'll be as blind as bats. They're from a race that cannot produce two extraordinary men in one generation. With Toussaint gone, they'll obey whoever holds power and fight each other to extinction. This whole violent generation of Negroes must be destroyed. We have five years to replace them by a new submissive population fresh from Africa. Then this colony will enrich the republic as it previously enriched the monarchy."

"And how are you going to get rid of Toussaint?"

"I have my plan."

On May 6, 1802, Cap-Français was in a festive mood with the streets decorated and church bells ringing. Toussaint rode in with four hundred horsemen from his honor guard's cavalry to make his submission to Leclerc. At the governor's palace, the French general went out of his way to make it appear as though nothing more was happening than the passing of power from one governor to another.

"General Louverture," Leclerc asked, "what are you going to do now?"

"I'm retiring to my home in Ennery to be with my wife, my children and my father."

"I've appointed General Brunet as commander of that area. Please, assist him with your advice."

"I'll be always at his disposal."

After an extravagant banquet given in his honor, Toussaint bid farewell to his men and dismissed them. They left the city in small groups. Toussaint, his two sons and Marcus were the last to leave Cap-Français. They decided to return to Ennery in easy stages, the first ending at the Breda plantation where they had all been slaves. They were received by the de Libertad family, to whom Toussaint had given back the management of the property. Of course, the rules had changed. Rather than slaves, there were farm workers who were entitled to one-third of the profits. The other two-thirds went to the state and the owner, respectively.

Toussaint and his group spent the night at Breda. Bayon de Libertad was different from the man they had known, no longer his old talkative self. Rocking back and forth in his chair, he seemed to barely notice the presence of his former slaves.

"What happened to your father?" Placide asked Michel.

"This is the way he's been since my mother's death. He's left the care of the plantation entirely to me and Gaële."

During this exchange, Isaac had managed to situate himself next to the de Libertad's daughter.

"Miss Gaële," he asked with a sly smile, "have you seen Monsieur Dubreuil again?"

"I am now *Mrs.* Dubreuil," she answered, showing the wedding ring on her finger. "We were married in the United States. When we left Saint-Domingue, we took refuge in South Carolina with my father's cousin who managed a plantation there. We were well received at first, but when we told them what had happened here to the colonists, their attitude toward us changed. They feared what might happen if their slaves knew the story.

"The three overseers who traveled with us had a particularly hard time. They were forbidden to talk to the slaves. But one day Antoine was caught doing just that. He would have been hanged without the intervention of my father and Michel. He was forced to leave the plantation, and Gaston and Didier decided to go with him. Over my mother's objection, Gaston and I were married before they departed. "

"Where did they go?"

"They were skilled seamen, so they went looking for work on a ship. They swore that they'd never be associated with slavery again."

"Have you seen Monsieur Dubreuil since then?"

"No, but I'm confident that God will reunite us."

After a pause, Isaac said, "I'm sorry to learn that your mother passed away. Was she ill?"

"Yes!" Michel answered abruptly, as if to signify that the conversation should not go further on that subject. An uneasy silence followed. Then the exhausted and expressionless voice of Bayon de Libertad rose on the veranda.

"My wife wasn't sick. She hanged herself, and it was all my fault."

"How awful!" a shocked Isaac exclaimed.

"Why do you blame yourself for such a tragedy?" Toussaint asked Bayon.

The Frenchman went back to his depression without answering, but Gaële thought that an explanation should be given to the visitors.

"My mother thought that we were in the United States only to wait for Saint-Domingue to return to its former state. We tried to convince her, without success, that her hopes were unreasonable. We had no information about what was going on here because the news from Saint-Domingue is strictly censored there. One day, a friend of Michel's who was secretly an abolitionist told us that the governor of Saint-Domingue was now a black general called Louverture. But the name meant nothing to us.

"A few months later, my father ran into the house brandishing an old newspaper and shouting that General Louverture was none other than Toussaint! Indeed, an article stated that the black governor spent forty years of his life as a slave on a plantation called Breda.

"My father decided that we should move back to Saint-Domingue. My mother disagreed. They fought every day and life in the house became unbearable. The day we were planning to sail, my father went to their bedroom and found that she had committed suicide."

"What a terrible dilemma," Isaac said. "I understand why Monsieur de Libertad wanted to return. Breda was his life. I also understand why your mother didn't want to. But why didn't you and your brother choose a place that is more peaceful than Saint-Domingue?"

"Breda is also my home," Michel said simply. "I can't be happy anywhere else, either."

"That's true for me too," Gaële added. "But I have another reason. My husband is on a commercial ship, and this colony is still very prosperous in spite of the war. Some day, his ship will land here and he will have the urge to see Breda again. It may be in a month or a few years, but I am certain that we will be reunited right here."

Toussaint and his entourage made four more stops on the way, arriving in Ennery fifteen days after they had left Cap-Français. They found that General Brunet was already in the area. Even before reaching home, the former governor had been receiving complaints against the French soldiers.

The population accused them of being brutal, of not paying for what they bought, and even worse, a French sergeant had insulted Mrs. Louverture in the market place. Knowing that the occupying forces were trying to provoke a reaction, Toussaint cautioned his sons to wait before acting.

At home, Suzanne confirmed that she had had a verbal exchange with a French soldier who said that soon he'd be able to buy her as a slave to do his cooking. Toussaint immediately sent Marcus with a formal letter of complaint to General Brunet, who had his headquarters in the main house of the George plantation about two kilometers from the Louverture home. The general made a verbal promise to look into the allegation.

Upon his return, Marcus informed Toussaint that Brunet didn't have more than a hundred soldiers with him, which was strange for a division general. Toussaint assumed that the greater part of the division was hidden somewhere in the area, and the general was waiting for a wrong move on his part as an excuse to massacre the population. Marcus asked for permission to search for the rest of the division, but instead Toussaint entrusted him with another mission.

"Return to General Dessalines," he said, "and tell him to start working on the alliance with the mulattoes."

Leclerc had already put his plan into action. The black and mulatto high-ranking officers had been positioned in those places throughout the colony where he expected the general revolt to occur. Christophe was sitting in the colony's high council in Cap-Français, Pétion was in Haut-du-Cap in charge of an infantry company, and Dessalines had been made district commander of the Saint-Marc area.

It would have taken Marcus just one day to cover the distance between Ennery and Saint-Marc if he had chosen to follow the main road on horseback. But a messenger from Toussaint to Dessalines would have been too obvious a clue for the French. So Marcus decided to dress like a simple farmer and to travel on foot through the mountains and gorges of the interior—a hike of eight days or more.

Taking leave of the Louverture family, Marcus said to his new companion, "I'll be back in about a month."

"If the curse of the pledge doesn't work," Placide teased.

"You shouldn't have said that," Marcus said sadly.

"Why not?"

"Old curses may remain dormant for a long time, but they wake up when people talk about them."

Placide apologized with faked embarrassment.

The rest of the May was uneasy for the Louverture family. As the French increased their harassment of the population, not one day passed without some abuse being reported to Toussaint. He carefully limited his reaction to notes of protest. The situation was further complicated by a series of sporadic revolts occurring in various parts of the colony, with bands of blacks attacking the French garrisons. Of course, Leclerc blamed Toussaint for the turmoil and asked him to use his influence to make the rebels accept Leclerc's authority. The former governor's response was that these groups had never been part of his regular army and that on many occasions he had been forced to fight them himself.

Finally, on June 7th, he received a message from General Brunet asking for a meeting in order to put an end to the situation once and for all.

Placide wanted to go with his father to the George plantation, but Toussaint refused, saying, "I am a citizen of this country, and I have the right to move about without an escort."

Brunet received him cordially, but during the meeting a group of French soldiers entered the room.

The French general said, "General Louverture, in the name of the Republic, I place you under arrest for rebellion. If you resist, you'll put your family in danger."

That same night, Toussaint was transported by coach to Gonaïves. There he was put on the ship, *The Creole Girl*, and sent to Cap-Français. When the ship arrived at that city, Toussaint was not taken ashore. Rather, he was moved to another ship called *The Hero*, where he found his wife and sons.

Watching his homeland disappearing on the horizon, Toussaint said, "They have only cut down the trunk of our tree of freedom, but its roots are deep and numerous. It will grow back."

For hours, Dessalines had been trying to find a way to break the news to Marcus that the whole Louverture family, with the exception of Papa Breda, had been deported to France. Finally he decided that the direct way was the only way and sent for Colonel Arada.

When Marcus entered the room he was surprised to notice, for just a brief moment, a look of affectionate concern on the fierce general's face.

"Get ready to travel," Dessalines said. "It's time to put old Toussaint's plan into action."

"Where are we going, General?"

"To meet Pétion in Haut-du-Cap. We must hurry, but we must also be careful. We'll take a land detour. Guides and horses will be provided for us on the way."

"Are we passing by Ennery?"

"No, we wouldn't find anyone there. Toussaint has been arrested and deported."

"And the family?"

Seeing that Marcus' eyes were filling with tears, Dessalines said, "My brother, we have a long and hard struggle awaiting us. Our enemies are strong and unforgiving. We have to keep our eyes dry so we can aim straight."

When the first stars appeared in the tropical night, three horsemen left Saint-Marc at full gallop: a guide leading the way, then Dessalines, and Marcus in the rear.

"The curse!" the African man was saying to himself as his tears fell, "The curse of the pledge!"

Chapter Ten

Three Abolitionists on a Slave Ship

Didier Godard woke up with a monumental headache. He was too experienced a sailor not to realize that he was on the high seas. But a putrid odor, not the fresh air he would have expected, was invading his nostrils. He identified the stench without hesitation. It was the smell of a slave ship. Not that he had ever been associated with that commerce, but every sailor could recognize the nauseating stink that followed the slave ships for miles: a foul mixture from vomit, feces, sweat and even dead bodies.

But what in the world was he doing on a slave ship? And where were his two friends? He tried to open his eyes but the brilliant sunlight entering through the porthole forced them shut immediately. Nevertheless, in that instant he had noticed two motionless bodies that seemed to have been just thrown into the hold with him. He crawled toward them and realized that they were still breathing.

"Gaston! Antoine!" he whispered, shaking them vigorously. "We've been kidnapped!"

The other two opened their eyes but it took them some time to come out of their stupor.

"What a stench!" Antoine finally said. "Where are we?"

"In the belly of a slave ship."

"How did we get here?"

For the next hour, through recollection and deduction, they pieced together the events that had led to the situation they were in.

They had been on shore leave in Kingston, Jamaica. It wasn't a regular stop for them, but their ship had come into port to wait out a tropical storm. The vessel needed some repairs and the captain decided it was as good a place as any to get the work done. The crew was allowed to go on leave for the whole month it would take to finish the job.

The three friends decided to explore the town, a busy port that was new to them. The docks were teeming with sailors of many nationalities and languages. A few days after their arrival, they met a tall black man named Leroy who could pronounce a few words in each of the languages spoken on the docks. He offered to be their guide and took them all over town and even out to the surrounding countryside.

When they were ready to eat, he brought them to a strange establishment that was part restaurant, part bar and part brothel. The ruler of this place was a mulatto woman so huge she could make a chair disappear by sitting on it. Leroy sat the Frenchmen at a table, then went and whispered in her ear while she kept her eyes glued to the three. Returning to their table, Leroy asked for their order.

"We don't drink alcohol," Gaston answered to Leroy's surprise. "We'll take any fruit juice, but papaya would be our first choice."

Leroy and the fat woman then disappeared into another room to prepare the juice for these strange non-drinking sailors. When he reappeared with three wooden plates and a bucket of goat meat—the specialty of the house—Didier invited him to share their meal. He declined, saying that he was a slave, the property of the fat woman he called Madame Inez, and that he couldn't sit at a table she was going to serve.

"You're very free for a slave," Gaston remarked.

"My job is to bring clients to this place," Leroy explained. "I also recruit sailors for Madame Inez's husband, who is a ship captain."

"Well, we're already engaged on a ship," Didier said.

"My job is just to bring you here to listen to what my master will propose. I'm not responsible if he can't convince you."

Leroy pointed out a group of men eating and talking boisterously. Their leader could easily be identified by the fact that, whenever he said anything, the others found it necessary to laugh loudly.

"Can I get him for you?" Leroy asked.

"You can," Antoine answered, "but it's not going to work."

The captain introduced himself to the Frenchmen saying, "They call me Clumsy."

"I agree," Antoine said. As a matter of fact, on his way to their table, the captain had knocked down two chairs and spilled a plate of food by bumping into a server. He was a big man, with profuse hair on his chest that showed through his unbuttoned vest.

He chose to ignore Antoine's remark and continued, "Gentlemen, it's getting harder for me to find skilled seamen. Because of the stupid French Revolution, nobody wants to sail on a French ship or under a French captain. I've decided to change my line of work, but before I do, I want to make a last trip that will bring me enough money to make a smooth transition. If you join me, you won't regret it. The merchandise I am after is the most expensive of all, and your share will be beyond your greatest expectation."

"What merchandise is that?" Didier asked.

"First let me explain why it's not going to be easy. As you know, France is at war with the world, so French captains and French ships are fair game for all the other nationalities. They steal our cargoes, sink our boats and kill us without mercy. To avoid them, we have to navigate away from the well-traveled lanes. When we're chased, we have to outmaneuver them. That's why I need experienced sailors. Our merchandise will be Africans. When we get on the high seas, I'll give you more details of my plan."

"You can keep the details for yourself, Captain. We aren't going," Gaston said firmly.

"Why not? This is a chance to make a fortune."

"We wouldn't mind being rich, Mister Clumsy, but we will not be associated directly or indirectly with slavery."

"In that case," the captain said, "I've been wasting your time and mine. Good night, gentlemen. No hard feelings." Then turning to Leroy, he called, "Go tell Madame Inez that the drinks for this table are on me."

Madame Inez came personally with three tall goblets of papaya juice, and that's the last thing the sailors remembered.

"We've been drugged and kidnapped," Didier concluded.

"I'm going to tell Captain Clumsy a thing or two," Gaston said, struggling to his feet.

"I'd strongly advise against that," Antoine warned. "We're completely at his mercy and there's nothing we can do. We can't seize the ship and turn it around. It would be us against the whole crew. We would need not one, not two, but a series of miracles. In the meantime, our task is to survive. Wouldn't it be wiser to pretend that we've accepted the situation? Let's go and congratulate the captain for his cleverness."

"How long will we have to pretend?"

"I don't know. Maybe until miracle time."

On the deck, the three friends were received with a roar of laughter from the crew.

"Ah, the sleeping beauties," the captain taunted. "Are you well rested?"

"We woke up with some aches and pains," Antoine answered, "but thanks to you, our sleep was undisturbed."

"I hope you realize that you're at my mercy."

"We do, Captain. Since we're here now, we'll serve you and the ship."

"Didn't you tell me you were against slavery?"

"We did, Captain. We also said we had no objections to being rich."

"You're here against your will. We're under no obligation to share our profits with you."

"It's true that we didn't choose to be here, but if we share your works and your dangers, we're entitled to our share of the profits."

"You're very smart, too smart maybe. I'll keep an eye on you. Remember that I may decide at any time to feed you to the sharks."

Then Captain Clumsy asked the whole crew to gather around him.

"It's time I told you what this expedition is about," he said. "Years ago, I was part of an outfit operating in Africa. We were in the slave business. We formed two groups, one to capture the slaves and the second to march them to the coast to be sold at the slave markets.

"As leader of the second group, I came to know many trails in and out of the interior, and also how to deal with the tribes that were found on the way. We're going to anchor the ship in a secluded cove I know, far away from the slave markets. We'll march to the interior and capture our own Africans, take them to the coast and load them on our own boat. All the pain, all the fatigue, all the danger will be ours, but so will be all the profits. We won't have to share anything with anyone. In four months, if everything goes well, we'll be back in Jamaica with at least five thousand pounds in everyone's pocket."

"Captain," one of the crew members asked, "you've explained the dangers we'll face on the sea. What dangers will we face on land?"

"They are insignificant—poisonous snakes, lions and so on. None of them will attack men."

"What about the people themselves?"

"What people? The Negroes? Nothing but cowards. Our greatest difficulty *would* have been to capture them. But we won't have to do that ourselves. We'll use one tribe to catch members of another. To answer your question directly, we will face no danger on land."

Didier asked, "If the Africans are such cowards, how do you explain the revolt of Saint-Domingue?"

"I don't have anything to explain!" the captain roared furiously. "Besides, we aren't going to Saint-Domingue, we're going to Africa! Let me warn you that any attempt to discourage the crew will cost you your head!"

Five weeks later, the ship reached the African coast. The crew went ashore except for Antoine, Didier and Gaston, who were left behind under the surveillance of five well-armed men.

Peace had returned to the Aradas' land and the old wounds from the raid had finally healed. Families that had been affected by the tragedy had developed new networks of relationships. The three villages had resumed their isolation from each other, so that the people of Kalame had to wait for the ceremony of the pledge to exchange information with Aradas in the other villages.

It could happen that, when something was of importance, messengers would be sent from one place to another. The death of Adegba was one of these rare occurrences. The king had to know of the passing of his trusted advisor and the other villages had to send delegations to the funeral, since the burial of the griot of the tribe required a formal ritual. But after this event, Kalame went back to the daily routine of Arada life. It was, therefore, a surprise when the sentries' drums signaled that a group of Arada men was approaching.

Bao, the village chief, Gaouno, the head of the defenders, and Bambolo, the griot of the tribe, went to the village gate to welcome the visitors. Another surprise awaited them. The leader of the visitors was none other than Bakao, the sacred singer who, many seasons before, had lived in Kalame.

He went straight to Gaouno and said, "I am honored to be the first to bow to the new king of the Aradas."

"What?" Gaouno exclaimed.

"I'm sorry to tell you that King Gaoube is dead," Bakao informed him.

"How do you know?" Bao asked, since Bakao was from Kilou and the king lived in Weewa.

Gaouno said, "Come to my hut and let's start from the beginning."

In the dwelling they found Maïle and her two boys, now adolescents, who greeted Bao and Bambolo with obvious respect and affection. They were more reserved with Bakao, whom they didn't recognize, since they had been babies when he left Kalame.

Everyone sat in a circle on the floor mat, including the youngsters. Gaouno wanted them to be present because their grandfather's death also concerned them.

"About twenty days ago," Bakao began, "two messengers came to Kilou from Weewa. King Gaoube wanted me to help bring him back to health. Until then, I hadn't known the king was ill. I left for Weewa the next morning. For eight days I worked with the king's healers, but his condition didn't improve. A few days ago, King Gaoube called the council of elders to his hut and declared that Gaouno is his only heir. He sent two messengers here asking you to come to Weewa."

"But no messengers arrived," Bao interrupted.

"We know. The two men returned and said that Gaouno had refused to come. The king was very sad at first, but later he refused to believe the messengers. He questioned them until they admitted they hadn't reached Kalame."

"Why?"

"They had been threatened to be forever cursed by the king's favorite wife and her father, who is the chief healer of Weewa."

"What did the king do?"

"He sent her and her father away with the interdiction never to set foot in Weewa again. Then he called me and told me in the presence of the council to go to Kalame with an escort of defenders. I am here to deliver his last order and his last wish to Gaouno."

"What is the order?" Gaouno asked.

"You have no choice but to accept to be the king of the Aradas."

"And the wish?"

"Your father wants to be buried in the sacred field beside Adegba. King Gaoube gave me those instructions in the afternoon and died during the night. That was two days ago, and here I am."

"I'll obey his last order and I'll grant him his last wish. As king of the Aradas, I order you, Bakao, to go back to Weewa and organize the funeral. Bring my father's body to the sacred field. I want a delegation from Weewa and another from Kilou to attend the burial. I'm giving you two days to do that. I'll be waiting for you at the sacred field with the delegation from Kalame. You may spend the night with your father and leave before dawn tomorrow. You may go now."

After Bakao had left, the circle of friends remained. The question arose as to whether Gauno should move to Weewa, but Bambolo reminded them that their kings used to live in Kalame. It wasn't until the fourth one after Gaou-Guinou wanted to be near his favorite wife, who was from Weewa, that they had begun to reside there.

"If we don't have to move from here, we won't," Gaouno said. "What do you think Bao?"

"I'm very glad you want to stay in Kalame. You'll be welcome as a king just as you were as a friend."

"Then it's settled. Now I need some time alone to reminisce about my father with my family. Tomorrow you'll help me plan for the king's funeral."

In Mboko's hut, the reunion of father and son was emotional. The healer couldn't hide the pride he felt in his son having worked with those who had taken care of the king. But Bakao had something else in mind.

"I want you to help me see Ganiloa," he said interrupting his father's ramblings. "I have to leave at dawn tomorrow, and I must see her before I go. Tell her to come with you to attend a sick person."

"I will not! She is Bambolo's wife and they have three children. You've had all this time to find yourself a wife and have children of your own. Even I have a new wife now. Your love for Ganiloa long ago faded away. What is left is your hatred for Bambolo. I am happy here, I am loved and respected. Don't expect me to compromise that by doing something as stupid as what you just proposed."

"I have neither love nor hatred in my heart. Anyway, I'm convinced that Bambolo is an impostor."

"Jealousy is speaking through your mouth, my son. If you think the griot is an impostor, why do you want to see his woman? Do you hope to convince her to follow you? I don't see any possibility of that happening. Then what? Are you going to provoke her husband? Suppose he beats you again like he did long ago? What will you do next? Return and try again when they have grandchildren? Your lingering jealousy is denying you the joy of playing with your own babies, of seeing their first steps, of watching them grow and supplying the village with the meat of their first kill. Your hatred is powerless against the chosen one, but not against yourself. It has already made you as barren as a savannah in the dry season."

"The chosen one! The chosen one! I have been hearing that since we came here for Nabo's funeral! What proof do we have, and who gave him the title?"

"Adegba did, and he was a wise man. I have no reason to doubt his judgment. I believe Bambolo is a chosen one because I have found no other way to explain how he could have described the village of Kilou or how, without ever leaving Kalame, he could have known the way to get there."

"That was a long time ago. What has he done since?"

"He has been training the defenders with the short spear. He is by far the best with that weapon. You can testify to that. But no one knows who trained him."

That was all Bakao needed to hear. He walked out. Striding along like someone who knew where he was going, he passed Bao without acknowledging the chief. Bao called to him, but he kept on walking.

By tradition a chief is the village's peacemaker. Realizing that something was wrong, Bao went to Mboko's hut and found the healer sitting with his back against the wall. In the dark, Bao couldn't see Mboko's tears.

"I just passed Bakao," Bao said. "He seemed very agitated. Did you two quarrel?"

"My son is a vulture," Mboko answered.

Fortunately Bakao wasn't present to hear his father's opinion, because calling an Arada a vulture to his face was the greatest of all insults. In the Arada culture, the vulture was the lowest of all animals. By flying high, it gives the impression of grace and power, but up close, it is ugly and clumsy. That makes it a liar. It is a flesh-eater but doesn't kill its own prey. That makes it a coward. It begs for food from the other flesh-eaters, yet when favored by numbers it steals from the others. That makes it a thief.

"What reason do you have to call your son a vulture?" Bao asked.

"He's still holding a grudge against Bambolo after so many years. He has no woman, no children. He is still hoping to turn Ganiloa away from her man, not for love of the woman but for the hatred he carries against the man. When I tried to reason with him, he preferred to walk out."

"That's not enough to call him a vulture."

"He *is* a vulture, I tell you, and you'd better tell Bambolo to keep an eye on him."

"Captain Clumsy," the sailor said, "we've been walking for nine days. Why do we have to walk another eleven before starting to capture slaves? There are Negroes all around us."

"Yes," Clumsy answered, "but they aren't quality merchandise. These people who call themselves Kaplaous are tall and skinny, as you can see. I want to capture Aradas. They're strong and well built. A single Arada can be sold for the price of two or three Kaplaous. You know that our ship is small and can't carry more than a hundred slaves, so they should be of the best quality."

"Thirteen or fourteen years ago," he continued, "we captured almost an entire Arada village with the help of these Kaplaous. That's why I came here."

"But their chiefs have been deliberating for hours," the sailor objected. "It seems that they're not finding it easy to reach a decision."

"They have no choice. Fourteen years isn't long enough for them to have forgotten what our weapons can do. Otherwise we'll give them another demonstration of our power."

The sailor was right. The Kaplaou council of advisors couldn't reach an agreement. They felt as powerless as the grass under the feet of two fighting elephants. On the one hand, they clearly remembered the last time their village was invaded by a group of white men. Mioc, the village chief, recalled how his father and the advisors of that time were killed without mercy. He realized that their lives were spared this time because the white men knew that the terror they had planted in the Kaplaous years ago was still vivid in their memory. On the other hand, they had the Aradas and their determination to avenge themselves.

"My friends," Mioc said to his advisors, "we are lucky to be alive. We might have been killed like our fathers. The white men have returned for the same reason they came before: to make us help them capture Aradas. But the Aradas will not be taken by surprise again. One cannot enter their territory without being spotted by their drummers. They will have enough time to flee and when we find only an empty village, the white men will turn against us. I'll be killed and so will you. The rest of our people will be taken away."

"I think I have an idea," one of the advisers ventured.

All heads turned toward the speaker. Hope was painted on every face.

"Speak," Mioc said, "and may our gods advise us through your words."

"There is one part of Arada territory that isn't well guarded. It's a large clearing in a forest where the Aradas gather at the beginning of each dry season. This is the only place we can enter their territory without being noticed."

"We are in the dry season now. Are you suggesting that we go to that clearing and wait until the Aradas to show up at the beginning of the next dry season?"

"Of course not. What I'm thinking is that from inside their territory it will be easier to spy on them and to determine which of the three villages to attack."

"But their king said that if we helped the white men again, they wouldn't leave one of us alive."

"We'll have to worry about that in due time. Today the danger is the white men. We should deal with that first."

Other suggestions were made during the meeting, including one that proposed making an alliance with the Aradas. They were all rejected as impossible or impractical. Finally the decision was made to take the white men to the Aradas' sacred field.

The next morning, fifteen white men led by Clumsy and more than a hundred Kaplaous led by Mioc left Bakou in the direction of the Arada territory.

For King Gaoube's funeral at the sacred field, there were only a hundred or so defenders from the three Arada villages, not the huge gathering that assembled at the time of the pledge. The men were wore loincloths and carried spears and shields. The new king was dressed the same way, but he had also a crown of black eagle's feather. Mboko, who was conducting the ceremony, wore a long white robe that hung to his ankles.

In accordance with Arada tradition, King Gaoube was put to rest in a sitting position while Bakao sang of his achievements. After the burial, a prayer asking their ancestors to accept the dead king into their ranks was recited by Mboko. He was standing on the mound beside his father, with the whole assembly facing him.

Bakao suddenly stopped singing and screamed, "Kaplaous!"

The Aradas swung around to see groups of ten Kaplaous coming at them, each led by a pink man. They were approaching cautiously, even with apprehension. Gaouno realized that the only chance some Aradas had to escape would be to fight their way between the enemy groups before they came closer and formed an impenetrable circle.

"Nguele!" the new king bellowed, and the Aradas sprang forward, but a volley of bullets sent half a dozen of them dropping to the grass. Again they tried; again, the same result. They ran back to the center of the sacred field in the greatest disorder. Now they were tightly surrounded by their enemies.

"Throw down your crown!" Bambolo hissed to Gaouno.

"Why?"

"You'll be killed if they know you're the king!" Then to Bakao, who was nearby, he said, "Look for your father and tell him to take off his robe!"

"You have no right to give me orders!" Bakao replied scornfully and turned his back to Bambolo.

Captain Clumsy crossed the space of about twelve paces separating the Aradas from their aggressors, entered the Arada ranks with no opposition, and dragged out the man with the white robe. He pulled a pistol from his belt and put it against Mboko's forehead. An explosion threw the healer backward. When he hit the ground, the top of his head was missing. A tall Kaplaou stepped into the space between the tribes.

"Mioc!" Gaouno whispered

"Disaster!" Bambolo groaned. "If you can recognize him after all these years, maybe he recognizes you too."

Mioc was accompanied by another Kaplaou, an interpreter through whom he said to his vanquished enemies, "Aradas obey, Aradas not be killed."

Captain Clumsy sent some of his men into the forest to cut long thin branches which were stripped of twigs and leaves to make long poles. The Aradas were gathered in single files of six with every line of men having a pole placed on their shoulders. Each prisoner was tied to the pole with a rope around his neck and had his hands tied behind his back.

Gaouno was the first of his column, immediately followed by Bambolo. The griot tried to keep his eyes on Mioc but it wasn't easy, since he couldn't turn his head. Bambolo was certain that Gaouno would be put to death if he were identified by Mioc or any other Kaplaou. When Clumsy gave the order to march out of the sacred field, Mioc and the interpreter passed Bambolo and walked on either side of Gaouno.

Bambolo's fear turned to panic when Mioc said to Gaouno through the interpreter, "Your name has never been pronounced in my presence, but I know you are the king's son."

"That's right," Gaouno replied. "You can call your pink friends and have me killed. I'm ready."

"My intention is not to have you killed," Mioc whispered, "but to help you escape."

"Why?"

"I want you to tell your father that we had no choice. After the white men leave, we should come together and find a way to defend ourselves. Tell the king that the Kaplaous want peace with the Aradas. The white men shouldn't see us speaking, so I'm leaving you now. But I'll return when we reach the forest. If your answer is favorable, I'll cut you loose. Your escape should be seen by your father as a gesture of our good will."

After the two Kaplaous moved on, Bambolo said, "I think you should accept."

"Of course," the king answered, "but I have my own condition. They must let you escape with me. The memory of the Aradas must not be lost again."

"I think you should ask for something more important: to bury our dead."

"You're right. I hadn't thought of that. But I still want you to go with me."

"We're in no position to pose too many conditions. And as far as I'm concerned, I feel that I'm under the protection of the gods. Tell Bao to take care of my family and tell Ganiloa never to despair of seeing me again."

"Are you still thinking of bringing Nguele back?"

"I don't know, but there must be a reason why I understand the language of these pink men."

Shortly afterwards Mioc and the interpreter returned for Gaouno's answer.

"I promise to talk to the king," he said. "But in order for me to convince him, you should bury our dead as a gesture of respect."

"Agreed."

The sea was calm and the breeze favorable. With all sails out, *The Sirène* was gliding effortlessly under a night sky so clear that the depth of space could be perceived by observing that some stars were closer to earth than others. But Didier Godart was too preoccupied to admire the view. He had in mind something he wanted to share with his friends. Since the sailing was easy, he passed the helm to a less-skilled sailor and went looking for Antoine and Gaston.

The three men had adopted a mode of conduct to avoid trouble. They were the busiest and most helpful sailors on the ship, didn't respond to provocations and avoided being seen together. Because of these precautions, they hadn't talked to each other in a week.

When Didier passed Gaston on the bridge, without stopping he said, "Meet me in the hold tonight. Tell Antoine."

"In the hold," Gaston thought, "among the Africans. Why didn't I think of that? Nobody there could report us to Captain Clumsy."

Later that night in the dark hold, the three had to be careful not to step on the captives who were chained by their feet to the floor. Finally they found a place to sit.

Didier started, "I'm convinced that the captain will have us killed before we reach land."

"You've heard something?" Antoine asked.

"No, but I've thought about our situation and have come to the conclusion that Clumsy has no intention to let us go free to tell about his crime. See for yourselves: We've been kidnapped to work on a slave ship, and every crewman knows that we're against slavery."

"So what?" Antoine interrupted. "We can't take him to court; slavery isn't illegal."

"Slavery, no," Didier continued, "but kidnapping is. If Captain Clumsy becomes known for kidnapping sailors to man his ship, he'll become a pariah among seamen. He won't be able to sell one bucket of goat meat in his restaurant."

"You may be right, but consider this," Gaston reasoned. "Half the crewmen on the ship are soldiers, here to man the cannons and defend the ship against attack. There are only a handful of real sailors, and we're the most experienced ones. If he kills us, who will steer the ship?"

"I don't think he'll try anything now. After he sells the slaves in Cuba, he'll still need us to navigate the Windward Passage between Cuba and Saint-Domingue on the way to Jamaica. But when we reach Kingston, he'll no longer have use for us."

"What do you suggest?"

"That we escape in Cuba."

"What about these poor souls? When we reach Cuba they'll be sold."

"Unfortunately, they will," Antoine agreed sadly. "However, our situation is far worse than theirs. They'll lose their freedom, but we may lose our lives."

"We have lost everything: wives, families, friends. Death would have been sweeter."

The voice was throaty and the accent heavy. Obviously it wasn't any of the three sailors.

"Who said that?" Gaston demanded.

"I did," the same voice answered. "I am Bambolo of the Arada tribe."

"How do you know our language?"

"That is not important. We should find a way to take control of the boat before we arrive in the place you call Cuba."

"There's nothing we can do before we reach Cuba."

"It will be too late for us then. If you are against slavery, you have to help us return to the place where we were free. You are right when you say that the captain wants to kill you. But it's not for the reason you think. He wants to keep something that is yours."

"It must be our share of the profits," Antoine said, "but how did you learn that?"

"Many people have come here to talk without being heard. You are not the first group."

"Have you talked to other people?"

"No. Each group has a different plan for the boat, but they all have the same plan for us. If I hadn't heard you, I never would have known there were white people opposed to slavery."

"We'd better go now," Gaston said anxiously. "Tell your people not to speak to the other groups."

"I'm the only one who can understand you."

All during this conversation, Bakao was listening. Of course he couldn't understand one word, but it became clear to him that Bambolo had certain powers. The doubts he had harbored about the griot being a chosen one evaporated, only to be replaced by fear.

"Bambolo," he said humbly, "you have reason to dislike me and power to destroy me. Why haven't you?"

"The gods never demanded that I kill anyone. Besides, they probably knew how useful you could be in a situation like this."

"What can I do?"

"I have an idea. You have to trust me and give me time to explain it to you."

"I know now that you are the chosen one. Speak, I will listen."

"The pink men have made one mistake, maybe more, and we should turn that in our favor. They should have mixed people of different tribes in this floating village. For some reason they didn't, and we can communicate. The pink men killed your father because he was wearing a robe. They thought he was the chief. They didn't want to have someone here who has the authority to tell us what to do and what not to do. So I've come to the conclusion that we need a chief among us."

"Who else but you can be our chief?"

"I am glad you think so. The people from Kalame will easily accept my authority, but those from Weewa and Kilou don't know me. I need your help there."

The Arada Pledge

"You can count on me."

"And you'll be my assistant."

"What will I have to do?"

"Sing."

"Sing?"

"Yes. As I've said, the pink men have made a mistake. Let's not make them aware of it by talking among ourselves. When I have to give a message, I'll tell you and you'll sing it. Other than that, all of us must speak as little as possible so they don't watch us more closely. You and I will just have to stay close to one another when they bring us up to walk and jump so we'll be chained here next to each other afterwards."

Coming out of the hold, the three Frenchmen went to the bridge and leaned against the rail. Didier and Gaston were facing the ocean as if they were admiring the splendor of the tropical night; Antoine had his back to the sea to make sure no one was eavesdropping.

"The situation isn't so desperate," Gaston said. "If Clumsy wants to kill us to keep our money, I suggest we let him know that we renounce our shares."

"I don't think it's that simple," Didier said. "Does Clumsy want to share our money with the whole crew, or does he intend to keep it for himself?"

"I don't see any difference for us."

"The difference is that if the captain wants to keep the money, as I suspect he does, only a small group, if any, is aware of his plan. In other words, we might find allies among the crew."

"But how would we know whom to talk to?"

This conversation had been taking place between Gaston and Didier.

Suddenly Antoine grabbed his two friends by the neck, pulled their heads close to him and whispered, "Wait for me. I know where to start."

Cautiously looking in all directions first, he sneaked back into the hold. Half an hour later, he still hadn't reappeared and his friends were starting to worry. Their apprehension turned to panic when they heard steps approaching, heavy steps announcing a huge man. Didier and Gaston tried to appear as casual as possible.

"Good evening gentlemen," a booming voice said. "Where's the other member of the trio?"

"He just left," Gaston answered.

"Too bad. I wanted to talk to all three of you."

"We won't keep anything from him."

"I know. I just wanted to see his reaction to what I'm about to propose."

The large man had a long dirty red beard, a patch over his right eye and a rapier hanging at his side. One-Eye Gaspar was the commander of the fighting men who defended the ship in the event of an attack.

"How would you like to take over the ship?" Gaspar asked, staring at the two friends with his solitary eye.

"Are you talking about a mutiny?" Didier asked.

"Of course not! Captain Clumsy has made it clear that he's had enough of roaming the sea and this is his last voyage. What is he going to do with the ship after we reach Jamaica? I propose that we buy it from him. I have fifteen soldiers on board and they've all agreed to give up half of their shares to acquire this ship. We'll need experienced sailors. If you're with us, one of you will be the captain and the other two his seconds. I'll keep my position as commander of the force."

"Why can't you be the captain?"

"I'm a soldier. My company is tired of the uncertainty of finding commercial vessels to defend. Sometimes we spend months without work. Our dream has always been to be permanently attached to a ship. Actually being the co-owners of the ship we are serving would be more than we ever imagined."

"What merchandise will you carry?"

"Whatever the new captain will decide."

"And if Clumsy refuses to sell?"

"It would be, for me and my men, a great disappointment."

"Couldn't you buy any other ship with your earnings?"

"We wouldn't have enough. We expect Captain Clumsy to offer a special price to the crew. Think about it and give me your answer tomorrow."

A few minutes after One-Eye Gaspar left, Antoine came out of the hold and rejoined his friends.

"You just missed the most amazing conversation!" Gaston said. "Where did you go?"

"To speak to the African. Remember that he said that other groups have come to speak in the hold? I wanted him to help me identify them so we could know with whom we could talk."

"What did you find out?"

"It's wasn't easy for the African to recognize people in the dark, but fortunately he was able to describe someone who wants to take the ship from Clumsy by giving him something in exchange. He said that it was someone very big. I concluded it was…"

"One-Eye Gaspar!" the other two said in unison.

"He just left," Gaston informed Antoine. "He proposed that we join with his soldiers to buy the ship from Clumsy with part of our shares. He also wants one of us to be the new captain. Our problem is solved."

"The African refused to speak," Antoine said, "until I gave him some information about Saint-Domingue. He knows that the blacks have been in rebellion there for some time. He also knows that we're five days away from Cuba."

The three men were about to go to bed when they heard a beautiful baritone voice floating out of the open hatch leading to the hold. Although they couldn't understand the words, they stopped to listen because the music was so captivating. To their amazement, there was one word they heard clearly in this strange song: Saint-Domingue.

The next day, One-Eye Gaspar burst of Captain Clumsy's cabin in a state of rage that he tried his best to hide. Gaspar's single eye was throwing flames but he talked to no one. His men carefully avoided him. They guessed what had happened and they didn't care to face one of his well-known fits of anger. The three French sailors also concluded that the captain's answer had been negative.

One-Eye Gaspar was a strange character. His reputation as a fierce fighter was established all over the Caribbean. He often bragged that no ship had ever been taken from him. The patch over his right eye attested to that. But at the same time, he was completely loyal and obedient to his captain, whoever that might be for the moment.

Clumsy knew this very well, which is why he had hired One-Eye Gaspar and why he had taken the risk of telling him that the ship had already been sold. However, he hadn't told his military commander that the new owner was an Englishman famous all over Jamaica for his opposition to the slave trade, an opposition so strong that the deal would be off if he knew what cargo the ship was carrying now. This was the main reason why the three abolitionists had to be sacrificed.

The situation was getting more complicated for everyone involved. Didier, Gaston and Antoine realized that their hope of survival had all but vanished. If the captain could refuse half the shares of the whole fighting crew, he was not going to be seduced by their three shares. Clumsy also realized that killing the three friends might not solve his problem, since the crew would know, sooner or later, who the buyer of the ship was, and they might spoil the lucrative deal by telling what the voyage was about. He started to doubt that Gaspar's loyalty would go so far as not to tell about the Africans.

After blowing off steam for the whole morning, One-Eye Garpar calmed down and decided to tell the bad news to his men. Of course he couldn't gather them on the bridge, so he called two of his closest associates and ordered them to pass the word, first to his crew and afterwards to Gaston, Antoine and Didier. Then he sat down to wait for their reactions.

He was ready to accept the lost opportunity, but his men refused to see it the same way. Their protests grew increasingly louder. After trying in vain to calm his troops down, Gaspar joined their chorus. They demanded a meeting with Clumsy but the captain refused because, in his opinion, negotiating with a group that had placed itself in a state of open insubordination would damage his authority. Instead, he decided to take a gamble.

He ordered the whole crew onto the bridge and told Gaspar to collect his men's weapons and place them in a barrel. To everyone's surprise, Gaspar obeyed and, although reluctantly, the men handed over their swords, rifles and pistols. The barrel was then brought down to the hold.

"Captain," Gaspar asked, "now that we're all disarmed, won't you explain to us why…"

"I don't owe you any explanation," Clumsy snapped.

"Why won't you sell the ship to us, Captain?" a sailor yelled.

Clumsy was going to answer, but a song rose from the hold. He held his breath and listened.

"Who is that?" he demanded.

"Don't change the subject!" another sailor said angrily.

Once again the African song arose, but this time it was not one voice. The song had become a chant repeated by all the Aradas.

Bambolo had told Bakao to prepare everyone for a fight.

"There is division among the pink men," he said. "Prepare your bodies and your minds. If we let them take us to this faraway land, our spirits will never join our ancestors. Our memory will be erased from future generations. It's better to die in combat. Death to our enemies!"

It was this last sentence that had become a refrain chanted by a hundred voices.

When it died down, Gaspar said, "We're still waiting for an answer."

"I don't owe an answer to anyone," Clumsy retorted. He was about to return to his cabin when the song started again, first with a single voice and then the chorus. Clumsy became enraged.

"I want that singing stopped immediately!" he commanded.

"Should we kill them all?" Gaspar asked sarcastically.

"No, idiot! Find the lead singer and hang him!"

"Wait!" Didier said. "I can try to make them stop. We don't have to kill anyone."

"I'll give you five minutes. Past that, the singer will die."

The captain didn't expect Didier to succeed. In spite of his need to reassert his authority, Clumsy understood the risk of sacrificing a member of the crew, but an African was expendable and his hanging could produce the same terrifying effect. He sat down, regained his composure and waited. Didier went straight to Bambolo.

"My friend," he said, "the captain is angry. If you don't stop the singing, he will have the leader killed."

"Will he send someone here to kill him?" Bambolo asked.

"No, he will be taken up on deck to be hanged."

"That's just what we want," Bambolo thought.

Didier went back up thinking that his mission had been accomplished, but as he was about to report his success to the captain, the song started again more powerfully than before. To everyone's surprise, Clumsy remained calm.

"You've failed," he said to Didier. "Now identify the singer and bring him to me."

One-Eye Gaspar took a few steps toward the open hatch, but the captain's voice stopped him.

"Where are you going?"

"To bring you the singing slave. I have the keys to the lock."

"I'm sure you want to retrieve your weapons. Give the keys to Monsieur Godart. I want four other men to accompany him."

"What is the punishment for mutiny?" the captain asked Gaspar.

"There was no mutiny. We voluntarily surrendered our weapons."

"I'll be the judge of that."

Everyone understood the seriousness of the threat. The punishment for mutiny was hanging.

The word of the captain was the law on any ship—military, commercial or pirate. The best vessel on the ocean was no more than a floating tomb without order and discipline, and maintaining them on *The Sirène* was Gaspar's responsibility. Although he bitterly regretted having surrendered his weapons, even now the idea of mutiny was repulsive to a man of the sea such as himself. He feared that his life wasn't worth a sou.

The Sirène hadn't been built to be a slave ship, but a commercial vessel. Captain Clumsy had made some changes to accommodate a captive human cargo. Two huge beams had been nailed to the floor of the hold the length of the ship and six feet apart. A series of rings were screwed into both sides of the beams and one more at each end. Then a chain was solidly attached at one end, run through the rings and secured at the other end by a lock.

When the captives were brought on board, each was fitted with an ankle bracelet welded to a ring of its own. By slipping the chain through both sets of rings, the Africans were maintained in captivity. Each beam held fifty captives, twenty-five on each side.

Bambolo had noticed that when the time came for exercising, twenty-five Aradas were freed by unlocking just one chain. If any resistance could be organized, he thought, that would be the time to start it. Even unarmed, twenty-five defenders could subdue the five crewmen who carried out this operation. But what about the rest of the crew? Bambolo knew that he needed an alliance, but with whom? The three abolitionists weren't enough, and Gaspar's group wasn't reliable, since they also were counting on the sale of the slaves.

He asked Bakao to beg the gods to send him a sign. When three crewmen brought a barrel full of weapons into the hold, the prayer was answered. From that moment, Bambolo's plan was ready.

He had had two major preoccupations. First, the revolt should occur when his row was freed for exercise so he could direct the operation, and second, it should also take place before the pink men resolved their differences, because obviously the weapons would then be given back to their owners. When

Didier told him that the captain wanted to kill the singer, he knew the time had come.

It wasn't difficult for the five sailors to identify the singer, since when Bambolo had seen them coming down from the bridge, he told Bakao to start the song again. Bambolo was the third man from the chain's locked end and Bakao was in the middle of the same row. He observed Didier Godart trying different keys to open the lock. Finally the Frenchman found the right one and freed the chain.

"Pull!" yelled Bambolo.

Since the beginning of the voyage from Africa, the crew had been used to the passivity and docility of the Africans. Thus they were stunned when the Aradas who were at the other end jerked the chain with such force that the first yank freed nine captives, Bambolo included. The Africans jumped to their feet and assailed the sailors. Two who were not subdued tried to flee, but the men still chained to the floor grabbed them by the ankles and tripped them. In less than a minute all the sailors were dead except for Didier. He was pinned against the wall with a sword at his throat.

Bambolo had run to the barrel of weapons, pulled a sword out of its sheath and immobilized the Frenchman. Without an order being given, the Aradas went to the barrel and armed themselves with swords. They threw the firearms through the porthole into the sea. Of the pistols at the bottom of the barrel, Bakao took two.

It took Didier only seconds to explain to Bambolo how the weapon worked, and Bambolo in turn showed Bakao. Didier was told to free the other Aradas. When this was done, they all gathered at the foot of the ladder waiting for a signal from Bambolo to storm the upper deck.

It was taking too long to bring up the condemned singer. Captain Clumsy quickly chose five more men, making sure they were not from Gaspar's group, and ordered them to see what was delaying the others. These five went to the hatch and leaned forward to see what was happening in the hold.

"Monsieur Godart," one of them yelled, "what's taking so long?"

The answer was a shot fired from below. A sailor fell, bleeding profusely from the left side of his neck.

"Nguele!"

The Africans erupted onto the deck and quickly surrounded the crew who, expecting to witness a hanging, had all grouped together. On a small upper deck overlooking the main deck Captain Clumsy stood with his two lieutenants, all of them armed. They pulled out their pistols and fired on the Africans. Three Aradas fell to the deck, but the effect Clumsy expected didn't occur. The captain was sure that the Aradas would panic and run back to the hold. Instead they increased the pace of the attack. Either they had decided to die fighting or they had learned that it takes some time to reload a pistol.

The Africans were upon the officers before they had time to draw their swords. With two Aradas holding the captain, Bakao pulled a pistol from his loincloth and applied it to Clumsy's forehead, just as he had seen him do to Mboko, Bakao's father, and with the same result.

One-Eye Gaspar was pinned against the mast surrounded by half a dozen Aradas, but his enormous fists kept them at bay. Each blow he landed lifted an Arada a foot into the air and send him crashing against others who were taken down with him as he fell.

"Nothing is lost!" he shouted to his men. "We only have to find the leader and kill him!"

Identifying the leader was easy. Bambolo was armed with a sword and shouting orders in all directions.

"It's this one," a sailor called, pointing to Bambolo.

"Throw me a sword!" Gaspar ordered.

Three swords lay on the floor near the bodies of the Aradas killed by the captain and his seconds, but they were beyond the reach of the crew, who were still completely surrounded. However, one of Clumsy's seconds had fled from the battle and taken refuge in the crow's nest high above. He heard

One-Eye's desperate call and dropped his sword at Gaspar's feet. The Aradas who were still trying to get at him backed out of reach. After witnessing what damage this man could do with his bare hands, they didn't care to know what he could do with a long knife. Guided by the crew, he moved quickly to kill the Africans' leader.

It became obvious to the Aradas that the big man with one eye was looking for their griot. Two of them tried to intercept Gaspar. It cost them their lives. Bambolo signaled to the others to let the huge man approach. They made way for Gaspar, who soon found himself facing the leader of the uprising.

"*En garde*," Bambolo challenged. An ugly smile spread across One-Eye's face. Without any preliminaries, he attacked.

Bambolo recalled Emile's lesson:

When facing a man who is bigger and stronger than you, expect him to use his height, weight and strength to overpower you. You must use your skill to end the fight quickly. Otherwise his powerful blows will tire you and he might even disarm you. Avoid his frontal charges and counterattack from the sides.

Three times Gaspar tried to overwhelm the African; three times he found nothing but air. At the third pass, Bambolo jumped aside and thrust at One-Eye's left side. The sword found its mark. One-Eye raised his arms to the sky as if to find something to hold onto. His weapon fell out of his hand and he collapsed heavily on the deck. The battle had lasted just half an hour. Six Aradas and eight crewmen had been killed.

Master of the battlefield, Bambolo had a serious problem: He couldn't run the ship.

"I am Bambolo of the Arada tribe," he said to the crew from the upper deck. "We don't want to be slaves. We want you to take us to Saint-Domingue. You may think that you can take this big canoe anywhere without me noticing it. But if we are not received by people of our own color, we'll kill you all. I want you to choose a new captain, but remember that I am the chief of this floating village."

Less than four days later, *The Sirène* reached the northern mouth of the Windward Passage with Cuba to the west and Saint-Domingue to the east. It was May 18, 1803. Captain Antoine Poussin engaged the ship in the channel, following the indented coastline of the French colony. His plan was to drop anchor at the island of La Gonâve, where the conflict between the colonists and their rebellious former slaves had never reached. A few hours after they sailed past the city of Saint-Marc, Antoine called on his two seconds.

"Didier, Gaston, what do you make of that?"

Didier took the binoculars first, and after looking where Antoine had indicated said, "They have weapons and uniforms, and I don't see one white face. This must be a stronghold of the rebel army."

Gaston agreed with Didier. They reported their finding to Bambolo, and the decision was made to try to make contact with the shore. Bambolo left to inform the Aradas of the situation.

"There's something familiar about that man's face," Gaston mused.

"I've noticed," Antoine agreed, "and I know what it is: the circle on his left cheek. Marcus had one like that."

Chapter Eleven

Flag Day

After traveling all night with stops near the Estère River and the outskirts of Gonaïves to change horses and guides, Dessalines and Marcus arrived in the town of Gros-Morne. It was a little after six in the morning. They were taken to a hut outside of town so they could rest a few hours before continuing their journey. Marcus was ready to fall asleep on the dirt floor, but Dessalines was pacing like a caged beast. He couldn't or wouldn't rest.

"General," Marcus finally said, "we still have a long way to go. You should try to sleep or at least relax. Besides, I feel like I'm betraying you by being so sleepy."

"If you knew what I'm thinking about," Dessalines responded, "you'd be as awake as I am."

"Tell me what's troubling you, and I'll be glad to keep you company."

The general stopped walking and sat down on the floor beside the doctor.

"I told you that I have to see Pétion, but I didn't tell you that I have to see Leclerc too. I received an order from him not to leave my command without authorization, and I'm trying to figure out beforehand what he wants from me."

"What he wants from you is simple: Are you sincerely on his side, or are you waiting for the best time to join the rebellion?"

"I want him to believe that I am on France's side. Otherwise, I'll be deported like Toussaint."

"May I speak to you frankly?"

"Of course."

"The French think of you as a brutal man with the intelligence of a rock lizard. This is the role you have to play for them. If you had been a slave on the Breda plantation, Toussaint would have taught you to make your face so blank that no one would have suspected you even had a soul."

"Is that what you did to cross the French lines at La Crête-à-Pierrot?"

"Exactly."

"How can one play stupid while wearing a French general's uniform?"

"The white man will believe anything that seems to prove his racial superiority. In spite of your victories over the Spanish, the British, the mulattos and the French themselves, they would never give you the command of a division where they think it would really matter—for instance, in Europe."

After a brief silence, Dessalines said, "You've given me an idea. "What I have to hide is my goal, not my intelligence. Besides, if I play too stupid they may not believe me."

A few hours later, they were riding toward Cap-Français, where they arrived the next day around noon. It was early October 1802.

Dessalines sent a message to Leclerc informing the general-in-chief that he was in the city. The courier returned with the order for Dessalines to wait for an honor guard to escort him to the palace.

The commander of the honor guard came with a new French officer's uniform, two gold-plated pistols and a dress sword for Dessalines. At the palace he was received by General Dugua, the most senior French officer. This veteran of the campaigns in Italy and Egypt ushered him into Leclerc's office.

After greeting him, the general-in-chief asked, "General Dessalines, do you like the new uniform I sent you?"

"As you can see," the black man answered, "I'm wearing it with pride."

"First Consul Bonaparte has another brother-in-law, a cavalry general named Murat. He is a very elegant officer and designs his own uniforms. You're wearing one of his creations."

"You gave me one of General Murat's uniforms?"

"Of course not. Murat is a tall man. I ordered my tailor to copy it from memory but to fit me. As you can see, we're about the same size."

"You tailor is a very talented man."

"General, you've probably guessed that we're not here to talk about uniforms. Have you ever heard of the United States of America?"

"Yes, General. It's a former British colony that has become independent."

"That's right. Did Toussaint want independence for Saint-Domingue?"

"I don't know, General. He never talked to me about it."

"That's hard to believe, since you were his second in command."

"General, I am a soldier. My task is to destroy whatever enemy my superior points out to me. Why he is an enemy is something I don't need to know. Ask me to bring him in chains, to bring his head, and that's what I'll do."

"And that's why you fought me so fiercely?"

"When Toussaint was my commanding officer, he ordered me to resist you, and I did. Now you are my superior. Why do you think I sent you Charles Belair?"

Belair was Toussaint's nephew. Dessalines' apparent reason for capturing and turning him over to Leclerc was because of Belair's plan to avenge his uncle.

Somewhat satisfied, Leclerc said, "General Dessalines, I'm facing a very strange situation. What is left of Toussaint's army has accepted my authority, but new groups of rebels have appeared everywhere. They've taken refuge on the peaks of inaccessible mountains from where they disrupt the normal life of the colony. What do they want? Could it be independence?"

"Impossible! They're common bandits who believe that work is slavery. They raid the plantations to take what they need without working for it. Colony or independent state makes no difference to them. They must be eliminated."

"What about you, General? Do you see any difference between the two?"

"It's not clear. Although the United States is independent, they still practice slavery there. I'd rather be in a colony where slavery has been abolished."

"I see that you are well informed."

"As a French general should be."

"What would be needed to eliminate these bandits?"

"An army of six thousand men, well trained and well armed."

"General, I order you to raise that army. I'll provide you with six thousand rifles. That will be all."

But Dessalines demurred.

"General Leclerc, I want to serve the Republic, but I would rather not do it in this way. May I be transferred to France with my family? I no longer know where I stand between the bandits and the mulattoes.

"General Dessalines, for the time being I need you here. Get rid of the bandits, and in six months I'll take you to France personally and introduce you to the first consul. Remember that I just gave you a direct order. Goodbye, General."

After leaving Leclerc, Dessalines paid a visit to General Henri Christophe, the second-highest ranking black general after himself. They had been comrades-in-arms since the early days of the revolt, rising side by side in the ranks with Dessalines having only a few months' seniority over his friend. He went openly in his new uniform and with his escort, knowing that the French had complete confidence in Christophe.

Indeed, Christophe had just sent his son Ferdinand to be educated in France. French General Boudet, who had just finished his tour of duty in Saint-Domingue, was the young man's guardian. Leclerc had interpreted this decision by the black officer as the highest proof of loyalty to the cause of France, but Dessalines knew better.

"Henri," he said, "you are aware, aren't you, that your son is now a hostage?"

"I had no choice now that I sit in the colonial high council. You know that the majority are old regime royalists with the motto, *No slavery, no colony*, and Leclerc is listening with sympathetic ears. A few days ago, I made a speech that I concluded with a veiled threat. I said, 'No freedom, no colony.' I thought I was going to be shot where I stood. After that I had to make an unequivocal gesture of allegiance to France. I wonder if future generations will understand what sacrifices we are making just to stay alive."

"But not only to stay alive. We're preserving our lives to accomplish something that will ensure the survival of our liberties. I came here to explain what happened with Charles Belair. As you know he was not a personal friend, but he was a comrade-in-arms. When he saw that the revolt was spreading, he proclaimed himself general-in-chief of the rebels. Leclerc sent me against him. He was captured and executed. I accepted this assignment for two reasons. First, it was not yet time. The rebel chieftains are not united as part of a national movement, and some of them will never be. Besides, the alliance with the mulattoes hasn't yet been made. Second, Belair didn't have the military skill to conduct and win a campaign against the French. If our descendants think that I sacrificed Belair to my personal ambition, so be it. I don't fight for fighting's sake; I fight to win."

Leclerc realized that Napoleon's plan for the colony wasn't working. Following the first consul's verbal instructions, the general had waited until he was in the bay of Cap-Français to open the papers given to him in Paris. They instructed him to use the mulatto officers traveling with the expedition only against Toussaint. But if the black general relinquished his authority, Leclerc should put them all on one ship and send them back to France. From there they would be exiled to Madagascar for the rest of their lives.

Whether or not he submitted to Leclerc, Toussaint should be deported to France. Then, with the French and mulatto officers commanding the expeditionary forces, the population should be disarmed and slavery reestablished. In case of resistance to the general disarmament, the rebels should be terrorized into submission, decimated and replaced by new and docile Negroes fresh from Africa. After the pacification, all of the rebels' superior officers, both blacks and mulattoes, should be deported or eliminated.

At first everything seemed to go according to plan. Toussaint had chosen to resist, so the mulatto officers were allowed to stay. After the deportation of Rigaud and Toussaint, Leclerc moved on to the next stage, the general disarmament. He assigned the task to the indigenous army so that he could keep the European troops in the cities.

He expected some sporadic resistance but nothing serious. He knew that there were more than two hundred thousand rifles and muskets in the hands of the former slaves. Using black and mulatto troops to collect these weapons would meet with less opposition, and if there were conflicts, the French army would be out of the turmoil. Only in the last phase of the operation would the European forces move in to capture the rebel officers and deport them. Napoleon, on the contrary, wanted the operation to begin with the deportations so that the population would be deprived of their leaders.

The first week went well. For more than ten years it had been common for black soldiers to carry their guns across their backs wherever they were—in the towns and villages, even while working the fields. They were easily disarmed of these conspicuous weapons. But after the first week, rifles and muskets disappeared, along with a large number of farmers who took refuge in the mountains to form armed groups. The maroons who had never accepted Leclerc's authority (or Toussaint's, for that matter) became their natural leaders. Fortunately for the French, these groups had no contact between them, no cohesion and no common goal. There were dozens of such groups in the northern province alone.

In his comfortable house in Haut-du-Cap, General Pétion was entertaining two visitors when he heard a knock at the door. His guests were asked to move quickly into another room. Then he blew out the lamp and peeked though the shutters. Standing outside was a man dressed as a farmer with the legs of his baggy pants rolled up, a loose-fitting jacket and straw hat with a large brim. Pétion armed himself with a pistol and opened the door.

"Who are you?" Pétion asked.

"Marcus Arada."

"Dr. Arada! Let me get some light."

The general disappeared into another room and came back with a candle whose flame he transferred to the lamp. Marcus noticed immediately the three half-empty glasses on the table and realized that Pétion had visitors.

"General," he said, "I see that I've interrupted a meeting. I'm sorry, but I won't be able to say what I intended to tell you."

"You may speak freely," Pétion assured him. "Only men with my complete confidence are allowed in this house. If you must know, General Clervaux and Colonel Geffrard, both old friends, are in the other room. Now what are you here to tell me?"

"General Dessalines is outside and wants to speak with you."

"Tell General Dessalines that I was praying for his visit."

Marcus went out and returned with a man also dressed as a peasant. The newcomer took off his hat and Pétion recognized him immediately.

"General Dessalines," he said, "it's an honor for me to receive you in my house. But you've taken a great risk by coming here. Are you sure you weren't followed?"

"Yes, I'm sure," Dessalines said. "I left Cap-Français late this afternoon after visiting Christophe. Then I stopped for a few hours at the Breda plantation where Marcus has friends. I'm supposed to be heading south right now with a small escort. Except that someone else is wearing my brand new uniform."

"May I ask why you're here?"

"For the same reason you were praying that I come."

"It's time we speak frankly," Pétion said. "We've fought each other for years, and we were both wrong. Our mutual enemy has created this division between us. If we don't erase that mistake today, I guarantee that neither of us will be alive in two months."

"You're right. I came here to convince you that Toussaint was correct when he said that the French expedition has only one goal: to reestablish slavery."

"I can prove that better than you can. Wait!" Pétion left the room and returned with a man dressed as a sailor of the French navy.

"May I introduce to you Colonel Geffrard. We fought against you in the Southern War. Colonel, please tell the general what you just reported to me."

"About a week ago, a ship arrived in the bay. That night five men swam ashore. They begged some fishermen to hide them because they were being deported from Guadeloupe where the French governor had just reinstituted slavery. They were all mulatto members of a group that had protested the measure. One of the fishermen came to get me and I personally talked to the escaped prisoners. I didn't know what to do, so I came here to ask for advice."

"You see, General," Pétion said to Dessalines, "you don't have to convince me about the intentions of the French."

Pétion opened the door to the next room and asked Clervaux to join them. Clervaux, like Pétion, was a mulatto general, but he had always been on Toussaint's side. After the authority of the old general had been turned over to Dessalines, he and Clervaux had fought together as allies in many battles.

"If you want me to speak first," Pétion offered, "I can tell you that by no later than the end of this month, Clervaux and I are going to raise the banner of revolt and join a rebel group operating in the outskirts of the city. What are your plans, General?"

"I'll do the same as soon as I reach my headquarters in Saint-Marc. But all that won't solve our two main problems: the unity of command and the unity of purpose."

"General," Pétion said enthusiastically, "you should be our leader. And the common goal is independence."

Dessalines agreed. "Now we have to convince and rally everyone who believes the French belong in France. I'll command the northern province. I want you, Pétion, to organize a meeting between me and the high-ranking mulatto officers in the west and you, Geffrard, with those of the south."

"I'll inform you of the date and place of the meeting as soon as I can, General, but it may take some time"

"How long?"

"Until April or May."

By the beginning of May 1802, the situation of the colony had already drastically changed. To begin with, only a few days after their conversation with Dessalines, Pétion and Clervaux had openly taken a position against the French. They moved their companies from Haut-du-Cap to an area called Morne-Rouge after taking captive about one hundred white soldiers they had surprised in one of the forts protecting the entrance to Cap-Français. In Morne-Rouge they met with Petit-Noël, a rebel chieftain who commanded a group of five thousand men, mostly farmers poorly trained, poorly armed and poorly led.

Less than a week later, Christophe joined the rebellion with the three battalions he commanded. When he arrived in Morne-Rouge, the whole movement almost collapsed, for Christophe and Petit Noël were sworn enemies. All the rebels of the northern province considered Christophe an agent of the French incapable of turning against his master. The two forces under their command would have fought each other if Pétion and Clervaux hadn't positioned their men between them. To try to save this already precarious alliance, Petit-Noël was proclaimed commander-in-chief.

In late October, a rumor spread that Leclerc had contracted yellow fever, an illness so virulent that it could kill its victim in only a few days. Moreover, the entire French garrison had been affected by this disease, and the morale of the troops was at its lowest. Petit-Noël wanted to take advantage of the situation, so his first decision as military head was to attack Cap-Français.

Pétion, Clervaux and Christophe tried to convince him that a city held by French soldiers couldn't be taken so easily, but the commander-in-chief was adamant. He was going to take the capital of the colony and end the conflict at once. It was a bitter defeat but not a rout, thanks to the experience of the other three officers and also to the inability of the French to pursue their enemies outside the city limits. It was obvious that Petit-Noël couldn't unify the movement, much less lead it to victory.

Clervaux suggested that the command be given to Dessalines, who was the highest-ranking and the ablest black general. However, Petit-Noël refused to step down. Realizing how important it was to give their troops an example of unity and good will, Pétion and Geffrard left Morne-Rouge to prepare the meetings Dessalines had asked them to organize.

On November 1st, General Leclerc died after designating Rochambeau as his successor. Dessalines was in the town of Verrettes when Marcus brought him the news. The general's apparent lack of reaction intrigued the doctor.

"General," he asked, "is this good or bad news?"

"It doesn't mean anything," Dessalines answered. "France can replace ten generals and send another expedition more powerful than this one. What happens to them or what they do is secondary to us. But tell me that Pétion has determined the date and place of my meeting with the mulatto officers of the west, and you'll see me jump up and down. That's what is important to me now, nothing else. Fortunately for us, the French have chosen to reject the mulattoes who came to help them. We have to open our arms to them and not give them even the chance to be neutral."

A few days later, Pétion arrived in Verrette but he didn't bring the news Dessalines was expecting. Instead he reported on the events at Morne-Rouge and the attitude of Petit-Noël. Dessalines decided that this group should be disbanded.

However, Pétion's main task of gathering the officers of the western province was harder to achieve. Not that any refusal was expected, but some of the officers being sought were in hiding and others were already scattered in the mountains throughout the province.

Since Pétion was known to be a poor horseman, Dessalines gave him ten messengers whom he sent in different directions with letters and the instruction to report back before the end of the month. It was the beginning of December, and Dessalines was tired of his inactivity in Verrette. He went north to help Christophe and Clervaux get rid of Petit-Noël. After a two-month campaign, the whole northern province recognized Dessalines' authority. Some of the chieftains joined the movement, while others had to be eliminated.

In mid-February 1803, Dessalines received the news he had been waiting for so impatiently. The meeting was to be May 17 to 19 in Arcahaie. In his letter, Pétion recommended that he come with some mulatto leaders of the north, and he described the mood of the mulatto leaders of the west as being favorable to independence and unity under Dessalines.

Rochambeau had been promised an additional ten thousand men from France with whom he expected to reconquer the whole colony. In the meantime, Dessalines had a free hand to strengthen the unity under his command.

The French had abandoned the interior to concentrate their forces on the coast so that they could receive supplies and reinforcements from France, and at the same time, stop the rebels from trading with England and the United States. But Arcahaie was one of the few coastal towns held by the indigenous army.

Dessalines arrived ahead of the mulatto generals on May 14. Beginning the next day, the other participants started to come alone or in small groups. Dessalines took advantage of the situation to have separate preliminary meetings with them as they reached town. He found that Pétion had been right in believing that there was a solid consensus on the question of independence and that everyone recognized Dessalines as a military strategist who had a good chance of leading them to victory. Since there was agreement on these main points, two other questions—army structure and shape of the military campaign—remained to be resolved.

The May 17th discussion on army structure resulted in Christophe being made commander of the northern provinces; Pétion becoming division general and given the western provinces; and Colonel Geffrard, although absent, being promoted to the rank of brigade general with the task of clearing the south of all French presence.

The following day, Dessalines was about to present his plan for the military campaign when Christophe arrived with important news. A British flotilla had blocked the port of Cap-Français, stopping all maritime traffic. This could mean only one thing: the Treaty of Amiens between France and England had collapsed. The two countries were at war again.

Everyone at the conference table immediately understood that quick action against the French army was needed, since it would receive neither supplies nor reinforcements in Saint-Domingue only for as long as the war lasted. The former slaves also realized that the British weren't interested in their independence but were acting in their own interests to prevent the riches of the colony from financing France's war against its European rival.

"Pétion," Dessalines said with his usual decisiveness, "I want you to encircle Port-au-Prince without attacking. That will allow Geffrard to pass behind your lines and start the liberation of the southern peninsula. I'll join you later and we'll unite our forces to take the city. Christophe and Clervaux will go north and wait for me in Gonaïves. Together we'll march against Cap-Français."

After a few hours of deliberation, every participant knew exactly what was expected of him. They were about to leave the house when Marcus burst into the room with another surprise.

"Gentlemen," he panted, "forgive the intrusion, but a ship is entering the bay!"

"Is it British?" Dessalines asked.

"I don't know. It isn't flying any color."

Everyone went outside to assess the situation.

"This is strange," Pétion said as he peered through binoculars. "There seem to be a lot of black men in loincloths walking freely on the deck."

"Maybe we should show our own colors, and these are no longer ours," Christophe said, pointing to a lone French flag flapping nearby in the breeze.

"You're right," Dessalines said. "Lower it and bring it to me."

He tore the white section from the center, put the blue part on his shoulder and gave the red to Pétion to lay across his. He inquired where a seamstress might be found and a passerby offered to show them the way. All the officers participating in the conference and their staffs followed the two generals to a house on the shore. It was the home of Catherine Flon, seamstress by trade and revolutionary by choice. When she saw who was calling on her, she couldn't hide her emotion.

"You cannot imagine the pleasure I feel seeing you together," she said to the two men in the lead.

"You see, I am the blue and Pétion the red," Dessalines said. "We are together because the white is no longer between us. I want you to sew these two colors together and create the flag of a new nation."

With the whole crowd looking on, Catherine stitched the pieces together and a few minutes later the new flag was floating over Arcahaie.

"Now that we are flying our colors," Dessalines said, "whoever is on that ship had better do the same. Let's give them one hour to do so. Past that, we'll send them to the bottom."

The Arada Pledge

Sitting on a rock by the sea, Pétion kept a close watch on the ship with his binoculars. Suddenly he dropped them and ran back to Dessalines.

"General," he gasped, "they've shown their colors."

"Is it a British or a French ship?"

"Neither! They're flying the flag you just created less than an hour ago!"

"I didn't even know we had a navy," Dessalines said wryly. "Christophe, would you please investigate?"

"They're probably French spies," Christophe objected. "If they can fly our colors, it's because they had a French flag on board. Let's just blow them off the water."

"And be the first to fire at our own flag? No, find out what this is all about."

Christophe assembled a group of volunteers, fixed the white section of the French flag on a stick and left in a rowboat for the suspicious ship. Those on shore watched as the boat reached the ship, Christophe spoke to someone on board, a ladder was lowered, Christophe climbed it and disappeared from view. He reappeared an hour later and returned to land.

"General Dessalines," he said, "it's a strange story. This ship is called *The Sirène*.

It's a commercial boat that was remodeled as a slave ship. The crew is mainly French and the Africans are all from the same tribe, the Aradas. They were to be sold in Cuba. I don't understand all the details, but it seems that the Africans took advantage of a mutiny to seize command of the ship. It also seems that they were helped by some of the crew. After they killed the captain and the master of arms, they forced the crew to divert the boat toward Saint-Domingue because they knew that this colony is the only place, besides Africa, where blacks can be free. All of this was possible because the leader of the Aradas could communicate with the other mutineers in French."

"Could he be a spy?"

"I don't believe so, since he was the one who killed the master of arms. He seems to be a fine duelist. He claims to have learned fencing and the language from a Frenchman who was captured years ago when they raided his village. I find that hard to believe."

"Why? Didn't we learn a language and military arts from our former masters? Haven't we also taken advantage of the conflict between French republicans and royalists to work our way into the position we're in now? These Africans had the advantage of being all from the same tribe. It has taken us longer to build our unity. It's significant that they've arrived here the very day we've consecrated our own unity. Their takeover of this vessel may be a sign that we are also going to seize a ship—the ship of state. Now we have work to do. Go tell the generals that we have to be out of Arcahaie within an hour and send me Dr. Marcus."

"Doctor," Dessalines said the moment Marcus arrived, "I can't spare any of my military commanders, so I'm leaving you here in charge of the ship in the bay. It's full of Africans and a French crew. Welcome them ashore and take care of their needs. This land must be a sanctuary for anyone looking for freedom. But be careful. There may be spies on board. If that's the case, don't hesitate to have them executed. I'll see you in Gonaïves."

"Why Gonaïves, General?"

"I expect to take Cap-Français by the end of this year. If everything goes well, independence will be proclaimed in Gonaïves at the beginning of next year. Be there and bring the Africans with you."

After the generals, their staffs and their regiments had left Arcahaie, Marcus allowed the travelers to come ashore. They disembarked to the acclamations of the whole population of the town, for their story had already become known. Marcus asked to see the captain of the ship. To his surprise, three men were introduced to him, the captain and his two seconds. Gaston, Antoine and Didier didn't recognize the quiet boy they had known on the Breda plantation, but Marcus easily identified the former overseers.

"Gentlemen," he said, "I'm disappointed in you. I wouldn't expect to find French citizens working on a slave ship."

"General, we weren't there by choice," Antoine explained. "We were kidnapped."

"I'm not a general. I am a doctor with the rank of colonel in the indigenous army. I didn't study in one of your schools of medicine, but so far my commanding officers have been satisfied with my services. But let's talk about you. What can you say to convince me that you aren't engaged in the slave trade?"

"You can ask the Africans. They appreciated our conduct so much that they protected us during the mutiny."

"So this would have been the second time that blacks in revolt have spared your lives."

"That's true… but… how did you know?"

"Because I drove the coach that took you to safety from Breda to Cap-Français. I am Marcus."

"Marcus! You know that we hate slavery! You know we're not lying."

"You could have changed."

"General… I mean, Doctor… uh, Marcus, we haven't changed. We really were kidnapped. We were forced to navigate the ship, but we didn't participate in any other operation. The leader of the Aradas will confirm that."

"Aradas! Did you say Aradas?"

"That's what they call themselves."

The Frenchmen were still in the room, but not Marcus. He was far away, roaming the savannah of his childhood. Names of places and people entered his mind as they hadn't for years: Kalame, the sacred field, Ganiloa, Bao, Eladjo, and the companion of his carefree youth, Bambolo.

"Marcus," Gaston asked, "are you all right?"

"Yes, yes… You may go now, but send me the leader of the Africans."

"He speaks with a heavy accent, but his French is passable."

"There will be no problem. I speak Arada."

"By the way," Didier said from the doorway, "He has a circle on his left cheek just like you."

"Bambolo?!"

"That's the name."

Chapter Twelve
Eladjo

James Little had come to Saint-Domingue with what he considered a brilliant idea. He wanted to make slave trading obsolete. Not that he was opposed to slavery as an institution, but a slave directly from Africa was very expensive. The price included the cost of purchasing the captives in Africa, the ship and its expenses, the crew and their share, food and ammunition. On top of all that, there was also the possibility of losing everything in a hurricane or in an encounter with a rival slave trader or a British warship.

So Mr. James Little conceived of a plan that would eliminate all these risks and expenses by raising the slaves himself. Since he couldn't have a slave farm in his native Boston, he decided to migrate to Saint-Domingue where slavery was booming. Arriving in 1760, he set out immediately to find land, but he found that the best soil in Saint-Domingue was not for sale. The fertile plains were all planted in sugar cane; every square inch was occupied. With the tremendous profits from sugar production, not a single colonist would agree to part with his property, not even a parcel of it.

Fortunately for Mr. Little, the topography of Saint-Domingue wasn't all flat. On the contrary, eighty percent of the territory was mountainous. As a matter of fact, before the country's name was changed to Hispañola by the Spanish and later to Saint-Domingue, it had been called *Haïti*, a word meaning *mountainous land* by its original inhabitants, the Taínos.

So James Little bought a plantation called Cap-Rouge overlooking the city of Jacmel in the southeastern part of the colony. The property was wooded and cool, ideal for growing the coffee that was fast becoming a cash crop. Mr. Little planned to raise the money to buy his first Negroes by growing coffee. Once he made this initial investment in Africans, besides the coffee that they would grow and harvest, his slaves would themselves also be merchandise. Therefore, he had no reason to work them so hard as to destroy their resale value. (The active life of a slave toiling in cane fields was no more than seven years.) Nevertheless, he had a small plateau of one acre planted with sugar cane where some Negroes were trained for the hard life that was awaiting them if they were to be sold to a cane grower. After all, if his slaves had the reputation of being lazy or unfit, his business would suffer.

It took Mr. Little years of planning and preparation, but his hard work paid off. By 1780, slaves raised on his farm were in demand all over the colony. He even sold a few to colonists in the surrounding islands. To upgrade his stock from time to time, he would send agents to the big slave markets in the cities to pick out some outstanding specimens, and that's how it happened that two of his men bought Eladjo in Cap-Français.

Eladjo arrived at Cap-Rouge after a twenty-day trek. The horse drawn carriage in which he was traveling had to be pushed when it reached a steep hill or came to a field of mud created by a flooding river. But physical fatigue wasn't Eladjo's main problem.

The African was the only black person with three pink men. One drove the horses, urging them on with a whip, and the others rode inside the carriage with him. Twice a day they stopped to eat and rest.

At one of these stops they picked up a beautiful black woman no older than twenty. The minute she was taken on board, the mood of the pink men changed. They became exuberant and loud, pointing at the woman and laughing. She remained calm and silent, and her face showed neither fear nor interest. But Eladjo saw the tears rolling down her cheeks.

When they stopped by a river that night, she was repeatedly raped by the three pink men without uttering a sound of pain or pleasure. This abuse was repeated on two other nights right in front of Eladjo, from whom she didn't seem to expect any help.

When they reached Cap-Rouge, the two Negroes were presented to the master, who by that time was sinking into old age. He examined his new acquisitions carefully with obvious satisfaction. The two captives were led to a secluded hut and locked in.

Then and only then did the woman release her anger and shame in uncontrolled sobbing. Eladjo tried to console her by wrapping his arms around her shoulders, but she pushed him away violently. After he had tried three times with the same result, he sat on the dirt floor and began to weep silently.

In his native land he used to feel not important, but useful. He could protect his herd against any flesh-eater, he could run as fast as a gazelle and make his spear find its heart on the first throw. He could dispute his kill against lions and hyenas. But the pink men had found a way to make him feel powerless. Powerless to defend his village and his people, powerless to protect Nguele, powerless to prevent what had happened to this woman and powerless even to comfort her. So lost was he in his grief that he didn't notice that her sobbing had subsided. Now it was she who came to sit next to him and put her arm around him.

They began to talk, each in a different language, but that wasn't important. The depth of some human feelings has yet to be explored by words. The voices were so soothing and the tone so compassionate that they understood each other.

Beyond the words, he heard her say, *It's not the first time I've been raped. But even though they use my body, soil it, I'll remain a virgin until the day I willingly give myself to a man of my choice. When that day comes, I'll be cleansed and I'll return to the innocence of my childhood.*

She also understood his feelings as if he had expressed them.

I'm from another land. I don't know where I am, I don't know why I'm here. I don't know what would have happened if I had tried to defend you. Would they have killed me, killed you, or both of us? I'm alone and lost. I need a friend and I have a lot of friendship to give.

At dawn the woman was up and about, but Eladjo was still sleeping. Having been in bondage all her life, she needed no reminder, no roll call, to know at what time a slave's day started. Although it was natural for Eladjo also to wake up at dawn, the last two months, and particularly the last few days, had been exhausting emotionally, mentally and physically. He remained motionless in spite of the roosters crowing furiously all around the hut.

The woman expected that at any moment overseers would burst into the hut to take them to work, with the help of a whip if necessary. But no one came until mid-morning, when she was brought to her new master. Crossing the yard, she noticed children of all ages and a lot of black couples. Men and women were well built and appeared to be in good health.

Mr. Little received her cordially.
"What's your name?" he asked
"My name is Magdala, Master."
"Do you like the man I've chosen for you?"
"Yes, Master."
"Did he have sex with you last night?
"No, Master."
"And why not?"
"I don't know. Maybe we were both too tired."
"Take your time," Mr. Little said, "and have all the rest you need. Have you had any religious instruction?"
"Yes, Master."
"Your man is a Bossale. He has never heard of the Word of God. I want you to take him to the chapel every Sunday.

Teach him to speak and help him understand the preaching of Father Murphy. You can go now."

Returning to the hut, Magdala tried to understand the situation. What kind of master, what kind of slavery was this? What was the catch? Many questions were dancing in her mind but she was too prudent to ask anyone. The only person with whom she could share her amazement wouldn't understand one word she might say. She decided to start teaching him her language that very day.

A week later, their situation still hadn't changed much. Little by little they were introduced to the work on the coffee plantation. The labor was light and would have even been boring if not for a minuscule red ant with a nagging little sting that could make you scratch for the best part of the day.

The other nagging sting was Father Murphy's preaching. He only developed four themes in his sermons: obedience, resignation, God's Chosen (that is, white) People, and life after death in a place called heaven, where your rewards would be proportional to your sufferings on earth.

No one knew where Father Murphy had been ordained. He was very sexually active with the women to whom he presented his favors as a shortcut to heaven. However, he was also very useful to Magdala in teaching the new language to Eladjo. After four short months, the African was able to carry on a conversation adequately. He would have made even more progress, but in this laid back kind of slavery, there was one rule that was strictly enforced: No gathering of slaves was permitted and no conversation allowed.

This isolation didn't bother Eladjo, but Magdala didn't like it at all. How long would it take her to figure out what this plantation was about without asking questions? Other slaves with whom she had worked in the coffee fields later disappeared. Where had they gone?

One night when she couldn't sleep, she heard voices in the yard. She went to the window and saw a group of black men, women and children being loaded into a huge cart to which were harnessed six oxen. She concluded that these slaves had been sold, a normal occurrence in a slave society, but not in such great numbers. At least thirty were being taken away. The fate of the children was particularly painful to her, for she was pregnant.

When he learned that Magdala was with child, Mr. Little gave her the light duty of cooking in the house. She gave birth to a lovely baby girl who was called Nora by the master, but in her parents' hut her name was Naïde. Eladjo also had been given the European name of Moïse, but except for his woman, everyone referred to him as the Bossale.

Naïde was three years old when the general revolt took place in the north. Mr. Little was elated. Everything was going his way. First, there was going to be a great massacre of blacks, and secondly, the slave trade from Africa had been reduced to a trickle with England policing the oceans. He assumed that this revolt couldn't last more than a few weeks at the most, and then his slaves were going to be in even greater demand.

He was wrong on all counts. Four years later the revolt was still going. The massacres of blacks did occur, but with corresponding massacres of whites. And no one wanted to buy slaves from Saint-Domingue, for they were no longer trusted in the other slave colonies.

Without his coffee plantation, Mr. Little would have been completely ruined. He was still selling slaves, but only an average of one a week. Meanwhile, the revolt was spreading to the west and south.

Nevertheless, Mr. Little remained confident that sooner or later everything would be back in place. All he had to do was to survive these bad times, so he decided to keep nothing but the good reproductive stock and to liquidate the rest.

Once Eladjo and Magdala had finally understood what the plantation was about, they lived with the fear that one day they would be sold. They also knew that they had almost no chance of being sold together. Magdala was expected to be the first to go, since on many occasions Mr. Little had said that one child in seven years was a waste of time and money. Thus, when two overseers entered the hut in the middle of the night to take her away, the couple was devastated but not surprised.

The night was very dark. With only a few steps, Magdala and her captors disappeared from view.

The men who took her had acted as if Eladjo and Naïde didn't even exist. They had no reaction to the begging of Magdala's husband or the desperate cries of their child. Eladjo and his daughter spent the rest of the night awake and holding one another as the last thing left to cherish.

In the days that followed, Naïde trailed her father wherever he was going, whether to pick coffee or to dry it on the flat surface in the yard. On the Sunday after Magdala's disappearance, Eladjo and Naïde were coming out of the chapel where Father Murphy had delivered a sermon about resignation when the same two overseers came and stood in their way. Sensing danger, Naïde jumped on her father, putting her arms around his neck and her legs around his waist in an embrace so tight that she had to be practically peeled off.

One overseer put a chain on her little wrist while the other held a rifle at Eladjo's head. Less than two minutes later, she was leaving the plantation in a one-horse cart. The man with the rifle pushed the African back to his hut and locked him in.

A few hours later the door was unlocked and a black woman entered.

"The master has chosen me to be your new woman," she said in an expressionless voice. "He wants us to produce one child a year."

"Do you have children?" Eladjo asked.

"Yes, two."

"Where are they?"

"They were sold."

"Why do they sell children?"

"To serve as playmates, as toys for white children. To train white children to act as masters. It seems that it doesn't come naturally to some of them."

"Do you want to have more children?"

"No!"

The next morning, the woman went to the master to report that the Bossale had left the hut the night before, she assumed to go to the woods to relieve himself. She had fallen asleep and when she woke up at dawn, she realized that he hadn't come back.

A manhunt was immediately organized, but Eladjo wasn't to be found. Only in the late afternoon did the overseers determine how he had probably left the plantation. The northeast corner of the property was closed by a small forest of bayahondes, a tree that produces a small yellow flower which attracts thousands of bees. The flower is surrounded by a crown of two-inch thorns. When the flowers develop into pods, the thorns fall to the ground to form a carpet that anyone barefoot would find difficult to cross. Since a cow was missing, Eladjo must have used it to ride over the thorns.

However, these findings were useless, for the African had at least a six-hour advance on his would-be pursuers. Moreover, Mr. Little and his party wouldn't leave the confines of the plantation because, for some time now, a group of rebel slaves had been operating in the area. The leader of this band, a tall, skinny Bossale known as Lamour Derance, had a solid reputation for cruelty. But Eladjo had no intention of joining a rebel group. He wanted to kill himself.

After crossing the two hundred meters of bayahond, he had freed the cow but took the rope by which it had been tied to a post. Finding a mango tree with a low branch from which he could hang himself, he climbed out onto the limb, secured one end of the rope, made a noose with the other end and put it around his neck. As he was about to jump, a doubt crossed his mind. Would his soul find its way back to the sacred field to join the spirits of his ancestors?

He climbed down and disappeared into the mountains, taking the rope with him.

Eladjo's escape had been fairly easy. Other slaves could have made the same attempt, but they were stopped by an obstacle more formidable than a small bayahond forest: the fear of being recaptured. Usually an escaped slave brought back to the plantation would have an ear, a hand or a foot cut off, depending on how many times he had tried. But Eladjo had lost this fear. His intention was to die outside of the plantation—to die a free man.

Knowing that the woman would report his escape for her own safety, he started walking as quickly as he could to put a safe distance between himself and the search party he expected to pursue him. By midday he was tired, hungry and thirsty. Having assumed that he'd be dead by now, of course he hadn't brought food or water.

Dozens of little brooks were running down the slopes, but what would he do for food? His weapon, the spear, could have easily been made here, for he was in a pine forest. But Eladjo's skills as a hunter had been acquired for the big game that roams the savannah, and in Saint-Domingue there was no big game.

The hundreds of guinea fowl running about and flocks of wild pigeons in the highest branches would be no easy targets for a spear. The brooks were too small and too fast for fish, and the pines had no fruit. By nightfall he still hadn't eaten.

Eladjo made a bed of branches right on the ground, knowing that in this country there were no flesh-eaters, no poisonous snakes. His only natural enemy was man. He dreamed that he was hunting on the savannah with Bao. They were after a baby antelope that they had isolated from the herd. Bao threw his spear, successfully bringing the animal down. When they reached their prey and were about to cut it up, the antelope changed into Naïde. Eladjo awoke breathless and sweating. Although dawn was still a few hours away, he got up to continue his march—not that he knew where he was going—but he was scared of dreaming.

The first rays of the sun found him on a mountain peak. The valley below was shrouded in fog, giving him the impression of being higher than the clouds. He waited and by mid-morning, the sun had lifted the fog and Eladjo could see a group of six huts near the bottom of the valley. He decided to go closer. Proceeding cautiously, he repeatedly hid behind one tree, then ran to another until he was a short distance from the closest hut.

"Where do you think you're going?" demanded a voice behind him.

"To find some food," a startled Eladjo answered.

"You're a thief."

"I'm hungry. I haven't eaten for two days."

"Are you a runaway?"

"Yes."

"From what plantation?

"Cap-Rouge."

The owner of the voice came out of the bushes behind Eladjo, passed without looking at him and simply said, "Follow me."

Minutes later, they reached the camp. Eladjo noticed that there were no women or children, only armed men. While he ate boiled plantains and smoked fish, the man who had brought him into the camp sat in front of him to observe.

"Where were you going,?" he asked. "Were you looking for us?"

"I don't even know who you are. I was just looking for food."

"Do you want to join us?"

"Tell me who you are."

"We're maroons. Our chief is Lamour Derance."

"What do you do?"

"We stay in the mountains and we fight anyone who tries to take us back to the plantations."

"I'm not a fighter."

"We don't only need fighters. We produce our own food, so we need farmers too."

"That I can do. But if one day I decide to hang myself, don't try to stop me."

Eladjo found himself in a group of twelve men who patrolled the western border of what they considered Lamour Derance's territory. They had many more stops to make because their responsibility was to guard an invisible line that ran from the city of Port-au-Prince to the town of Jacmel. After two weeks of walking and sleeping in temporary shelters, the patrol left the border and moved deep inside their own territory to replenish their food supply. A half day's walk over mountainous terrain took them to a small plateau superbly cultivated with bananas and plantains, manioc and malangas. Eladjo was to remain there with the three men and three women who attended this mini-plantation.

After eating and filling their bags with vegetables, dried cod fish and smoked herrings, the patrol left to continue its surveillance. Eladjo, tired of walking, was glad to stay behind. He was welcomed by his new partners for whom an escaped slave was some kind of hero. In conversation with them, he began to gain a general view of his situation.

When Lamour Derance had arrived in these mountains a few years back, he found a community of maroons already established there. It was said that some of these black men and women had never been enslaved. They were, as they said, 'born on the slopes.' Happy not to be slaves themselves, still they had no desire to fight slavery. To avoid capture by the colonial army, they led a nomadic life, moving from temporary camp to temporary camp. Occasionally they even crossed into Spanish territory, since their main area of operation was on the border mountain of La Selle, whose other side in the Spanish colony was called Bahoruco.

Next to the French colonists, their main enemy was hunger. To be self-sufficient in food, they established dozens of mini-plantations. When Lamour Derance became their leader, he instituted the patrols and also created a village he named Grand-Doco. The site of this village was a secret so well guarded that even some maroons thought it was a myth. The French organized many expeditions against it, but Grand-Doco was never found.

Eladjo also became more informed about what was going on in the entire colony. Every time a patrol came to resupply, they would bring news of revolts, battles, tortures, massacres and finally, the abolition of slavery. In spite of all these events, the mountain remained relatively peaceful.

Four years later Eladjo was still at the same station. In 1799, a rumor predicted that a war was about to break out between Toussaint Louverture and Andre Rigaud. The rumor was well-founded. Toussaint's army invaded the southern peninsula, Rigaud's stronghold. Toussaint decided first to occupy the town of Jacmel to avoid being attacked from the rear. His army was commanded by Dessalines and Christophe, while Pétion was Jacmel's chief defender.

Although Lamour Derance embraced Rigaud's side, he didn't participate in the fighting. He watched passively as the northern army encircled Jacmel. He did nothing to prevent Toussaint's soldiers from bringing their artillery up the slopes and submitting the town's garrison to a night and day bombardment. When finally Pétion succeeded in breaking away, Derance created no diversion to help Pétion's column to escape.

After the fall of Jacmel, the war moved farther and farther away as Toussaint's army pushed Rigaud's forces west down the peninsula. Eladjo returned to the routine of his life as a farmer. News and hearsay continued to reach him: Rigaud fled to France with his principle lieutenants, Toussaint became governor-general, Toussaint annexed the eastern part of the island.

Later he learned about the French expedition and the deportation of Toussaint. Still Eladjo remained indifferent. Like the maroons around him, he experienced slavery as a personal misery rather than as a social injustice. In Kalame, he had been grounded in a sense of community, a place where he belonged, but in Saint-Domingue he felt nothing of the sort.

With the whites, the mulattos and the blacks coming from so many tribes, he was lost.

Too, the loss of his wife and daughter left no room in him for any other preoccupation. Their absence, and the fact that he didn't even know their fate, left him with a numbness against which he had no strength to react. His days were filled with regret and his sleep with nightmares. Slowly the idea of suicide returned.

One afternoon he decided to end his meaningless life. Leaving the banana field in which he had been working all day, he started toward his hut to get the rope. Before he reached the hut, on the plateau appeared a patrol, a team coming to replenish their food supply. As usual, they would spend the night and depart in the morning. The leader of the group approached Eladjo.

"Where are the other farmers?" he asked.

"They're still in the field."

"Go get them to prepare some food. We're hungry."

Eladjo was neither relieved nor disturbed by their arrival. It merely meant that his plan was postponed for a day. Two hours later, farmers and warriors were sitting around a campfire eating and talking.

"Hey, Bossale!" one of the patrolmen called, "Didn't you say you were Arada?"

"Yes, I am."

"A group of your tribesmen seized a slave ship at sea and landed in Arcahaie. That was about three months ago."

"A group of Aradas? Where did you learn that?"

"We were patrolling near Port-au-Prince when we met some soldiers. They were with an army sent as reinforcement to General Geffrard, who's fighting the French in the south."

"Do you know anything else? A word they said, the name of someone or some place?"

"Yes," another patrolman said, "a soldier told me that some of them came from a place called Calamity or something like that."

"Calamity? Calamity…? Kalame! That's my village! They really are Aradas! Where is Arcahaie?"

"Do you want to go there?"

"Yes!"

"But you have your duty here."

"When I came, I told you that I had no more taste for life. I asked you not to stop me if I wanted to kill myself. Now I want to leave. It's just about the same thing."

"Go north from here until you reach Port-au-Prince. After you pass the city turn left to the sea, then follow the shore. You'll pass the small town of Cabaret. Continue on, and the next town is Arcahaie. Take my bag with some food. It's far."

At dawn Eladjo was on his way.

Chapter Thirteen
A Ship Renamed Haïti

Fifteen days after leaving the farm, Eladjo reached Hospital Mountain, which overlooked the city of Port-au-Prince. He would have gotten there sooner, but he'd become lost many times and, being barefoot, he had cut himself descending into a ravine.

As he did every night, he found a place to sleep. Cannon blasts awoke him. The city was under attack.

Since he had left the maroons' camp, Eladjo had carefully avoided encountering anyone. Whenever he had heard voices, he had left the path to hide in the bushes. But now, with his bag of food going empty, he had to find a supplier. As he watched near a well-traveled mountain path, he could see but not hear groups of black people who passed from time to time. Some stopped for a while to observe the battle going on below, and Eladjo became curious about what was happening in the city. Who was fighting and why? Deciding to let himself be seen, he went to a flat rock beside the path, sat down and waited.

The first passerby who came along was a crippled man walking with a crutch.

"Good morning," Eladjo said.

"Good morning my brother."

"Do you understand what's happening down there?"

"I do, indeed. General Dessalines and his army are attacking the city. They started about a week ago, and now the residents have no food or water. Just a few more days and Port-au-Prince will fall."

"How do you know?"

"Some soldiers going to the front told me yesterday. I used to be a soldier myself. I fought in many battles without being wounded until I took a bullet in my knee. Now I can't bend my left leg."

As he spoke, the man approached and sat on the rock beside Eladjo.

He was relieved to be off his feet for a while.

"My name is Clovis," he said. "What's yours?"

"Eladjo."

"Is that an African name? Are you a Bossale?"

"Yes, I am Arada."

"I heard something about Aradas lately. What was it again? Oh, yes! A boatload of Aradas landed in Arcahaie last April or May—I don't remember exactly."

"That's where I'm going. But I don't know the way and I'm low on food."

"I can find some food for you and I can tell you the way to Arcahaie, but first I must know if you're a deserter."

"What's that?"

"A soldier who abandons his unit without permission."

"I've never been a soldier. I'm a farmer."

On their way to his hut, Clovis noticed that Eladjo was limping slightly. He persuaded the African to remain with him for three days to allow his foot to heal. By the fourth day, Eladjo was eager to be on his way, despite his foot still being tender. A crude bandage was fashioned by Clovis from an old shirt, and Eladjo was sent off with the advice that he walk slowly if he wanted to reach his destination.

When he arrived at Arcahaie, he was disappointed and frustrated to learn that the Aradas had stayed in the town for an entire month and then had sailed to Gonaïves. He was taken to Catherine Flon for more detailed information, and she noticed the bad condition of Eladjo's left foot. The bandage had worn off and the foot was badly swollen. Once again Eladjo experienced the kindness of a stranger when she put him to bed and took care of his wound herself.

Port-au-Prince fell to the indigenous army, leaving only a few coastal towns in French hands. Each time the black army overran another settlement, what was left of the town's garrison retreated toward Cap-Français.

In November 1803, General Rochambeau fortified Cap-Français with a series of forts overlooking the only road leading to the city from the south. He knew that losing the capital meant losing the colony. Each time that possibility occurred to him, he panicked. What would happen to his career? What would happen to his family's reputation if he returned to Europe with the shame of being the commander of a French division who had lost a war to some disorganized subhumans?

He remembered his father, who had fought in the War of American Independence, telling him that when the British lost the last battle there, the English general tried to surrender his sword to the French general, whom he regarded as his equal, instead of giving it to the American commander, a colonist considered unworthy of that honor. But at least that colonist was white! Here in Saint-Domingue, he was facing the possibility of surrendering to a Negro, a slave.

Dessalines, on the other hand, was confident that the final victory was his. This self-assurance worried Pétion. Following the fall of Port-au-Prince, the two black generals had a strategy meeting to plan the rest of the campaign.

"Pétion," Dessalines said, "now that the center of the country is firmly in our hands, I want you to stay here to protect both my rear and Geffrard's. I'm going north to take Cap-Français."

"I know how Rochambeau thinks," Pétion cautioned. "He's experienced, brave and cruel. It's not going to be easy to dislodge him from Cap-Français."

"Rochambeau is a very able general," Dessalines agreed, "but he's blinded by racial prejudice. He refuses to believe that we have a strategy. We'll have three times his ten thousand men, and he's going to think that I'll just hurl our forces against his in order to overwhelm him. And at first I'll give him the impression that he's right. Then I'll change tactics in the middle of the battle. By the time he realizes it, the most important element in his defense system, Fort Vertières, will either be destroyed or in my hands."

"Do you really believe that after the battle of La Crête-à-Pierrot any French commander would still underestimate you?"

"They'll underestimate us for years to come. We have to make that our strength by talking stupid and acting smart. I expect you to be in Gonaïves on January 1st for the proclamation of independence."

The next day Dessalines, with a small escort, left Port-au-Prince for the northern province. Two days later he reached Gonaïves where Christophe and Clervaux were awaiting him with their divisions. Soon two more divisions from the Artibonite Valley joined them, bringing the army to a total of twenty thousand men.

In the beginning of November, the march to Cap-Français began. The first rest stop was made at Ennery, where Dessalines visited the George plantation, site of Toussaint's arrest. From there they passed Mt. Puilboreau and stopped in Plaisance. Three days' rest and they were on the move again. It took one day to pass Mt. Bedoret and reach the town of Limbé. There their number was again increased, this time by a division from the northwest, bringing their strength to twenty-seven thousand.

The last leg of the march was the thirty-five kilometers separating Limbé from Cap-Français. This distance could have been covered in a day, but it was the rainy season. The northern plain was transformed into a sea of mud. Dragging artillery pieces through the muck was possible only for those who knew that freedom was at the end of their efforts.

On November seventeenth, the indigenous army encircled the city of Cap-Français. As the bugler was awakening the French garrison with reveille, Clervaux's division opened fire.

When Gaston, Didier and Antoine left the room, Marcus went to the window. His heart was beating uncontrollably because he knew that the next person to enter might be Bambolo.

The door opened behind him and a voice said in French, "I am Bambolo, griot of the Arada tribe. You sent for me."

Not recognizing the voice, Marcus turned slowly to face his visitor. The last time he had seen Bambolo, they were both in their early adolescence. Fifteen years had passed, but there are aspects of a person's features that age without really changing. He recognized his childhood friend, ran to him and embraced him.

With his arms stiffly at his sides, Bambolo was trying to understand why this black man disguised in pink men's clothing was pressing him so tightly to his chest.

"Bambolo," Marcus exclaimed, "don't you know who I am?"

Bambolo noticed something familiar in the voice, a resonance that lingers in spite of the years.

"Look!" Marcus said, removing his three-pointed hat and turning his left cheek toward Bambolo. "Don't you remember this circle? I'm Nguele!"

Bambolo's eyes opened wide and he sank to the floor. The gods had guided him to Nguele.

So this was the reason for each unusual event, for every bit of knowledge he had acquired, for all his training—his ability to go on Gaou-Guinou's Mountain, the language, the fencing, being captured at the sacred field—they all were serving the same purpose: to find Nguele and bring him back to Kalame.

Marcus was puzzled by Bambolo's reaction. He sat on the floor facing the griot.

"You don't seem to understand," he said. "I am Nguele, your friend. We were called the Mischievous Pair, remember?"

"Yes. Yes, I do. I recognize you now."

"You don't look happy."

"I am happy beyond words. I knew that you were alive but I never expected to find you this far from Kalame."

"We have so much to talk about."

"That's what I'm afraid of."

"Afraid? Why?"

"Because the first thing I have to tell you is that I've betrayed our companionship."

"How did you do that?"

"I took into my hut the woman who was supposed to be yours."

"Who is that?"

"Why, Ganiloa, of course."

"Is that it?"

"Isn't that enough?

"Listen, Bambolo, I am so happy to see you that I am ready to forgive anything you might have done against me. But you haven't wronged me. I have a wife and children here. When we took the pledge on our own, we were children playing. Once the attack on our village separated us, our future no longer was in our hands. There's nothing we could have done even if we had taken the pledge as adults. I also did something of the same nature. I took the pledge with another companion. He protected me when I needed a friend. I don't consider that betraying you. I had to live my life where I was."

Bambolo was relieved to know that Nguele wasn't angry with him, but his friend's forgiveness forced him to muffle his own anger that Nguele had chosen a new companion.

"Who was he?" he asked.

"Who?"

"The man with whom you took the pledge."

"He was the son of a great chief named Toussaint Louverture."

"Where is he now?"

"I don't know. The whole family was sent away by the white men. This family claimed to be descendants of an Arada king."

"It's possible. Don't you remember that King Gaou-Guinou's son was taken away in the pink men's first attack?"

"Yes, I do remember. I believed that the Louvertures were descended from Gaou-Guinou because there's no other way they could have known about an Arada king who died so long ago."

"Where are all the people who were captured with you?"

"I have no idea. We were mixed with many other tribes and put on different boats. Some of them probably landed in this country, but the boat that took me had only two Aradas: Eladjo and me."

"Eladjo? Is he alive?"

"I don't know. We were separated the day we arrived here."

It was the first week of December. The night was cool and comfortable, but Eladjo couldn't sleep. Too much noise. The streets of Arcahaie were crowded with people walking or running in all directions. Soldiers, civilians, men, women and children carrying hundreds of torches were kissing, embracing and shaking hands all over town. Dozens of drummers beat African rhythms.

Catherine Flon's house was a two-story structure, with Eladjo's room on the second floor. Hopping on his good foot, he went to the small balcony to have a better view of the street and to learn what was going on.

"What are you doing on your feet? Go back to bed!"

It was Madame Catherine playing at being angry, but the glow on her face betrayed her real feelings. She was elated.

"I can't sleep with all that noise."

"I didn't ask you to go to sleep. I want you off that foot. I myself don't intend to close my eyes for a second. This is a night for celebration! General Dessalines has taken Cap-Français after a battle that lasted only eleven hours. We're no longer a colony; we're a nation! On January 1st we'll proclaim ourselves independent."

Eladjo couldn't share Catherine's enthusiasm. The concepts of colony and nation left him indifferent. His dream didn't go beyond a primitive village where everyone knows everyone else. He hoped to find the Aradas who had been in Arcahaie recently and recreate with them the life they had known in their homeland. His only interest in the victory by the black army was the possibility of obtaining an old plantation where an Arada village could be built.

He had talked to Catherine about his idea and she had encouraged him with her belief that there should be plenty of plantations available. The white owners were leaving the country as quickly as they could find passage on a ship. She also suggested that Eladjo look to Dr. Marcus for help.

"Who is Dr. Marcus?" Eladjo asked.

"He's the chief doctor of the army and personal physician to General Dessalines. The general is suffering from malaria and Dr. Marcus knows how to bring the fevers down. Dessalines will drink nothing from anyone else's hands. If Dr. Marcus agrees to help your project, you can consider it done."

"Why would he want to help?"

"Because he is Arada too. He was brought to this country about fifteen years ago. I don't recall exactly how, but he is related to the man who led the revolt on the ship. They must be brothers or cousins, because they have the same circle on their left cheeks."

"They aren't related; they're companions. You see this snake on my forearm? Someone in Kalame has one just like that… if he's still alive."

This conversation led Eladjo to reminisce about his homeland: his companion Bao, the sacred field and Kalame. Little by little, as his memory became sharper, it left generalities to dig out specific scenes. He seemed to hear Bao's laughter when he had embarrassed himself in front of some women standing naked on the river bank near the sacred field. He also remembered those two mischievous boys who took the pledge all by themselves. He had found them in the bushes bleeding from circles they had cut on each other's cheeks. He reviewed the life he had known, he recalled that a boy from Kalame had traveled with him on the same slave ship, and how he had carried him ashore because of an injured ankle. What a painful moment it had been when he realized that he was no longer a man but a slave unable to help a child who should have been under his protection. That child's name remained engraved in his memory: Nguele.

How many times he had been awakened by a nightmare in which a boy was drowning. Tied to a tree, he was unable to save him. The boy's face was not always Nguele's, but he always had a circle on his cheek. Eladjo would wake up screaming that name.

The nightmare began when he learned that a slave arriving in the colony in a condition that didn't allow the ship captain to sell him immediately was considered damaged merchandise and thrown into the sea. Eladjo thought often of the terrible fate of that boy who had grown up on the African plain, loved, happy and free, and who had died so young, so alone and so far away from whoever had known his name. Now, an idea was taking shape in Eladjo's mind: Dr. Marcus was an Arada. He had arrived in this country about fifteen years ago and had a circle on his cheek. Could it be possible that Nguele had survived?

"Madame Catherine," he asked, "what else do you know about Dr. Marcus?"

"Not much. He grew up on the Breda plantation near Cap-Français. He was raised and trained by Toussaint Louverture himself. He joined the revolt…"

"Do you know his Arada name?" Eladjo interrupted.

"What do you mean?"

"Marcus is a white man's name. Have you heard the Aradas call him something else?"

"How would I know? I don't understand their language. When they speak, I only hear an succession of sounds. I wouldn't even be able to separate one word from another. Why did you ask?"

"Besides myself, there was only one other Arada on the ship that brought me here. He was a young boy named Nguele. He had a circle on his cheek. The chain had cut his ankle so deeply that he couldn't walk, so I had to carry him off the ship. I was wondering if by chance Dr. Marcus weren't Nguele."

"I heard him say that Toussaint Louverture saved his life by healing a badly infected wound he had on his foot when he came out of the slave ship."

"He survived! My little brother survived!" Eladjo exclaimed. "Madame Catherine, how soon can I leave?"

"What's your hurry? The Aradas can't vanish into thin air. Your foot is doing fine, but you're not yet ready for a long walk."

Although the French had lost the battle for Cap-Français, it was not a complete rout. Actually, they still held the city itself, but they had lost all the fortifications that were supposed to protect it. Rochambeau, realizing that there was no way he could resist a general assault by the indigenous army, decided to negotiate. He sent an emissary to Dessalines to ask for a delay of eight days to evacuate the city. Dessalines agreed but notified the French general that in eight days he would occupy the city of Cap-Français peacefully or by force. Rochambeau took advantage of this delay to negotiate his surrender with the British commodore commanding the flotilla that was blockading the port. On November 29, 1803, the indigenous army entered the capital of the colony.

A month before Eladjo reached Arcahaie, the Aradas had left the town for Gonaïves. Marcus had accompanied them on *The Sirène* because Dessalines wanted them to be present for the independence proclamation. The general-in-chief arrived in Gonaïves a week before the celebration. In a good mood after so many years of fighting, he immediately sent for Dr. Marcus.

Gonaïves was a city in ruins. Fewer than a hundred structures were left standing after a series of battles between the French and indigenous armies for the control of the area. Nevertheless, thanks to thousands of tents left behind by the departing French divisions, Gonaïves was transformed into a vast military camp.

The Aradas were given two huge tents across from the house where Dessalines had taken up residence. Marcus never left his tribesmen. He ate with them and slept with them, always at Bambolo's side.

The general-in-chief wasn't alone when Marcus was brought to him. Christophe and Pétion were sitting with him around a small square table. The doctor was invited to take the fourth seat.

"How are the Aradas?" Dessalines asked.

"They're doing well, except that they want to return to their village."

"They're dreaming! How are they going to reach Africa?"

"Why not? They have the ship and the crew."

"The crew is French," Christophe added. "They might sell the Africans instead of taking them to Africa."

"The Frenchmen are disarmed. Only the Aradas have weapons."

"I meant that the Aradas have no knowledge of navigation. The crew can take them anywhere and they would realize it wasn't Africa only when it's too late."

"General Christophe," Marcus replied, "I know that we can't trust the French, but I personally know the boat's captain and his seconds. I assure you that they will take the Aradas to Africa."

"What makes you so sure?" Pétion asked.

"These men were themselves slaves on ships, and for three years they endured what we've suffered here. They developed a strong hatred for slavery. They were later hired as overseers on the Breda plantation. When the general revolt occurred, Breda was declared a sanctuary because of these three men and the de Libertad family. The other overseers were expelled from the plantation to find their own way to Cap-Français. None of them survived, but I was ordered by Toussaint himself to take these three to safety."

"Do you believe that?" Christophe asked Pétion.

"It's possible. In every slave society, there have been white people who opposed it."

"If Dr. Marcus is right," Dessalines objected, "what were they doing on a slave ship?"

"I think they're the only ones to answer that question."

"You're right. Bring me the Frenchmen."

Minutes later, the three sailors were facing the general-in-chief.

"Marcus told me that you're against slavery. Is this true?" Dessalines asked with his characteristic abruptness.

"Yes, it's true," Antoine answered.

"Nevertheless you are the captain of a slave ship. Why?"

"I became the captain only after the mutiny."

"What were you doing on the ship in the first place?"

The Arada Pledge

"We were drugged and kidnapped in Jamaica."

"What do you plan to do now?"

"The ship is legally yours, but the crew would like to buy it for commercial purposes."

"Do you have the means?"

"No, but we were hoping to pay in terms."

"My decision isn't yet made but I may have a deal to propose you. You may go now. Marcus, bring me the leader of the Aradas."

Bambolo had hoped to meet the leader of the indigenous army. To prepare for that eventuality, he had obtained from Marcus a large piece of white material to drape himself from his waist to his feet. Bakao had been asked to make an amulet that the griot intended to wear for the occasion. When Marcus came looking for him, Bambolo was ready. It was as the griot of the Arada tribe that Bambolo appeared before Dessalines.

"I am told," the general said, "that you want to return home. Is this so?"

"Yes!"

"Do you realize the dangers you will face between here and Africa? Do you know that every nation, every ship, every piece of floating debris on the sea will be an enemy?"

"Yes, I know."

"Why do you still want to go?"

"Because I am the griot of the Arada tribe. I am the memory of my people."

"Very important, General," Christophe interjected. "If the story of our struggle is not told, future generations will never understand the hardship of slavery, the sacrifices we had to make, and they may never hear the name of Jean-Jacques Dessalines."

"What do you think, Pétion?"

"I completely agree with Christophe. You should allow the griot to go. He will tell the Africans what their descendants have accomplished here. We have demonstrated that the Europeans are not invincible and we have proven beyond any doubt that we are not of an inferior race. If we don't tell our own story, our enemies will. They'll suppress and distort it to make it sound like an epitaph."

"I understand you, gentlemen, and I agree. Now I want you to understand my concern. Suppose the crew finds a way to kill or to sell the Aradas before reaching Africa? How would we know?"

"General," Marcus said, "after these three men were protected by the slaves on the Breda plantation, they had to leave the United States because they were accused of being too friendly to slaves there. They helped the Aradas seize the boat and brought them here, the only place where they could escape slavery. Why shouldn't we trust them?"

"They are French and I don't want to trust them. But I trust you, Dr. Arada. If you can assure me that the ship will be returned with something that can be found only in Africa, I'll let them go."

"I'll give you my answer tomorrow, General."

Then, turning to Bambolo, Dessalines asked, "Why do you want to leave so quickly? You are free in this land. You don't seem to appreciate what we just accomplished here."

"I am fully aware of what you have done. You have filled me with admiration and pride. But to some degree you are right: There are things I don't appreciate here."

"What?"

"You speak and dress like the pink men and, even worse, you seem to have become as violent, as cruel as they are."

"That's true, but as slaves we had no choice. We couldn't choose our clothing or keep our languages. They were chosen for us. As far as violence is concerned, let me show you something."

Dessalines took off his overcoat, untied his red neck scarf and lifted his shirt over his head. He stood bare chested facing his visitors. He was in his early forties, of medium height and well built with powerful muscles. Slowly he turned and put his hands on the wall above his head. His back was criss-crossed by long scars left by the whip. Some were so deep that the skin had never recovered its original color. The brownish pink gave the impression that they were fresh wounds.

"You see," he said to Bambolo, "this is how hatred was taught to us, and lessons like that cannot be forgotten."

On January 1, 1804, Gonaïves was teeming with people. The ceremony for the declaration of independence was to start at seven. In the main square of the city, a wooden platform was built around a royal palm, the symbol of freedom for the black population.

A few minutes before seven, Dessalines, surrounded by his generals, left his residence to go to the national altar. When they had taken their places on the platform, the general-in-chief signaled that he wanted to speak. The crowd became silent. Dessalines' voice couldn't reach everyone, but those who were close enough heard him speak of the violence and humiliation inflicted on the black and mulatto peoples, the atrocities committed by the French during the three centuries of slavery in Saint-Domingue. That was the explanation and justification for the violent means used in seeking their independence.

Then one of Dessalines' secretaries read a proclamation by the general-in-chief to the nation. He also read the declaration of independence, which Dessalines then signed. Everyone on the platform did likewise. After that, Dessalines asked them to pledge allegiance to the new nation, to fight to the death for its independence and to renounce France forever.

That night, there was a banquet at Dessalines' residence. Marcus and Bambolo were invited.

During the dinner the general-in-chief asked Marcus, "Do you have my answer, Doctor?"

"Yes, General. I've asked one of the Aradas who is a sacred singer to make me a drum without the skin on it. When the ship returns with the drum it must be covered with a fresh zebra skin. This animal cannot be found anywhere outside of Africa."

"And how can you ensure that the ship will return here?"

"I have a plan, but I have to go to Cap-Français to know if it will work."

"Cap-Français?" Dessalines asked, "Where is that?"

Seeing that Marcus didn't understand, he explained.

"This country is no longer a French colony. Therefore, we can't have a city called Cap-Français. From now on it will be called Cap-Haïtien because we have changed the name of our country from Saint-Domingue to Haïti."

"Very well, I must go to Cap-Haïtien before I can assure you that the ship will return."

"May I ask you a question, General?" Bambolo interrupted.

"Of course. What is it?"

"How long do you think this country will remain independent?"

"Forever, I hope. Why did you ask?"

"I was thinking that we have the same enemies: every other nation, every ship, every piece of floating debris, as you said. But there are differences. My boat is small; yours is big. My boat can run; yours cannot, and they all know where it is. I have more chance of reaching Africa than you have of staying independent."

After a brief silence, Dessalines conceded, "Come to think of it, you're right. Very well, you win. You're free to go. But Marcus, if you find a way to make the ship come back, do it so we will have news of our friends."

Three days later, Eladjo entered Gonaïves at dusk. The town had returned to normal. Although the generals, the soldiers, the farmers and even the tents were gone, it was still a place ravaged by war. He immediately started to ask around about the Aradas. He was told that they had left that very morning for Cap-Haïtien. For the second time since he had started his search, Eladjo felt discouraged.

Was there really a group of Aradas who had seized a ship on high seas and landed here? If the story hadn't been confirmed everywhere he had stopped, he would have had serious doubts about its truth. Since it was now dark, he went to the port and fell asleep on the sand near the pier. Eladjo thought that the most likely people with information about the Aradas would be those loading and unloading ships.

In the morning he approached a group of men who were repairing a fishing net. They were fishermen part-time and longshoremen the rest of the time. They confirmed that the Aradas had left for Cap-Haïtien. One of the men said that he had overheard a conversation between two members of the crew. They were talking about bringing the Aradas back to Africa after the ship spent a week in Cap-Haïtien to take on food and water for the trip.

"How do I get to Cap-Haïtien?" Eladjo asked.

Epilogue

The *Sirène* docked in Cap-Haïtien the day after it sailed from Gonaïves. Early in the morning, Marcus assembled the crew and recommended that they not leave the boat. A group of Frenchmen in a city just liberated from the French army would have created a commotion. Alone, Marcus went into town to purchase supplies for the voyage and came back two hours later on horseback, accompanied by a dozen other riders. Soon after, the loading of the boat began.

"This is our escort," he said to Gaston Dubreuil.

"Our escort? Are we going somewhere?"

"Yes, to Breda. We're going to see your wife."

"What?" Gaston cried. "Gaële is here? But how was the plantation not destroyed with the battle that just took place around here?"

"Breda is intact and the de Libertad family is still managing it. Let's go."

They arrived at Breda at midday. The de Libertad family's lunch was interrupted by a white servant announcing Marcus, who had gone alone to the dining room. Gaële received him at the door.

"What brought you here?" she asked politely but without enthusiasm. Before he could answer she saw over his shoulder Gaston dismounting in the yard.

"My darling husband," she screamed. "I was right! I knew you'd find me here!"

Gaston let go of the horse's reins and ran to embrace his wife.

"My beloved," he said, "I only knew this morning that you were here. Otherwise I would have come sooner."

Gaston and Marcus were invited to the table and Gaële took visible pleasure in serving her husband personally.

"Poor Gaële," Michel teased. "She has waited so long to play the role of a wife."

"Starting today," Gaële stated, "this is the only role I want to play in life."

"I'm glad," Gaston said, "but you will not start today."

"What do you mean?" Gaële asked anxiously.

"I have to leave again on a special mission. We're going to return the Aradas to their homeland."

"But the ship has a crew!" Gaële protested. "One man can't be indispensable."

"You're right. The boat can go without me, but I want to be part of the voyage. I want to be able to say to my children—to our children—that I helped return some Africans to their land. It's a small compensation for the evil we've done in this place."

"How long will the trip take?"

"Four months at the most. We've waited for years, and four months will go by very quickly. Besides, now I know where to find you."

Marcus had heard what he wanted to hear. First, Gaston wanted to take the Aradas back to Africa, not for financial gain, but from personal humanitarian conviction; and second, the love between Gaston and Gaële was strong enough to guarantee the return of the ship.

He then felt free to say to Gaston, "General Dessalines authorized me to offer you a deal. The ship is legally the property of this nation, but if you take the Aradas to their land and return here with the proof that it was done, the vessel is yours."

"What kind of proof will convince the general?"

"Don't worry about that. The Aradas know exactly what to send back."

Marcus wanted to return immediately to Cap-Haïtien, but Gaston begged him to stay longer.

"It will take about two full days to load the boat with food and water enough for the voyage," he pleaded.

Marcus relented.

When the two men and their escort returned to Cap-Haïtien, the boat was fully stocked and Bambolo was becoming impatient. From the ship's deck he saw the horsemen enter the vacant lot adjacent to the wharf. He left Bakao, with whom he had been talking, and descended the plank to meet them. Bakao followed him ashore, but at a distance.

"The captain told me that everything is ready," Bambolo said to Marcus. I told him that we would leave when you returned, because the gods had sent me here to bring you back to Kalame."

"The gods must have something else in mind," Marcus replied, "because I'm not going with you."

"What?" Bambolo exclaimed. "Are you telling me that everything we've done was in vain?"

"No, I'm only saying that my place is here. My wife and children are here, and now I'm no longer only a member of a tribe, although of course I will remain an Arada all my life. I've chosen that name for my children to carry from generation to generation. But I just helped to create a nation. Before all else, I am now a Haïtian. The gods could not have brought you all the way here only to return me to Kalame."

"What other reason could they have had?"

"Maybe they want you to tell the Aradas that you have been to a place where all the tribes are united. Ibos, Congos, Kaplaous, Mandingos, Aradas and other tribes whose names I don't even know have come together, learned to use the white men's weapons and defeated them. Tell them that all these tribes have abolished slavery and claimed the country for themselves."

"Maybe you're right. I'm a storyteller. My responsibility will be to tell everyone of your struggle and your victory. Unless… it is to reconcile the Aradas with the god of the salty water."

"What do you mean?"

"Adegba told me that King Gaou-Guinou angered the god of the sea. To have appeased him, the king would have had to send boatloads of young Aradas out to sea to put themselves at the god's mercy. I'm convinced that the pink men were just the instruments of the god to collect his due. If a boat returns with survivors, it will mean that the god is satisfied. I'm also convinced that the price has been paid because we're going to be taken home by pink men."

"I hope you're right, but what I see as your mission is more important. Think of it, Bambolo, this place where we stand used to be a slave market. The ship that brought me here anchored where this ship is now. I was burning with fever, and my ankle was so painful and swollen that I couldn't stand. Eladjo took me in his arms and carried me ashore. He put me down just about where Bakao is standing. We stayed together only for a brief moment and then he was taken away by two white men. He felt that he was abandoning me. I wept to see him go, and that image of him being taken away has stayed in my mind ever since. Think of it, Bambolo! No one will ever be sold here again."

"And you never knew where Eladjo was taken?"

"No. Do you see that man limping toward us? That's where I was when I saw him for the last time."

"Could he be still alive?"

"It's possible, but I have no way of knowing."

"Promise me to look for him. I want to go with the hope that he'll be found to live under your protection."

While this conversation was taking place, the limping man that Marcus had noticed was painfully approaching the group. When he got to within twenty paces or so, he stopped, either from respect or fatigue. He then sank to the ground and sat in the dirt. His eyes remained fixed on Marcus and Bambolo, but he didn't utter a word. The doctor and the griot didn't see him because they had turned toward the ocean, but Bakao did. Thinking the man was in some difficulty, he ran to him.

"Can I help you?" he asked in the only language he knew.

He was surprised when the man answered in the same language.

"I want to see Dr. Marcus if he is here."

"He's here. You see those two men standing over there? Dr. Marcus is the one in the pink men's clothes. Let me get him."

"Tell him I am Eladjo."

It was a very emotional reunion with tears, sobbing and laughter. Eladjo was transported to the shade of a tree where Marcus carefully examined his foot. He concluded that there were no broken bones but a very bad infection. He cleaned the wound, applied ointment and bandaged it with clean material.

The three Aradas spent a good part of the day filling each other in on the parts of their lives the others didn't know. Three amazing trajectories that had started in a peaceful African village and had converged some fifteen years later in a former slave market of a former colony recently liberated from slavery.

Eladjo's story was the saddest. He just wanted to spend the rest of his days in the company of Aradas in a village that would recreate in this new land the life he had known before his brutal capture. But when he realized that his tribesmen had not only the will to go home but also the means, he adhered wholeheartedly to the idea.

"Take me with you," he begged. "Take me away from this hell."

"But we are free now," Marcus said.

"Maybe, but you will spend the rest of your life defending your freedom. The white man will never leave you in peace."

"We know that, and we're prepared to resist. When he comes to take your land in Africa, will you be ready to defend it? I heard Toussaint once say that the white man will conquer the world or destroy it. Wherever he set his foot, he takes possession. Everything must be his: land, rivers, animals, even people. One day he will invade Africa. You will not be safer there than we are here."

"By the time they get to the Aradas' land, I'll have enjoyed some times of peaceful freedom. Take me to the boat, please."

Bakao leaned forward to pick Eladjo up, but Marcus stopped him

"It's for me to do that."

Before starting their voyage the next day, Bambolo gathered the Aradas on the deck of the ship and had them sit around him in a circle.

The Arada Pledge

"Aradas," he said, "today we're going home. When we were captured in the sacred field, we didn't know why. When we marched through the forest, we didn't know where we were being taken. When we got on this ship, we had no idea of the size of the salty water or how long the voyage would take. We were in chains and frightened.

"Today, everything is different. We know where we are going, and we know how long it will take. We are not in chains and we are not afraid. Now we know about freedom because we lost it. We also know what it takes to regain it. What was accomplished here must be known, not only by Aradas, but by other tribes, too. If we don't tell that story, our enemies will tell it their own way, and future generations will never know the truth."

Then Bambolo invited Marcus to join him inside the circle. They knelt facing each other. Each placing his right hand on the other's left shoulder, once again they took the Arada pledge, but the words this time were different.

"Repeat after me," Bambolo said. "I have chosen you as my companion for life. We will not work together, we will not hunt together. I will not bring your body back to be buried. I won't even know when you die, because soon there will be great distances between us: the salty water, the forest, the swamp and the savannah. But my children and my children's children will know your name and your story. Your memory will be in my family for generations. Remember, don't ever let your enemy tell your history."

Just then a one-horse carriage entered the empty lot. It was driven by Gaële Dubreuil, who had come to say goodbye to her husband. She was immediately admitted on board. Shortly after noon, Captain Poussin politely asked Gaële and Marcus to leave, as the ship was ready to raise anchor.

"Chosen one," Bakao said to Bambolo, "may I leave with them? I desire to stay here."

"Why?" Bambolo asked.

"I have nothing to return to. My father is dead and the woman I want has chosen another man. Maybe I can start a new life here if Dr. Marcus would take me under his protection."

"I'd be happy to help you," Marcus said, "if Bambolo agrees."

"You may stay," Bakao's old rival agreed.

All sails out, the boat renamed *Haïti* slowly moved away from the pier, pushed by a gentle but steady breeze. From the shore Marcus, Gaële and Bakao were waving. On the ship the blue and red flag of the new nation waved back at them.

When Marcus' arms grew tired, he looked for a special place and sat down. It was the exact spot where Eladjo had put him down when they arrived in the colony, the place where they were separated and where Toussaint Louverture had rescued him.

Looking at the ship that was now almost out of the harbor, he repeated to himself, "Don't ever let your enemy tell your history."

www.ingramcontent.com/pod-product-compliance
Lightning Source LLC
Chambersburg PA
CBHW022003160426
43197CB00007B/250